ALLAH, J

MW01487949

To
Annette
Enjoy!

Jordan
Harris

Prometheus Unbound

To suffer woes which Hope thinks infinite;
To forgive wrongs darker than death or night;
* To defy Power, which seems omnipotent;*
To love, and bear; to hope till Hope creates
From its own wreck the thing it contemplates;

* Neither to change, nor falter, nor repent;*
This, like thy glory, Titan, is to be
Good, great and joyous, beautiful and free;
This is alone Life, Joy, Empire, and Victory.

by
Percy Bysshe Shelley

Allah, Jesus, and Yahweh

The Gods That Failed

by

Gordon Harrison

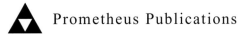 Prometheus Publications

Copyright © 2013 by Gordon Harrison.

Published by: *Prometheus Publications*

                Peterborough, Ontario
                Canada

Allah, Jesus, and Yahweh: The Gods that Failed. All rights reserved. No part of this book may be reproduced or transmitted in any form or by any means, electronic or mechanical without written permission from the publisher, except for inclusion of quotations in a review.

Library and Archives Canada Cataloguing in Publication

Harrison, Gordon, 1936-
    Allah, Jesus, and Yahweh : the gods that failed / by Gordon Harrison.

Includes bibliographical references and index.
ISBN 978-0-9879596-0-7 (pbk.)

    1. Religions. 2. Religiousness. 3. Religions—History.
4. Religious ethics. I. Title.

BL85.H37 2013   201   C2013-902294-5

Cover design by Jason Alexander; Senior Graphic Designer,
                Expert Subjects, LLC.
Printed in Canada

To my partner Evie and my daughter Jennifer
— in all possible universes I would hold you close.

CONTENTS

PREFACE

Has there ever been a society which has died of dissent?
Jacob Bronowski

We left paradise when I was five, and moved to the city to live with my mother's sister. As I learned later, there were two reasons for this move: so that my parents could find work and I could attend school. My mother was sympathetic toward my desire to return to the farm, so every Dominion Day, July 1, she took me back to paradise for the summer months.

Not long after our move, my aunt thought that her son, my city cousin, and I should go to Sunday school. Where she got this novel idea, I will never know. Now my cousin and I reasoned that five days of school were quite enough, and Sunday was a *special* day reserved for road hockey and for exploring a large undeveloped beach park nearby. Nonetheless, she sent us off in our best clothes with money for something called the collection plate and with instructions to behave. Since my cousin was older, he was put in the senior and I in the junior Sunday school class. This religious schooling went on for a few weeks until one fateful Sunday, the last time I attended. The teacher had been reading a story about a great leader called Moses who took his people into a desert while trying to get to someplace called the Promised Land. He wandered in this desert for forty years *killing* everyone he met.

Then came the teacher's inevitable questions. She seemed to be reading from a special book—we had no books at home, just newspapers. First, she asked *me* who Moses should turn to for help. With childlike innocence, I replied, "He should have asked the people for directions instead of killing them—that's what my mother would do—then he wouldn't be lost." I got stunned looks from my classmates and a look of withering disdain from the teacher who quickly turned away from me to ask another student the same question. So next Sunday I suggested to my cousin that we skip class and spend the coins destined for the collection plate on ice cream. For several weeks that's what we did until discovered. My aunt stoically accepted her failure at turning us into saints. My mother only smiled but never mentioned it.

When I was in primary school, we were always lining up for one reason or another. We wiggled and squirmed and the line wavered as we attempted to contain the irrepressible energy of youth. In one particularly long lineup leading to an elderly man seated behind a school table, I could overhear him asking each boy a few personal questions. One of these disturbed me greatly. "What's your religion, son?" he asked repeatedly. My extended family was neither religious nor irreligious and despite my abortive Sunday school career, I was clueless. So embarrassingly, I was stuck for an answer. At that time I didn't realize that Catholics had their own school system, and almost all the families in my neighborhood were Protestants—a word I had rarely heard. I decided on the spot that that's what I would be. Never was a boy so quickly and easily converted. As I stepped forward, he asked me, "What's your religion, son?" "I'm a pro-**tes'**-tant, sir." He looked at me kindly and smiled at my mispronunciation and said, "I bet you are."

Afterward, an acquaintance from my Sunday school days told me the man behind the table asking questions was from the Gideons, and that they gave New Testaments to all grade five Protestant students. He suggested I take two.

As I grew older these minor contacts with religion receded from my memory, but major concerns also arose. I came to understand, it's not so much that religion—all religions—are parochial and false, but it was the tremendous *moral harm* they did which exasperated me. Ever since I recognized this, I have been a true pro-**tes'**-tant, and this book is the outcome of that dissent.

OUTLINE

Scattered throughout my text are appearances by two legendary characters: Epios from the *Iliad* and Phemios from the *Odyssey*. I use them to carry my narrative forward and symbolize science and art respectively—two Greek gifts. They often make reference to Odysseus, the hero of Homer's epic, and the stress he puts on individualism and intelligence.

To borrow an adjective from biology, freedom is a keystone concept for happiness, democracy, and Western Civilization. Without it, you may as well live in present-day North Korea or

Saudi Arabia or medieval Europe. We will explore freedom's origin in Chapter 1, and although freedom has many tributaries, its Greek source is clear. Major contributors are the Age of the Enlightenment plus the United States Declaration of Independence, with its "life, liberty and the pursuit of happiness."

Perhaps you feel that freedom once won will always be with us. If so, then Chapter 2 is for you. Both psychology and history teach us how quickly it can be lost. Freedom is a river but rivers may be dammed and blocked, and their turbulent creative waters turned into compliant lakes bent to a single purpose. Waterways once full of teeming, divergent life morph into dreary pools of monotony and conformity. We will investigate this perilous danger in with an eye to avoiding it.

Some believe that religion and science can't be in conflict because their areas of interest and expertise don't overlap. Chapter 3 exposes this myth by comparing and contrasting the research methods of biblical scholars and scientists as they both seek to discover the beginning of time. Their conclusions are astoundingly different; each will be fully analyzed. For both groups and people everywhere, their results have far-reaching consequences. Whichever path you follow—religious or scientific—will profoundly influence all aspects of your life. Even if you are unaware, you doubtless have already made your choice—however tentative or firm.

For all those who believe the Bible is an unerring source of perfect morality, I suggest they read Chapter 4, "On human Bondage." This chapter concentrates on one great moral failure in the Bible and the Qur'an: both are pro-slavery from beginning to end. Not a word, not even a murmur, against slavery, much the opposite. Although the modern churches re-write history to cover their moral embarrassment, we must not let them whitewash their pathetic past. Unless you believe in the bankrupt idea of ethical relativism, this was a great moral catastrophe.

This chapter also exposes why the Catholic Church invented a new form of bondage, one usually reserved for rebellious farm animals: castration. In a sixty-year period, they gelded approximately a quarter of a million boys in Italy alone. This "holy work" was accomplished to be in agreement with a verse of St. Paul's found in I Corinthians.

The final page of this section reveals the first person in recorded history to speak out against slavery—he *was not* a member of the Abrahamic religions.

Chapter 5 discusses numerous topics found nowhere else in the anti-theistic writings I've read. For example, the Roman God Mithras was *the* model for Jesus and church ritual! Since both Mithras and Jesus were saviors, celebrated the Eucharist, and had identical birthdays, this parallelism disturbed early Christians. This chapter discloses who Mithras was and why he became the archetype for Jesus and church ritual. Remarkably, the early Christians built their church (now the Vatican) on top of the largest Mithraic temple of the ancient world.

After the triumphant early Church eradicated Mithraism, they turned their weapons inward to stray Christian sects, like Gnosticism. This group had some intriguing ideas on the origins of the name *Jesus* and his number, a subject called *gematria* mentioned nowhere else in today's literature.

We'll discover little known biblical patterns and puzzles. The Qur'an had similar riddles. The curious relationship between Shakespeare and the 46th Psalm deserves investigating.

The truly bizarre legend of the Wandering Jew will amuse us.

We end this entertainment with a full course of bubbly, hot, cheesy Pastafarianism with meat balls plus a side order of quotations from their sacred text, *The Loose Canon*.

Chapter 6, God's Messengers, gives the reader a hilarious look at the second, more recent, team of God talkers: Muhammad and Joseph Smith uncovering delusion and fraud respectively. Mark Twain, who owned a copy of The Book of Mormon, wrote, "It is such a pretentious affair and yet so slow, so sleepy, such an insipid mess of inspiration. It is chloroform in print." Unfortunately, this dreary book also offers support to racists and slave owners.

But comic relief is close at hand with the magic underpants Mormons wear and their penchant to polygamy. Evidently, with thirty-seven wives, Smith didn't have his magic undies on most of the time. In Mormon cosmology we are told of the planet or star Kolob (Smith confused these) where God has his permanent residence and keeps his spirit (or is it spirited?) wives. But the winner in the absurdity sweepstakes is when Jesus returns he will keep a summer home in Jackson County, Missouri, the original Garden of Eden *don't you know.*

This chapter also explores the recent work of V. S. Ramachandran—listed in *Time* magazine as one of the world's most influential thinkers. His research points to Muhammad suffering from a peculiar form of *temporal lobe epilepsy* that accounts for his visions and many aspects of his behavior. Moreover, history records powerful evidence that the author of the priestly parts of the Torah, St. Paul, Ezekiel, and even Moses had this form of epilepsy. This new line of research called neurotheology offers exciting prospects to explain religious behavior beyond deception.

For all those who falsely believe we would be running naked through the streets without the God-given morality of holy books, I recommend Chapter 7, Morals and Man. We can do better—we have done better—than an Old Testament that descends to the level of stoning children to death for disobedience or women for a little dalliance.

Curiously, my wildlife photography of bears and wolves provided a bizarre extra-biblical source for morality. Over the years, I have observed that these supposedly *fierce animals* show surprisingly moral behavior within their species, and occasionally even to other species. Why such pro-social conduct? This chapter will answer that question.

A close reading of the New Testament reveals a side of Jesus rarely mentioned. He was not always a paradigm of great moral conduct! Jesus has two faces—the one presented in Sunday school and from the pulpit and a terrifying, implacable face presented in the Gospels. Other writers have only alluded to some of this, but with exact verse references, this chapter develops the idea in convincing detail.

Cultures in Collision, Chapter 8, is a poem in praise of the *moral benefits* of science. In the wrong hands, of course, bad actions can come from science, just as in the proper hands good things can flow from religion. But everyone plays the odds. Nobel laureate Steven Weinberg said it best to *The New York Times,* on April 20, 1999:

With or without religion, you would have good people doing good things and evil people doing evil things. But for good people to do evil things, that takes religion.

Who are the heroes who created the greatest moral advances in all of human history? Why have we forgotten them? This last chapter answers these questions. These few men and women wrought more miracles than all the prayers ever mumbled by priests, rabbis, and imans. Recall the church fought anesthetics, women's rights, the theory of germs, vaccination, birth control, Darwin, the civil rights movement, emancipation of blacks, and this miserable, ignorant list goes on. Presently the churches, mosques, and synagogues are still fighting stem-cell research, family planning, Darwin, gay rights, etc. It will take more than amazing grace to save those wretches, both papal and public, who oppose such reforms!

Come, walk with me through these pages and see the glory and the horror we have created. Hold my hand. From religion to science, it has been a long night's journey into light.

ACKNOWLEDGEMENTS

The genesis for this book has been a lifetime. I have always considered myself to be fortunate, especially so in having an excellent editor, Julia Kuzeljevich. She went through the entire book, word by word, offering innumerable improvements. I owe her a great debt. In writing this book, I have also been fortunate in having many friends who offered suggestions that have greatly improved the text: Lois Raw, John Shepley, and others. My partner, Evelyn, has been an important sounding board and a source of ideas and unending support. My daughter has listened to me rave about the book and has always been encouraging. And in his enthusiasm, Larry Keeley has led me to believe this book is better than I would have imagined. I am grateful to everyone.

An old proverb affirms, "Luck never gives; she only loans." But in the writing of this book, I've been Lady Luck's major beneficiary, and these gifts she can never take away.

The majority of the photographs are from Google images; all have been Photoshopped. Every reasonable effort has been made to contact holders of copyright for the images used here. The author will gladly receive information that will enable him to rectify any inadvertent errors or omissions in subsequent editions. All the diagrams, however, and many of the photographs are my own.

Grateful acknowledgment is made to the following for permission to reprint:

Page 21: Pheidippides on Marathon Road from the website Hammer of the Gods27

Page 76: The James ossuary was on display at the Royal Ontario Museum from November 15, 2002 to January 5, 2003.

CHAPTER—1

THE CHILDREN OF ODYSSEUS

This is the story of a man, one who was never at a loss.
First sentence of the *Odyssey* translated by W.H.D. Rouse

We are on the beach at Marathon; it's 490 BC, the eve of history's most momentous conflict—the battle for the future. This is where slavery and the hive mind first confront European ideals of freedom and individuality.

Two elderly Greek men—who occasionally converse in an ancient Hellenic dialect—are dressed as warriors and are apparently ready to do battle with the Persians massed on the beach below. Epios, the larger of this unlikely pair, is an engineer and boxer while his smaller friend Phemios is a poet and minstrel.

Greek Soldier

Odysseus would be proud of them in a way he never was of himself at Troy. He was the only hero who did his best not to go to war, but once there, he did everything possible to end the conflict. Odysseus devised the stratagem of the Trojan horse, and then he directed Epios to build it. And when the epic wanderer returned home and slew all his wife's suitors, he spared the poet-minstrel Phemios but killed the priest, saying he could not slay a man of God. Odysseus avowed:

All men owe honor to the poets—honor
and awe, for they are dear to the Muse
who puts upon their lips the ways of life.

These two ancient friends have always credited their great longevity to Odysseus' blessing—he called them his two sons, science and art. This night they're watching for Persians reconnoitering Greek numbers and preparing for tomorrow's battle. Let's listen in and hear what they are saying:

"Stay near, Phemios. There's danger here!"

"Where?"

"Over that low ridge I saw a Persian patrol just a minute ago."

"Shouldn't we warn our encampment about them?" Phemios asked.

"No, no, the generals want the Persians to realize how few of us there are. That works to our advantage. Once your adversary mistakenly thinks you're weak, you have the upper hand."

"Upper hand be damned! You have a sense of humor, Epios. You've seen how many Persians are on the plain below—like locust come to eat us mere blades of grass. Hippias, that bastard tyrant we drove out of Athens, is with these Persians as their new toady. And I bet he advised them to land here so as best to deploy their cavalry—of which we have none. Just a week ago, these hordes destroyed nearby cities; killed the men, and enslaved all the women and children. I'm telling you, these multitudes of Darius, have a right to be arrogant."

"Don't despair, Phemios, we sent Pheidippides to Sparta a week ago asking for their assistance—they'll greatly increase our numbers. Our generals are delaying the battle only because the Spartans haven't arrived yet."

"You don't know do you? They're not coming! That's right, they're not coming! Some superstitious nonsense about waiting until the moon was full before they could leave. At times I wonder if Spartans are truly Greek. The only allies we have are 1,000 from loyal Plataea, and they came without being asked. Together with our 10,000 Athenians, we are still outnumbered by at least ten to one. And worse yet, our leader Miltiades has convinced the other generals, we should attack tomorrow. We're to attack! That's madness! Thrace, Macedonia, the entire Ionian coast, all the islands of the Aegean, plus Cyprus and Corinth have fallen. Yes, these Persians or Medes, as they sometimes call themselves, have good reason to be arrogant. No one has ever defeated them. And you say we have the upper hand? From India to the Aegean, Darius is emperor of the earth. We're alone, Epios—truly alone! And the beast's minions, Datis and Artaphernes, have come to eat us. By this time tomorrow, we'll all be dead if we're fortunate, slaves if we aren't.

"Even the great Odysseus, the man who was never at a loss, couldn't help us here. And, Epios, that wooden horse you built for him at Troy would be useless as well. The Medes would split that monster into myriad pieces to stoke their campfires star-scattered on the plain below."

"I can't argue with you. I'm terrified too. Still, I know that tomorrow when we march beside our companions in formation with our shields and long spears, we will both conquer our fear and put panic in their hearts. These haughty barbarians will see Greek pride when we charge their ranks at a full sprint. You and I have lived longer than anyone else has here. If we must die, this would be the time and place of my choosing."

"Ever the heroic warrior, eh, my friend. It's never a good day to die. Yet I believe some causes are better than others. And this must be the best of them!"

THE PERSIANS

These two Greek soldiers, Epios and Phemios, had little idea of the momentous occasion upon them—our contemporaries have little more. This was to be history's first pivotal battle with the most astounding consequences. The fate of European civilization teetered in the balance. It is no exaggeration to say that you are able to read this page, at this moment, only because the Athenians and Plataeans triumphed with an inconceivable victory.

What was the root cause of this initial conflict of East versus West? There were many, but every imperialistic power is fueled by *testosterone*—the mother of all arrogance. The proof? Lower or eliminate testosterone in species after species and levels of aggression plummet. Restore normal levels with injections of synthetic testosterone and aggression returns. Every great power will find or manufacture a "noble" cause to invade another country: the destruction of Sardis, the Sudetenland, and the Gulf of Tonkin. These were the supposed causes of Darius, Hitler, and Lyndon Johnson, respectively, going to war. The memorials to the dead, however, will be remembered long after the spurious reasons for going to war are forgotten. Dress your motives however you wish; they all feast on a raw banquet of arrogance.

Others find motives in money. Karl Marx argued that the Trojan War was not about the abduction of Helen (their noble cause). Rather, the Greeks sought to freely trade in the Black Sea region without paying a tax to a strategically-placed Troy, which lay at the entrance to the Hellespont. Still others find motives in love and altruism. Religions mistakenly claim these domains as their sole preserve.

Motives exist beyond biology (testosterone), economics, and ethics. Each of these causes seems to be necessary but hardly sufficient. Consider biology. If it were sufficient, then fatalism would be the only true philosophy, and we might as well build statues to pedophiles as to poets. Humans dissipate, sublimate, or repress testosterone/arrogance by playing sports, intellectual activity, entertainment, and so on. Humankind *has the capacity* to rise above biology and reach rational decisions—we call it freedom. For the Hellenes, freedom was the very air they breathed. This was what Epios and Phemios were willing to die for at Marathon.

What was the Persian attitude or mind-set toward freedom? Herodotus (c. 484-425 BC), history's first historian, answers this question in his famous *Persian Wars* (also called *The Histories*). His is the single greatest source we have on this clash of civilizations. He tells us that in the reigns of the Persian emperors Darius and Xerxes (father and son), Greece suffered more than in the twenty generations before.

Consider one of these revealing occasions recorded by Herodotus. When Xerxes was on his way to Greece to punish the Athenians for aiding the Ionian revolt, he passed through Lydia and a man named Pythios magnificently entertained him and his entire army. Pythios offered all his money for the war effort but Xerxes declined to take it. Instead, he praised the Lydian exceedingly and said he had done what no other person in his kingdom had, and Xerxes named him his "guest-friend." On this occasion, the host asked for nothing. But some time later after Xerxes had had his engineers build a pontoon bridge over the Hellespont (Dardanelles) and was about to cross over from Asia to Europe, Pythios asked the king to grant him a small request.

"Master, I would desire to receive from thee a certain thing at my request, which, as it chances, is for thee an easy thing to grant, but a great thing for me, if I obtain it." Then Xerxes, thinking that his request would be for anything rather than that which he actually asked, said that he would grant it, and bade him speak and say what he desired. He then, when he heard this, was encouraged, and spoke these words: "Master, I have, as it chances, five sons, and it is their fortune to be all going together with thee on the march against Hellas. Do thou, therefore, O king, have compassion upon me, who have come to so great an age, and release from serving in the expedition one of my sons, the eldest, in order that he may be caretaker both of myself and of my wealth: but the other four take with thyself, and after thou hast accomplished that which thou hast in thy mind, mayest thou have a safe return home." [1]

Xerxes was furious. He called Pythios a wretched little man to have the impudence to ask such a favor. The king reminded him that he was *a slave* and that it was his duty to come with his entire household, including his wife. Nevertheless, he said, your eldest son shall not come with us. Instead, he will be cut in half and the two pieces will be put on either side of the road for all to see as we march between. And those of the king's men, who were responsible for such gruesome duties, executed it. In the lands of Xerxes, everyone was a slave—whose life was forfeited on the least whim. This included even his wife and children.

Herodotus gives many reports of this conflict between East and West, some more horrific than that of Pythios. In one case, a father was made to eat his son and had to comment—to save his own life—that whatever pleases the king pleases him. All Persians were slaves; so-called, and so-treated—even the governors of his provinces. This struggle between Greece and Persia was beyond flesh and blood, rising to a colossal clash of values and ideals: freedom versus slavery, human worth versus trash—individualism versus the hive mind.

BATTLE OF MARATHON

Julius Caesar in his *Commentaries* tells us that all Gaul was divided into three parts. The divisions in the forms of government are even fewer: you live either in a democracy or in a non-democracy. Initially these two divisions appear flippant like saying you are either a toad or a non-toad. Further assessment reveals this not to be the case.

Consider the non-democracies. All have a common pattern that has persisted over vast stretches of time and across all continents except Antarctica. I call it the *priest, potentate, peasant* model, or PPP in short. Now the peasants were as a rule powerless, but the priests might occasionally vie for power with the potentate. This form of government describes the whole of the non-Greek world. Egypt was the prototype for PPP. The pharaoh played potentate doing as he pleased: building pyramids, carving mammoth statues, and waging war on neighbors. And from time immemorial, the peasants did as they were told. What did the priests do? Why, they kept the peasants ignorant, hence fearful and thus easy to control. Thereby they guarded their position of power—the classic PPP plan.

In a long dreary list of pharaohs, only Akhenaten did anything original with respect to religion. He introduced a form of fanatical monotheism doing away with usual half-man half-animal deities. The priests, the lords of conservatism, bided their time and when Akhenaten died, they erased everything he had changed. Everything! The power behind the throne, the priesthood, always takes the long view of history.

The 20th century is a horrific catalogue of non-democracies. Consider Nazism. Der Führer is the potentate, the SS (in particular Reichsführer Heinrich Himler's occult faction) is the priesthood, and the obedient millions we have seen so often shouting "Heil Hitler" are the peasants. This is an archetypal case of a multitude following a maniac to do evil.

The Roman Catholic Church is also an ideal example of the priesthood that works inside many governments—mostly non-democracies. As an easy task, I'll leave it to the reader to make the associations between it and PPP.

In these non-democracies, the power and roll of the potentate and priests were mostly constant. But the power of the peasant could vary from slave to a citizen of sorts—with a general improvement from the ancient to the modern world. Slavery is a shape-shifter. While coping with just Cro-Magnon instincts, we are tempted by ideologies new and old and modern abundance that urge us to morph into new forms of enslavement. Although, as Herodotus recorded, the slaves in ancient empires were mere property to be discarded as the potentates or priests preferred. The serfs of our time are soldiers in war machines, suicide bombers, children in madrassa, sheep in megachurches, and workers in multinational sweatshops. They live but are not alive!

In the hills surrounding the plain of Marathon, the situation facing the Greeks in September of 490 BCE[*] was whether they should offer the Persians earth and water—their religious symbols of submission—or take up arms against a sea of enemies. Was Greece to become another despotic Persian province or the shining symbol of everything we value in art, literature, poetry, politics, mathematics, and science? A decision had to be made.

Herodotus records the details of the war committee that made the decision. The Athenians were divided into ten demes (townships). Each deme had to mobilize 1,000 soldiers and had to appoint a general as their leader. So the army comprised 10,000 soldiers and ten generals. Aristides and Themistocles, both of whom would gain fame in later battles, were two of the ten. Now these ten generals were evenly divided, five for a direct confrontation with the Medes and five who counseled against such seeming madness considering the enemy's size. A tie-breaking vote was needed. Because all decisions were voted on, the city of Athens appointed a "polemarch" (literally a war ruler), who also had a vote, to break parity. At this time the polemarch was a man named Callimachos. It is no exaggeration to say that the vote of this one man determined the fate of European civilization—the Butterfly Effect in action where small deeds have enormous consequences. The Greek commander Miltiades realizing some part of this spoke passionately to Callimachos:

> With thee now it rests, Callimachos, either to bring Athens under slavery, or by making her free to leave behind thee for all the time that men shall live a memorial such as not even Harmodios and Aristogeiton [two Athenians famous for tyrannicide] have left. For now the Athenians have come to a danger

---

[*] To avoid religious parochialism in dating, I will hereafter use BCE, meaning *Before the Common Era* for BC, and CE, meaning *Common Era* for AD.

the greatest to which they have ever come since they were a people; and on the one hand, if they submit to the Medes, it is determined what they shall suffer, being delivered over to Hippias [former tyrant of Athens], while on the other hand, if this city shall gain the victory, it may become the first of the cities of Hellas. [2]

Speaking thus, Miltiades convinced Callimachos to vote for a direct confrontation. A momentous decision—particularly for him because he was killed in the subsequent battle. This was the decision Phemios had reported to his friend previously.

On judgment day at Marathon, the Persians deployed as they always did: elite troops in the middle, weaker troops on the wings. It was a winning formation—after all, they had never lost a battle. Miltiades did the precise opposite! His center was weak to draw out the enemy hordes allowing the Greek soldiers on the flanks to cut them off from the remaining Persians. Divide and conquer. Miltiades' craftiness was reminiscent of Odysseus.

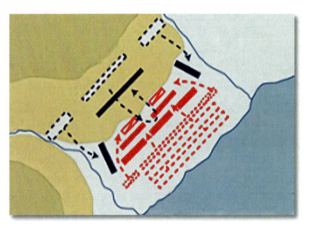

The Battle of Marathon

Greeks   Persians

When the Greeks came down from the hills and the Medes saw they had no cavalry or archers, they considered them lunatics facing utter destruction. The generals Aristides and Themistocles went to the center of the plain with very few troops. After they had marched some distance toward the enemy—to the astonishment of the Persians—the Greeks broke into an all-out sprint shouting "On sons of Hellenes! Fight for the freedom of your country."

Although Aristides and Themistocles' men fought bravely, the sheer numbers of the Persian troops forced them to retreat—as planned. The Persians, by chasing the Greek center, were drawn out so their inferior guards had to move into position to cover the flanks of the elite troops. When Miltiades saw this, he ordered the bulk of his soldiers to charge into the Persian sides (*see* diagram above). This maneuver split their center and as a result, the Athenians surrounded the elite troops. Although trapped they fought fiercely, but these previously invincible forces finally turned and fled for the safety of their ships. And *panic* ensued among the Persians. The Greeks chased them to the beach where the hardest fighting took place. Here Aeschylus' brother was cut to pieces and the polemarch Callimachos was slaughtered. Nevertheless, the Greeks drove the Persians from the plain of Marathon and captured seven ships in one of the greatest upset victories in human history. Historians believe these "elite" Persian troops were the "Immortal 10,000"—

The Burial Mound at Marathon

On white marble is an inscription by the poet Simonides:

*Fighting in the forefront of the Hellenes, the Athenians
at Marathon destroyed the might of the gold-bearing Medes.*

the same ones who fought at Thermopylae. The name arises in a remarkable manner. Any Immortal killed or injured was immediately replaced, so the *number* was kept constant at 10,000. Yet, as the Greeks demonstrated, the *number* might be immortal, but not the actual Persian troops.

After every battle comes the arithmetic: the body count. Herodotus tells us the Athenians lost 192 men, the Plataeans 11, the Persians a staggering 6,400. The Athenians buried their dead on the plain in a mound that still exists and serves as the starting point for their modern marathon races. Not since the days of the Trojan War were Hellenic men buried outside their city walls. But all Greeks treat this plain as virtually holy ground. The Plataeans interned their dead in a smaller mound near the foot of Penteli Mountain. It was the Persian custom, however, to leave the enemy dead as food for vultures, wolves, and lions. So these invaders were amazed when they learned that the Greeks had buried all 6,400 Persians on the plain itself, a grave where each had fallen. This was a sign of respect for a fellow warrior, but more a show of deference for the dead and an indication of the value for *all* human life.

THE DEAD AND THE BURIED

"God damn you Persian bastards—stay and fight!" Epios raced to clutch the stern of a ship just as it pulled out of his reach and away to deeper water. "We kicked your sorry asses! We won! Free men always win—tell Darius that the Athenians did this to his army and to send real men next time, not slaves!" The old warrior roared after them and banged the butt of his spear into the sand, just as an angry stag stamps his hooves.

"You sound like Odysseus taunting the Cyclopes Polyphemus. Calm down. They'll be back, you know. There will be another time. Arrogance always needs a second lesson.

"I'm exhausted. This damn running up and down the plain with this massive spear and heavy shield. I'm too old for this nonsense," his small friend panted while staggering to cast his equipment aside. Adding, "It's fortunate you didn't reach that ship."

In a quieter voice Epios said, "Rest here on this rock."

"I said it's lucky you couldn't reach that ship. Aeschylus' brother caught one and a Persian leaned over the side and cut off his hand, so he bled to death. Up the beach near the captured ships, some fellow warriors have gathered his pieces and laid them out."

"Does Aeschylus know?"

"I think so. He's nearby. I saw someone gather the gory pieces and put them on the beach," Phemios replied.

"I'll find out. You rest here."

Epios was gone for some time but the minstrel could see him up the beach talking to various soldiers. Phemios stretched and flexed his cramped fingers fearing he might have permanently ruined his musical ability by carrying the massive 12-foot spear. From fatigue and thirst, he sank into a reverie on life and death all around him. He was aware of the epic scale of the Athenian triumph, and that the death of these Persians gave freedom and a future to all Greeks. But here he was sitting in the sunlight at the seashore, waves gently lapping at his feet, birds singing overhead, while blood, gore, and corpses were everywhere. "What a strange, horrible, marvelous world this is," he thought. Then anger entered his mind—a bright, fiery anger toward the vengeful lunatic Darius whose arrogance had caused all these Athenian, Plataean, and Persian deaths. After this his fury softened while reflecting on the ephemeral nature of human life; a poem by his friend Simonides drifted through his mind:

> Long, long and dreary is the night
>   That waits us in the silent grave;
> Few, and of rapid flight,
>   The years from death we save.
> Short—ah, how short—that fleeting space;
> And when man's little race
> Is run, and Death's grim portals o'er him close,
> How lasting his repose!
> Simonides (translated by J.H. Merivale)

"Phemios, are you all right?'

"Yes, yes. Just resting." Then he added, "What a short, miserable life these poor Medes had. No wonder their officers must literally whip them into battle. Why should they fight—they have nothing to live for or dream about. Why is life so incredibly unfair? I can rationally understand it, but I can't emotionally accept it. It's immoral. Any god who would allow this to happen is either impotent or wicked.

"We'll discuss philosophy later—I have news. Miltiades has already left for undefended Athens racing to arrive before the Persians in their ships. We're to stay here with our deme of Themistocles and that of Aristides as a reward for carrying the weight of the battle today. And—you'll love this—we can take whatever we want from the dead Medes, but Aristides has been put in charge of all the wealth found in their tents."

Phemios slouched down, "I refuse to take trinkets from the dead. But thank Zeus we don't have to quick march to Athens—I wouldn't make it."

"Don't celebrate yet. We are to collect, count, and bury our dead in a single mound as a memorial. And we're to bury their dead as well, all of them—it's the only decent thing to do."

THE MARATHON

The deeds of the Children of Odysseus at Marathon still inspire writers, poets, and artists even after more than two millennia. The English poet Robert Browning was particularly impressed with the legendary runner Pheidippides who after the battle still had enough strength to run the 26 miles to Athens and proclaim their victory. What follows are the last two stanzas of Browning's poem "Pheidippides":

Yes, he fought on the Marathon day:
So, when Persia was dust, all cried "To Acropolis!
Run, Pheidippides, one race more! the meed [reward] is thy due!
'Athens is saved, thank Pan,' go shout!" He flung down his shield,
Ran like fire once more: and the space 'twixt the Fennel-field
And Athens was stubble again, a field which a fire runs through,
Till in he broke: "Rejoice, we conquer!" Like wine thro' clay,
Joy in his blood bursting his heart, he died—the bliss!

So, to this day, when friend meets friend, the word of salute
Is still "Rejoice!"—his word which brought rejoicing indeed.
So is Pheidippides happy forever,—the noble strong man

Who could race like a god, bear the face of a god, whom a god loved so well,
He saw the land saved he had helped to save, and was suffered to tell
Such tidings, yet never decline, but, gloriously as he began,
So to end gloriously—once to shout, thereafter be mute:
"Athens is saved!"—Pheidippides dies in the shout for his meed.

The God referred to in line twelve was Pan, whom Pheidippides encountered during his earlier run from Athens to Sparta and back (240 miles) in two days. Pan was the God of shepherds' fields and wild places where the night noises of owls and wolves and other creatures can induce a feeling of panic—the same *pan*ic the "invincible" Persians felt during their absolute rout by the Athenians.

Browning's poem "Pheidippides" inspired Baron Pierre de Coubertin, the founder of the modern Olympic Games, to create a footrace of 26 miles called "the Marathon." The ancient world had no such event.

All this is a wonderful story, but that's all it is. We know Herodotus wrote of Pheidippides dash to Sparta and back to Athens, but there isn't a word about his Marathon sprint. And this is too significant a story for the great historian to have overlooked. This victory was such an unexpected outcome that it inspired later authors, like Plutarch and Lucian, to bring out the tall tales. Nevertheless, there is much to learn here. Let's see what it is.

Every one of my readers doubted part of this story—yes that means you! What part is that? Why, the anecdote about Pheidippides meeting the pastoral deity Pan. All modern readers are *atheists* with respect to this field God or all other gods—myself included.

Pheidippides on Marathon Road

We are certain Pan was an invention from the mind of the oxy-gen-deprived runner. Oh, how easy it is to view other cultures' truths as mere myths. Would that we could do the same with our sacred "truths."

THE GOLDEN AGE OF GREECE

Rewriting history is a hobby for many dictators, most cultures, and all religions. In this wild maelstrom of fiction and fact, how can the reader stay afloat? Modern historians seem to enjoy downgrading the Greek victories over the Persians as recorded by Herodotus. After all, they say, Herodotus was Greek and the Persians wrote no histories—but what do we know *positively*? This period of history gives us two great truths. The first is a succession of Hellenic victories whenever Greek met Persian in a major battle:

Marathon—Triumph on land in 490 BCE by Miltiades
Salamis—Victory at sea in 480 BCE by Themistocles
Plataea—Victory on land in 479 BCE by Pausanias

As Phemios said, "There'll be another time. Arrogance always needs another lesson." Sometimes a third, it seems. Even in defeat, the world regards the heroic stand of Leonidas at Thermopylae a victory. It's noteworthy that Herodotus, the father of history, made every effort to be evenhanded by showing both sides of the war. This is something the authors of the Old Testament never did. It was white hats and victory for the Hebrews, black hats and death for everyone else. Herodotus set a higher standard.

These three battles *were not*, to contra quote Matthew Arnold's poem "Dover Beach," a case "Where ignorant armies clash by night." The future of European civilization hung in the balance. Far from offering the Persians earth and water—their Zoroastrian religious symbols for submission—the Greeks gave them spears and swords and that made all the difference. Those who submitted would have recognized Persian power and do-minion over everything—even their lives would belong to the emperor. Furthermore, had Darius won the Battle of Marathon or Xerxes Salamis and Plataea, the reader would probably be a

Zoroastrian worshipping under the monotheism of Ahura Mazda. Sound familiar? I think not and happily so.

So in retrospect it wasn't just the Persian military victory that was feared. Rather, it was their monotheistic religion: an early form of Zoroastrianism that mandated top-down servitude. This would have prohibited the freedom and creativity necessary for art and science, philosophy, sports, and politics. Persian concepts of a single God, judgment, heaven and hell heavily influenced the Abrahamic religions. Assume for a moment that the Persians had defeated the Greeks. Certainly at some later date, with its empire in decline, the Persians would have withdrawn from Greece to their home territory. Yet the virus of their monotheistic religion would have remained with its moral and intellectual baggage preventing the Golden Age of Greece.

I mentioned above there were two great truths we know from this period in history. The first was the trinity of astonishing victories at Marathon, Salamis, and Plataea. After this, the Persians never returned to *mainland* Greece—arrogance had learned its lesson. The second truth was the inspiring effect these military triumphs had on Greek society, especially Athenian. To understand something of how these Children of Odysseus felt, imagine yourself having won the Nobel Prize for your ideas or an Oscar for your acting. The Greeks sensed they had won both, but now what were they to do? Quite simply, build a new world of ideas in art, science, mathematics, music, writing, sculpture, and architecture. Percy Bysshe Shelley said it best:

> The period which intervened between the birth of Pericles [495 BCE] and the death of Aristotle [322 BCE], is undoubtedly, whether considered in itself, or with reference to the effects which it has produced upon the subsequent destinies of civilized man, the most memorable in the history of the world. [3]

This was the Golden Age of Greece.

As an example of Shelley's Hellenic passion consider the following. So certain were the Persian generals Datis and Artaphernes of their triumph over the Athenians that they brought their own marble for a victory monument in one of their 600 ships. In contrast to this monument that never was, the

Greeks built the ancient world's greatest structure—the Parthenon. The creative energy for this momentous undertaking was their victory over the Persians. Some Greek scholars believe it is significant that apart from the charioteers, precisely 192 male figures adorn the cavalcade on the frieze, which is the same number of Athenians killed in the judgment at Marathon. The Parthenon Frieze is unique. Created in the most original and expansive era in European art, it has no equal in size and complexity throughout the ancient world.

This Golden Age gave the modern world democracy and the concept of human rights. From Aristotle and others we learned empirical science. From Hipparchus and others we acquired our basic knowledge of astronomy. Aeschylus, Sophocles, and Euripides gave us not only the concept of tragedy but also some of the world's greatest plays. Athens gave us Pericles, the undisputed champion of democracy and the arts in the ancient world. From Socrates and Plato we were educated in philosophy and the life of the mind. Herodotus and Thucydides gave us history. From Phidias we acquired architecture and the world's most elegant structure, the Parthenon. From Pythagoras to Euclid we learned deductive reasoning and developed the mathematics that unfolds our empirical science and explains the world. And lastly, all Greeks gave us the Olympic Games and the exhilaration of competitive sport. In contrast, the Persian Empire gave us Darius, Xerxes, Artaxerxes (I, II, and so on), and a whole gang of sociopathic butchers. Despite all this, and more, periodically some damn fool will say or imply that our heritage is entirely Christian. The English philosopher Alfred North Whitehead stated, "I consider Christian theology to be one of the greatest disasters of the human race." [4] Better we had our religion from the twelve Olympian Gods; at least they provided some comic relief, unlike the entirely humorless Bible or the angry Qur'an.

Western civilization has endured this Christian religious burden since declaring the twelve Olympians myths. Yet almost everything of value in our modern society had its origin in Classical Greek thought. Even the word *democracy* is Greek and means rule by the people. We stress individualism and intelligence. Odysseus, the hero of Homer's epic poem, was the archetypal for these qualities, the man who ended the Trojan War with a stratagem and got home safely to his wife and son. In some very real sense, you and I are the Children of Odysseus. We are the heirs of the Greek ethic of individualism, democracy, and freedom. We come from Athens not Jerusalem!

After visiting the Hawaiian Islands and observing the work of the missionaries, Mark Twain drily noted, "How sad it is to think of the multitudes who have gone to their graves in this beautiful island and never knew there was a hell." The Classical Greeks were like the Hawaiians before the missionaries came, happy without hell. This could have been our heritage, but then St. Paul arrived.

There is something yet to say about Aeschylus, this towering Greek genius. Fighting, for him, wasn't a matter of pressing buttons, or pulling triggers. His was the hand-to-hand combat

Aeschylus

he experienced at Marathon, Salamis, and perhaps even Plataea. So when he wrote about such things, they were real, they were personal. History says he wrote 90 plays, but only seven survive—the one I find most remarkable is *Prometheus Bound*. This tale tells of the Titan in the title defying Zeus and giving humankind fire, writing, mathematics, medicine, science, and the arts of civilization. Prometheus spoke reason and compassion to power and suffered horrible consequences. Aeschylus' dramas were trilogies plus a satyr or short farce at the close. The second play of this trilogy is lost, but history calls it *Prometheus Unbound*. (Shelley, quoted earlier, wrote an epic drama of the same name as if to complement Aeschylus' vanished work.) By his actions at Marathon, the tragedian had shown what he thought of dictators and slavery, and this meant more to him than all his immoral dramas. When he died, his tombstone said only this:

I fought at Marathon.

I Would Choose

Plato said, "I thank God that I was born Greek and not barbarian, freeman and not slave, man and not woman; but above all, that I was born in the age of Socrates." These were his values—we almost certainly wouldn't agree with all of them. Time changes *some* values. You may disagree and desire to totally adhere to biblical or Qur'anic values? Read the Pentateuch or the Qur'an and try to hold fast to their values of stoning and killing. See how long it is before the authorities incarcerate you as a homicidal maniac.

Not all values are equal. I would choose freedom over servitude. I would choose truth over falsehood. I would choose compassion over cruelty. I trust you would too. This has *nothing* to do with race, but everything to do with culture and religion—skin color is skin deep. Genetically all peoples are created equal. We haven't had time to differentiate significantly since we came out of Africa 75,000 years ago. There is no such thing as a Muslim child, a Catholic child, or a Seventh-day Adventist child. This labeling is child abuse—a value I also do not adhere to. As Rousseau declared, "Man is born free, but everywhere he is in chains." How eagerly society forges these chains to shape a child into a communist, a Nazi, a Christian, a Muslim, a Jew, or whatever. Where is their compassion?

Not all cultures are equal because not all values are equal. I would choose Greece and not Persia. I would choose Athens and not Sparta. I would choose America and not Nazi Germany. I would choose Europe and not the Middle East. I trust you would too.

Number Nonsense

As we have seen in this first chapter, the Athenians and Spartans repelled the Persians saving Greece for the flowering of her Golden Age. Nonetheless, a profound Asiatic influence came into Hellenic culture before Marathon from one of her own: Pythagoras. He was possibly the first genius of Western culture, with his blend of high intellect and high idiocy. To paraphrase Bertrand Russell: when he was good, he was very, very good, but when he was bad, he was dreadful.

Pythagoras was born (c. 570 BCE) on the Greek island of Samos, which is one mile off the coast of Asia Minor (modern Turkey). His culture was that of the Ionian Enchantment with reason and science. This is where *abstract* reasoning began—that is reasoning with numbers. Rest assured that millennia before him the Babylonians knew of hundreds of particular triangles (e.g., 3, 4, 5) where his famous theorem was true (i.e., $3^2+4^2=5^2$). So, what did he do? Pythagoras proved *for all time* that the truth of the theorem bearing his name depends only and always on the triangle being right-angled. This was history's first instance of anyone proving anything. It was a remarkable achievement!

This legendary intellectual hero learned much of significance from his Asiatic neighbors, one mile off the coast of Samos. But he also imbued their mystic tendencies that ran all through his work and left a bizarre legacy. The mystic element entered Greek philosophy by his invitation. Russell summed up Pythagoras' weirdness in his *History of Western Philosophy*:

> Pythagoras is one of the most interesting and puzzling men in history. Not only are the traditions concerning him an almost inextricable mixture of truth and falsehood, but even in their barest and least disputable form they present us with a very curious psychology. He may be described, briefly, as a combination of Einstein and Mrs. Eddy [Mary Baker Eddy, creator of Christian Science]. He founded a religion, of which the main tenets were the transmigration of souls and the sinfulness of eating beans. His religion was embodied in a religious order, which, here and there, acquired control of the State and established a rule of the saints. But the unregenerate hankered after beans, and sooner or later rebelled. [5]

Pythagoras' strangeness encompassed much more than beans. Russell lists a few of his taboos: not to break bread, not to walk on highways, not to pick up what has fallen, and so on.

The man behind these rules is not the austere logician we learned in secondary school. This individual is a devotee of the occult. Oh, that our teachers had revealed this underside of Pythagoras, so we might have shown more interest in his theorem. Yet as youthful rebels, we would have said that he was not so much out of his tree, as driving away from the orchard at warp speed.

Modern apologists for Pythagoras' obsession with bean abstinence cite the blood disorder favism caused by ingesting fava beans. This is reminiscent of the 4000-year old Jewish ban on pork, often incorrectly reported to be an avoidance of the parasitic disease trichinosis. Yet, all religions have strange dietary laws, which they later try to justify on scientific grounds. But let's be honest, heaven just hates ham and apparently beans too. Sadly, there will be no pork and beans in paradise!

Mathematics can lead to mysticism and it did with the Pythagoreans. I'm not writing about trifles like magic, lucky, or evil numbers; nor magic squares, whose modern incarnations, Sudoku puzzles, appear in the daily newspapers. I also don't mean tedious numerology nonsense—although we'll see some of this in a later section on a subject titled gematria. Let's call all this the lower foolishness.

How does mysticism arise in mathematics, our most rigorous and respected enterprise? Consider geometry, the preeminent domain of the Greeks. Geometry concerns itself with *perfect* circles, *perfect* lines, and *perfect* polygons. But surely no matter how sharp your pencil, how exact your compass, or how precise your straight edge, *you cannot draw anything perfect*. No such sensible objects exist. Magnification will expose their unruliness. As Bertrand Russell says, "This suggests the view that all exact reasoning applies to ideal as opposed to sensible objects; it is natural to go further, and to argue that thought is nobler than sense, and the objects of thought more real than those of sense perception." [6] And intuition is superior to observation. This door, once opened, lets in other goblins. The idea of the eternal comes from numbers that go on forever and are neither destroyed nor created. Integers are eternal; exist outside of time. And where would that be? In the mind of God, of course! Let's refer to this as the "higher foolishness." Judge the following two famous quotations illustrating this point: God is a geometer (Plato) and God does arithmetic (Carl Gauss).

I could have listed exactly 7 such examples in the previous sentence. This number 7—not the quotations themselves—is part of the lower foolishness found throughout Western culture. The following cases show an ancient fondness by the Greeks for using 7 as a quantity implying *completeness*:

- The 7 Wise Men
- The 7 Wonders of the World
- Odysseus spent 7 years as a prisoner of the nymph Circe
- *Seven Against Thebes*, a play by Aeschylus
- The 7 Sisters, daughters of Atlas
- Even their horses' iron shoes were fastened with 7 nails.

From time to time, the keepers of lists changed particular Wise Men and certain Wonders of the World by deletion and addition. Yet, the outstanding point is that the number of each was always kept constant at 7. This implies the greater priority of the list's total over who or what might actually be in it (like the 10,000 Immortals). The Romans had their own 7 Sages, not to be confused with the Greeks' 7 Wise Men. Legend says 7 followers of Romulus raped 7 Sabine women and afterward took them for brides. (This is the basis for the Broadway musical *Seven Brides for Seven Brothers*.) Since the Romans built their city on 7 hills, they could hardly avoid this number. Recall the passage about the Harlot of Babylon (Rome):

> *This calls for a mind with wisdom.*
> *The 7 heads are 7 hills on which the woman sits.*
> Revelation 17:9

Our Western culture is adorned with a great variety of 7s. We see 7 colors in the rainbow. The beautiful constellation of stars called the 7 Sisters or Pleiades consists of only 6 naked-eye objects. Yet we insist, to keep the number right, that the 7th is hiding. On more earthly matters, biologists divide the animal kingdom into 7 parts. Musicians sing do, re, mi, fa, so, la, ti and start the scale over with another do, an octave higher. Writers pen plays about the *7 Ages of Man*, and sailors speak of the *7 Seas*. Movie producers say, and legends affirm, it is always *Snow White and the 7 Dwarfs*. Everyone considers 7 to be a lucky number. To be born the 7th son of a 7th son of a 7th son is said to be a triple blessing. I'm sure the reader can add to this already extensive inventory.

The Islamic people, the descendants of Abraham and Hagar's son Ishmael, have also inherited this peculiar number tradition.

Their religion tells them they must—at least once in a lifetime—go to Mecca and circle their sacred cubical rock (the Kaaba) exactly 7 times. And the central prayer of Islam, the Fatihah, has 7 verses.

Although we are barely aware of it, in Western and Islamic society the number 7 represents *completeness* of a list or a task. Remember the Creation week in Genesis had 7 days. Curiously, centuries ago Shakespeare knew all this harmless foolishness. In his celebrated play *King Lear*, there is a scene where the Fool and the King discuss the number of stars. These are probably the 7 stars of the constellation Orion referred to in Revelation 1:16: "In his right hand he held 7 stars."

The Fool speaks first:
The reason why the 7 stars are no
more than 7 is a pretty reason.
And the wise King replies:
Because they are not 8.
The Fool says:
Yes indeed. Thou wouldst make a good Fool.

Shakespeare's wise Fool said it exactly right. We should not force our cultural predispositions on the natural world.

All literature is culturally influenced. But surely it greatly detracts from the divine origins claim of the Bible and the Qur'an to give a mundane number like 7 such prominence. God, Allah, and Yahweh were all, apparently, arithmetically challenged and culturally influenced. Or one would almost believe these Holy Scriptures were purely a product of human invention!

After this tour of the low lands, let's return to the higher foolishness of mysticism and mathematics. Russell accurately informs us that this potent mixture originated with the Pythagoreans but it stamped itself on the religious philosophy of Plato, St. Augustine, Aquinas, Descartes, Spinoza, and Leibniz. This intellectualized theology is an unusual feature of Western thought and quite different from the simple mysticism of Asia.

The idea that the eternal and the perfect are revealed only to the intellect and never to the senses has been a destructive force ever since Pythagoras. And Pythagoreanism in its many incarnations was active for hundreds of years. Most Greeks would not dirty their hands in the real world of the senses—this was the realm of slaves and servants. Deduction of a purely intellectual kind can lead to mysticism; induction by examining the real world usually leads to science. The Greeks generally preferred the former. When you have the science of the Industrial Revolution, you don't need slaves.

RELIGIOUS INVASIONS

There is no time and no place in history when you can say these peoples were entirely Asiatic and those were wholly European. The peoples of these two continents have been intermingling deep into prehistory. All Europeans must have come from or passed through Asia to reach Europe. This is not the problem.

There have been *at least five* major *religious invasions* from Asia into Europe. In particular, Mesopotamia or the Middle East seems a virtual hatchery for faith and fanaticism. It's the birthplace of Judaism, Christianity, and Islam not to mention the earlier Zoroastrianism or the much later Baha'i Faith plus a plethora of minor cults and lunacies. This is the problem. It appears the Middle East could sell franchises on religion. What follows is a chronological list of these intrusions:

ASIATIC RELIGIOUS INVASIONS OF EUROPE

   I   The Pythagoreans and their secret society

   II   The Persians and their Zoroastrianism

   III   Judeo-Christian invasion

   IV   The first Islamic invasions of Europe

   V   The second Islamic invasion of Europe

We have explored the initial two on this list, and in subsequent chapters, we'll make an inquiry into the remaining three. The final one is of particular moment—the modern immigrant and refugee invasion from the Middle East. The parlance in vogue for this fifth invasion is a *clash of civilizations*—East versus West! But this is not the case. There is a clash, but we have confused the combatants. Many in the West do not intend to fight for the preservation of Christianity; some in the East feel the same about Islam. Let the devil take them both. What we will defend are freedom, democracy, and the values of the Enlightenment* versus submission, dictatorship, and the ideals of the Dark Ages. This is the old battle of the Children of Odysseus versus the Army of the Night. I would make my stand in the light. I trust you would too.

---

* The Enlightenment was a movement of the 18th century Europe that emphasized the use of reason to examine accepted doctrines and traditions such as religion, and that brought about many humanitarian reforms.

CHAPTER—2

FREEDOM AND AUTHORITY

Freedom is the battle cry of the oppressed. Freedom is the wellspring of creativity. Freedom is the most emotionally charged word in the English language. At Marathon, Aeschylus says the Greeks advanced upon the Persians shouting:

For freedom, sons of Greece,
Freedom for country, children, wives,
Freedom for worship, for our father's graves.

The philosopher Jean-Jacques Rousseau declared, "Man was born free, and he is everywhere in chains."

What is this thing called freedom? Who are these oppressors? How does freedom engender creativity? Why should we care? Freedom can also be the battle cry of the scoundrel. And the oppressors may see themselves as paternal liberators bringing "truth" to the masses. Furthermore, authorities often view creativity as a threat to social stability. Paradoxically, after one or more generations as slaves or free men, we often don't comprehend our condition—we think this is the natural order of things. Those new to freedom will die to keep it; those long enslaved often don't realize it. Slavery can be as much a state of mind as of body. By propaganda and half-truths, the majority of slaves can be convinced of anything. Goethe said, "None are more hopelessly enslaved than those who falsely believe they are free."

Make no mistake, freedom is at the core of democracy; it is the center of our happiness and reason. This rich soil gives birth to the greatest art and science. Lose it and you are just another slave in Siberia's gulag archipelago.

History is a *written record* of the past—everything else is prehistory. This record is one long, remarkable drama, worldwide, terrifying, horrible, but occasionally heroic and compassionate. Great historians are seldom read today even by scholars because their works are too long, too tedious, and often too dull.

Moreover, we cannot begin to cope with the voluminous productions of modern historians whose works (in all languages) presently surpass 10,000 tomes per year. How can we hope to learn anything of the past in this immense tangle of facts, lies, distortions, and incomplete truths?

The situation is far worse than the previous difficulty implies. Chaos theory tells us that events *never exactly repeat* themselves. Consider two raindrops on a windowpane. These will always traverse different paths downward—always. The probability of the two drops having the same number of molecules— about one in a gazillion—is vanishingly small. This number determines the drop's mass and hence gravity's pull. Even if their masses were the same, they couldn't be at identical heights on the windowpane. Why? Precision depends on the measuring instrument, so *all* measurements are approximate numbers. If we grant even this, the glass pane will have different contours at the microscopic level, determining the course of the drops, just as the Earth itself does, establishing the route of rivers.

In the early 60s Edward Lorenz, a meteorologist with mathematical inclinations, made a landmark discovery. He found that no matter how much data he collected, his weather predictions— and everyone else's—would *never* be accurate in the long run. And the cliché *in the long run* could mean as little as a few days. This is not a matter of refining our models or discovering new ideas; it's part of the nature of things. Neither the awe-inspiring power of the Cray supercomputers, nor the mythic reliability of the *Farmers' Almanac,* nor the alleged absolute verisimilitude of your Aunt Mildred's corns will prevail! In the end, the unpredictability of the weather will always triumph.

Into this universe, and Why not knowing,
Nor Whence, like Water willy-nilly flowing;
And out of it, as Wind along the Waste,
I know not Whither, willy-nilly blowing.
Omar Khayyám: *Rubáiyát 29*

A folk wisdom resonates to the beat of the butterfly's wing, an echo we can all hear. Had I not gone to that party, I would never have met my wife. Had I left the house a few seconds earlier/later, I would have been involved in the car accident. Had I not taken my daughter to the dentist that morning, I would have been at the World Trade Center.

In Benjamin Franklin's *Poor Richard's Almanac* for 1758 you can read:

> And again, he, Richard, adviseth to circumspection and care, even in the smallest matters, because sometimes a little neglect may breed great mischief, adding, for want of a nail, the shoe was lost; for want of a shoe the horse was lost; and for want of a horse the rider was lost, being overtaken and slain by the enemy, all for want of care about a horseshoe nail.

In this homily, *For Want of a Nail*, we hear a clear reverberation of the Butterfly Effect. Similar earlier versions predate Franklin by at least 150 years; some are probably centuries older.

Ideas gain power when they're clearly articulated and used: Edward Lorenz did this for the Butterfly Effect. This power is a broad indication of an idea's worth and longevity. New visions are then created; former structures are rebuilt; others demolished. History is one such house.

Human history is an excellent example of non-periodic behavior. Civilizations may rise and fall, but *events never happen in the same way twice*. Small actions can change the world—such as the birth of a new virus! Some historians thought that the heroes and despots of previous ages controlled the unfolding of events. Others considered that these defenders and destroyers were really carried along by the flux like wood chips in a great whirlwind of waves and water. Sensitivity to initial conditions— and there is a near infinite regress of these—speaks more positively of this second view. But truly, neither alternative commands history: minuscule actions and/or broad events often rule for a while until shoved aside by new usurpers.

By finding patterns in time's passage, men and women thought to understand the events of the past. They longed to give existence meaning by discovering cycles and consistency in their lives, in the life of their country, and in the lives of previous civilizations. From Daniel in the distant past to Arnold Toynbee in our time, historians have known this to be their major task: find history's design. Down through the centuries they have pursued this chimera only to have it vanish in the flap of a butterfly's wing.

Oh, like the weather we may know the seasons, different climates, and the average of this and that but never any of the intriguing details and definitely not the long-term outcome.

The 5th century BCE Greek philosopher Heraclitus in his maxim "Man never bathes in the same stream twice" [*] immortalized this constantly changing cascade of events (chaos). So complete was Heraclitus' belief in the flux that he declared the sun to be created new each day like the morning's cooking fire. For him the only unchanging thing was change itself.

Nothing ever truly repeats. History lives in the same house as weather. Every path is unique; every event, distinct; every life, original! Finding patterns where none exists is part of our biological heritage. We often see more than is there. Humans are not passive observers of the landscape, but active participants in it. We dance, but we dance together. The power of the scientific method is its ability to disentangle the dancers: the subjective from the objective. This gives us freedom.

FREEDOM AND OBEDIENCE

Everyone has a half-dozen or so favorite movies they will always remember, ones that affected them emotionally and perhaps intellectually. One of mine is *The House on Garibaldi Street* adapted from a book of the same name written by Isser Harel, the head of Mossad, the Israeli secret intelligence service. This is a spellbinding account of the Israeli capture of Adolf Eichmann, written succinctly by the man who led the operation. In 1960, the Mossad apprehended Eichmann—hiding under the alias Ricardo Klement—in Buenos Aires, and spirited him away to

---

[*] Some wit remarked, "Not even once."

Adolf Eichmann

Israel disguised as an El Al crewmember to stand trial for war crimes and crimes against humanity.

Eichmann stood in judgment before an Israeli court in 1961. The trial, with its recitation of the horrifying crimes the Nazis had committed against Jews, homosexuals, gypsies, and others, brought out a riotous emotional response among the Jewish people—many of whom had had their entire family gassed. What follows is from the Jewish virtual library on Eichmann:

Memories that had been repressed burst forth in the courtroom. People screamed and cried and wanted to attack and kill Eichmann in his bulletproof glass box. The whole story of Eichmann's directing the "Final Solution" came out into the open. He asked for understanding and mercy from the Jewish people—claiming that he had acted "under orders," that he was just a "cog in the machine," that he had only done as he had been told—that it was the Nazi government's fault, and not his own for what had been perpetrated on the Jewish people.

The mantra of the monsters at the Nuremburg War Crimes Tribunal was always the same: "We were only following orders." It became a common refrain, one that Eichmann used repeatedly, and one we will investigate shortly. The strutting arrogance of the man cited above with his jackboots, high hat, uniform, leather coat, and medals was now gone. The fawning minions ready to execute his every wish had vanished. The Übermensch of the "Final Solution" was now Ricardo Klement, the man pictured at the right, obsequious, willing to please, and begging for mercy. Under the pen

Ricardo Klement

of political theorist Hannah Arendt, Eichmann/Klement's personality at the trial gave rise to the infamous phrase "the banality of evil." *Obersturmbannführer* Adolf Eichmann, SS number 45326, architect of the Holocaust, was dead.

Eichmann received more mercy than he ever gave—his trial lasted several months. He was executed by hanging on May 31, 1962, and his ashes broadcast into the Mediterranean Sea far off the coast of Israel. His last words were "I die believing in God."

There exists a deep paradox in this portrait of Eichmann. Before joining the Nazi party in 1932, he was a none-too-bright salesman for the Vacuum Oil Company. Life offered him few opportunities because he had dropped out of high school and failed at vocational training. When the prosecutor revealed these facts during his trial, he blushed—having previously presented himself as an intellectual of sorts. After the war, and living in Argentina as Ricardo Klement, he had a variety of jobs: laundryman, rabbit farmer, and such. What could possibly have transformed the demigod of the death camps into this milquetoast? Was he a rotten apple? Was he in a rotten barrel? Or was it both? What in the human psyche could permit such a complete character transformation?

Stanley Milgram

Enter Stanley Milgram, the man who discovered the answer. Milgram was born in 1933 to Jewish immigrants in the Bronx, New York City. Despite the rough neighborhood and his poor family, he excelled academically, constantly winning scholarships. Ultimately, he became a professor of social psychology at Yale University where he conducted his most famous and controversial experiment.

In July 1961, three months after the start of the sensational Eichmann judgment at Jerusalem, Milgram began his experiment. This was to devise a study to answer the question "Did Eichmann and his accomplices have a *mutual* intent with regard to the goals of the Holocaust?" In other words, Milgram thought that perhaps their mantra of "I was just following orders" might be true—at least in their minds.

Let's describe the setup of his experiment. It involved three people: the experimenter (the authority figure in the white lab coat), the learner (an actor), and the teacher (or mark if you wish). The authority figure and the actor were always the same two people. However, Milgram recruited the teachers through newspaper ads offering $4.00 for an hour of their time—remember this was 1961.

Everyone met and the experimenter had the other two draw lots to determine who would be the teacher and who the learner. But both pieces of paper were marked teacher. Of course, the actor always said his lot read learner—so the cover story developed. The actor/learner went to another room to be strapped into a chair with electrical wires, but was sure to tell the teacher he had a heart condition. The experimenter then gave the teacher a 45-volt shock to appreciate what the learner would *supposedly* receive. With a list of word pairs in hand, the teacher began reading these to the learner/actor. The initial word of each pair was read followed by four likely answers. By pressing a button, the learner indicated his response. If *incorrect*, the teacher gave the actor a shock, with the voltage increasing in 15-volt increments. If *correct*, the teacher would read another word pair. The electro-shock generator had nowhere to go but up—up to a stunning, if not lethal, 450 volts.

Fortunately, unknown to the teacher, the learner/actor received no shocks whatsoever. After the actor went into the room by himself, he set a tape recorder integrated with the electro-shock generator, which played standard responses for each voltage level. After several voltage increases, the actor would begin banging on the wall separating him from the teacher while screaming, ostensibly, in pain. Eventually after thumping on the wall several times while complaining about his heart condition, all responses would cease. The experimenter instructed the teacher to interpret this as a negative response and to continue with the voltage increases.

Milgram designed the protocol between teachers (marks) to be rigorously similar. If the teacher indicated he was reluctant to continue, the experimenter gave him the following standard responses, in order:

1. Please *continue.*
2. The experiment requires you to *continue.*
3. It is absolutely essential that you *continue.*
4. You have no other choice, you *must* go on.

If the teacher still wished to cease the experiment after all four verbal prods, the experimenter halted. Or else, it was stopped after the teacher had given the maximum 450-volt shock *three times* to the now silent actor.

To know how meaningful his results were, Milgram had to establish a baseline. So, before running his experiment, he polled senior Yale University psychology majors—people who should know what the results might be. All speculated that only a few, about 3 percent or less, would go all the way to a near-lethal 450 volts. Recall household voltage is about 120 in North America, and that really hurts.

In his first of 19 such experiments with variations, 65 percent (26 out of 40) teachers gave the final massive 450-voltage shock *three times.* They obeyed the authority of the man in the white lab coat even when the actions insisted upon went against their deepest moral convictions not to harm others. Only a single person steadfastly refused to go beyond 300-volt level. Let us call him a Milgram hero.

Milgram summarized all this in his 1974 article, "The peril of Obedience."

> The legal and philosophic aspects of obedience are of enormous importance, but they say very little about how most people behave in concrete situations. I set up a simple experiment at Yale University to test how much pain an ordinary citizen would inflict on another person simply because he was ordered to by an experimental scientist. Stark authority was pitted against the subjects' [teachers'] strongest moral imperatives against helping others, with the subjects' ears ringing with the screams of the victims, authority won more often than not. The extreme willingness of adults to go to almost any lengths on the command of authority constitutes the chief finding of the study and the fact most urgently demanding explanation.

> Ordinary people, simply doing their jobs, and without any particular hostility on their part, can become agents in a terrible destructive process [enter Adolf Eichmann]. Moreover, even when the destructive effects of their work become patently clear, and they were asked to carry out actions incompatible with fundamental standards of morality, relatively few people have the resources necessary to resist authority. [1]

Each repetition of the experiment, regardless of time and place, confirmed the previous ones with remarkable consistency. With women participants, obedience levels did not differ meaningfully. These results revealed something deeply disturbing about most of us: *Homo sapiens* were behaving badly. It gets even worse! Stanley Milgram told the following to his friend Philip Zimbardo, a psychologist at Stanford University, about those who refused to administer the final shocks:

- None insisted that the experiment be stopped.
- None left the room to check on the condition of the victim without first requesting permission from the experimenter.

It seems even the heroes were in some form of obedience mode.

THE LUCIFER EFFECT

The idea that we are so obsequious in the presence of authority—much more than anyone previously realized—needs to be examined. Furthermore, it needs to be used in society and history to really come alive. Otherwise, it's an inert idea of limited usefulness, a dull daydream on a lazy afternoon. Undoubtedly, it explains much about Nazi cruelty arising from a great and sophisticated society that gave us Bach, Beethoven, and Brahms. Philip Zimbardo calls this the *Lucifer Effect*.

Consider Lord Acton's famous statement, "Power tends to corrupt, and absolute power corrupts absolutely." This appears to be an alternate statement of the Lucifer Effect—one is the right hand, the other the left hand of evil. They are a potent pair. And what organizations have such power and authority? You know who they are. The three most prominent are the military, political, and the religious. The latter controls this life and claims the same for the next.

Yet what is isn't what has to be. History and myth record any number of heroes. To rebel against perceived truth or supreme authority takes a great force of character. Prometheus of Greek legend had such, and if such heroes are not real, we will invent them. He is said to have brought fire and freedom to all peoples and for this, the gods had him chained to a rock where every day an eagle came and feasted on his liver.

Punishment is what gods do best. In case you have forgotten Yahweh's incredible outbursts of fury and rage, consider Zephaniah 3:6-8 (NIV):

"I have destroyed nations; their strongholds are demolished. I have left their streets deserted, with no one passing through. Their cities are laid waste; they are deserted and empty.

Of Jerusalem I thought, 'Surely you will fear me and accept correction!' Then her place of refuge would not be destroyed, nor all my punishments come upon her. But they were still eager to act corruptly in all they did.

Therefore wait for me," declares the LORD, "or the day I will stand up to testify. I have decided to assemble the nations, to gather the kingdoms and to pour out my wrath on them—all my fierce anger. The whole world will be consumed by the fire of my jealous anger."

Now that's what I call a truly angry deity. Clearly, he missed his Prozac that morning and maybe his breakfast too. Moreover, he has this wicked habit of periodic genocide. Recall Noah and the flood when he drowned every living thing except the fishes and eight people: Noah and Mrs. Noah, their sons Shem, Ham, Japheth, and their wives. (Women weren't considered important enough to have names of their own other than Mrs.) All this burning, drowning, and slaughter imply Yahweh doesn't abide by any moral standards whatsoever. As with all dictators and despots, God thinks he is above the law. Christians, Muslims, and Jews explain this by saying God moves in mysterious ways—like all sociopathic killers. Lord Acton explains it differently.

When Hollywood wished to portray God, they cast him as George Burns, the famous American comedian. Yahweh may be many things but funny he is not. The deity is *so miscast* that these movies work to hilarious effect. At one point in the film *Oh, God!* Burns, a.k.a. God, complains, "It's true. People have trouble remembering My Words. Moses had such a bad memory I had to give him tablets." Burns could have added that Moses had to go back up the mountain a second time because he smashed the original tablets in a fit of rage. Seemingly, both God and Moses had anger management issues.

Let's return to our listing of heroes: those who defy men in white lab coats, black jackboots, and red cassocks. I would recommend *Spartacus*, who led a slave revolt against the Roman Republic and was either slain in battle or afterward crucified. I would recommend *Socrates* as portrayed in Plato's dialogues. He gave the world the Socratic method of reasoned debate by question and answer. For this, the Athenian authorities accused him of corrupting the city's youth and sentenced him to death by hemlock. I would recommend the Dominican friar *Giordano Bruno* as a proponent of infinite space where every star is a sun. For this, his church burned him at the stake. I would also recommend *Galileo Galilei* for challenging the church's position on geocentrism. After being shown the instruments of Inquisitional torture twice and forced to recant, the Church placed him under house arrest for the rest of his life. I would recommend *all those* involved in the forty-two attempts on Adolf Hitler's life. And I shudder to imagine what happened to those the Gestapo captured. I would recommend *Ayaan Hirsi Ali* for confronting Islamic misogyny and the old men with long beards, flowing robes, and twisted faces while thriving under their death fatwas. Whom would you recommend? There is danger here. Because the hero having survived the Lucifer Effect and winning his/her battles, must guard against being seduced by their own success to the tyranny Lord Acton noted.

Why are heroes important? Quite simply because they profoundly inspire us. Why are wimps important? They also inspire us but in a negative way—by example they lead us to do evil. Two of Stanley Milgram's nineteen experimental variations are pertinent to these points. By changing one variable in each experiment, Milgram could tease out the relevant forces. In one variation, the teacher (mark) witnessed two previous teachers rebel. In this case, compliance fell to a mere 10 percent. Alternately, when the teacher saw just one other participant go all the way to 450 volts, compliance rose to an astounding 90 percent. Aristotle wrote that we are social animals. He could have more accurately said that we are *herd* animals. We will all go together even if it's over a precipice. You cannot be free when you are obediently following the herd. Undoubtedly, we are more sheep than goat; that's why God calls us his flock. Moreover, sheep can be sheared at any time.

What follows is a small table summarizing Milgram's most important results. They imply, among other points, that outside forces often determine whether we act as wimps or heroes—the situation is situational.

TEACHER WITNESSED	COMPLIANCE LEVELS
Heroes	10%
Neither	65%
Wimps	90%

Authorities whether military, political, or religious dislike heroes and love wimps. Heroes cause problems; shake up the status quo and interrupt coffee and cigar breaks. The powers that be loathe *anything* they can't control. The single paramount technological event in the history of humankind is the Internet. Governments are always trying to censor it, control it, or shut it down—dictatorships have nightmares about it. Conservatives petition us to avoid sex sites, Wikipedia, foreign sites, free music download sites, and now WikiLeaks, and so on. Often their motivations seem unclear as with Wikipedia. Are they trying to control information and free thought? Perhaps they want us to use Conservapedia, which I'm convinced is a joke or so highly biased that psychological help is needed for its writers.

THE BANALITY OF HEROISM

An old French adage says, "To know all is to forgive all." Nevertheless, this cannot be entirely true. *Understanding is not the same as excusing.* Why?—because it takes no account of human freedom, that 35 percent refusing to go all the way in the Milgram experiment. Human freedom is always an element in any situation. Just because we know the forces shaping Eichmann's actions, doesn't imply we can forgive him. He is the only criminal an Israel civilian court ever sentenced to death. If we are not accountable for our actions, then we may as well build statues to Adolf Hitler as to Abraham Lincoln.

As we know, if Milgram's 35 percent had witnessed a rebel first, then their refusal rate rises to 90 percent. Conclusion: we need more heroes. As Philip Zimbardo states, we must celebrate the *banality of heroism.*

Heroic behavior spreads quickly like a chain reaction. In 1940 when the Nazis put Denmark under their protectorate, the Danes refused to cooperate in the deportation of Jews. I suspect a few heroes spread their refusal by example across this small nation. Even the Danish courts severely punished what little anti-Semitism there was. Miraculously the Nazis backed off, at least temporarily, on their solution to the "Jewish problem." However, the German defeat at Stalingrad and in North Africa in 1943 emboldened the Danish resistance; this in turn led to a Nazi clampdown and ultimately the resignation of the entire Danish government. The beasts in Berlin now put Denmark under their direct rule and the Nazi answer to the "Jewish problem" went into overdrive. Some Danes went through their telephone books to warn those with Jewish-sounding names to go into hiding. Most hid for a week or two before being smuggled to Sweden, which offered asylum to all Danish Jews. Remarkably, more than 99 percent of Danish Jewry escaped the Holocaust. Some reached Sweden's shores in kayaks and rowboats. This is what heroism can do!

Philip Zimbardo encourages the *heroic imagination*[*]. These acts may be social as well as physical: Socrates or Spartacus,

---

[*] *Google* "The Banality of Heroism".

whistleblowers or warriors. Athletes often visualize themselves executing a perfect pitch, jump, or catch, and this improves their actual performance. Zimbardo is suggesting we do the same for any socially or physically dangerous situations we will face during our lives. But I'll let him speak for himself:

> The banality of heroism concept suggests that we are all potential heroes waiting for a moment in life to perform a heroic deed. The decision to act heroically is a choice that many of us will be called upon to make at some point in time. By conceiving of heroism as a universal attribute of human nature, not as a rare feature of the few "heroic elect," heroism becomes something that seems in the range of possibilities for every person, perhaps inspiring more of us to answer that call.

> Even people who have led less than exemplary lives can be heroic in a particular moment. For example, during Hurricane Katrina, a young man named Jabar Gibson, who had a history of felony arrests, did something many people in Louisiana considered heroic: He commandeered a bus, loaded it with residents of his poor New Orleans neighborhood, and drove them to safety in Houston. Gibson's "renegade bus" arrived at a relief site in Houston before any government sanctioned evacuation efforts.

Modern society often celebrates the anti-hero, and Hollywood encourages us to identify with him/her. This protagonist usually has some contemptible character traits, and producers and directors manipulate the audience to espouse his/her cause. If we let racist or homophobic comments go unchallenged, we become *bystanders* to prejudice. When your Aunt Martha says such people weren't allowed in the neighborhood in her day, you should respond (gently but firmly), or you become a participant in racism. In the case of the movie, you can simply leave the theater, press the off button, or read the reviews first. This is not censorship but merely the exercise of your free will.

What section of modern civilization demands sweeping conformity in thought? We all know the answer is religion—any religion. Show me the country with the most devout, the most pious, and you will have found the most conformist, least happy, least creative, least rational, and most socially disadvantaged group of people on earth. Consider Somalia. Yet everyone in this group will be absolutely convinced they are correct, God's chosen people. Their "spiritual" leader will claim infallibility on matters of doctrine, and by this action alone, he is already mistaken.

The bottom line of science is "We may be wrong; let's look at this again." Contrast this with religion, which claims it is *never* wrong because it has God's holy word in a book. Ecumenicalism is a farce since every religion "knows" theirs is the one *true* faith. Whether Pope, Archbishop, or Imam, these are the clerics with absolute power and knowledge, the disciples of Lord Acton, and their faithful are those who complied in the Milgram test. With so many in obsequious obedience, the compliance levels rise to 99 percent and beyond. We must have challenges to Catholic and Islamic claims of omnipotence and omniscience.

We need individuals with heroic imaginations like Ayaan Hirsi Ali, who wrote the bestseller *Infidel* about her extraordinary struggles to leave Islam and enter the Western Enlightenment of reason. At great personal cost but with brilliant success she has accomplished both, with death fatwas trailing behind her. It's noteworthy that after Hirsi Ali escaped from Islam she did not take up Christianity but rather the Western intellectual tradition.

Ayaan Hirsi Ali

As Mikhail Bakunin wrote in *God and the State,* "The first revolt is against the supreme tyranny of theology, of the phantom of God. As long as we have a master in heaven, we will be slaves on earth." Compare her smiling, free face (no burka here) with the abject genuflections shown on the next page— and this ignoble knee bending and head hammering must be done five times a day, every day. In all this sea of bended bodies, there isn't a single woman. Why? Islam subjugates women to second or third class status, so they must pray out of sight in a separate room or in a basement. The Muslim religion is a club of misogynists, run by greybeards full of hate always worrying about the next world while their present world is in anarchy. (I will return to the topic of Islam in Chapter 6.)

Muslim Men at Prayer

Freedom isn't a gift; it's a birthright! Yet we must be ever vigilant in order to keep it. Your parents restricted your freedom when you were young to keep you safe. When you become an adult, anyone usurping your freedom usually does so for his or her own benefit. Of course, if you don't wish to be free—and there are such people—your choices for servitude are everywhere. The prime usurpers of freedom are a master triumvirate of military, political, and religious forces. (And some people would include the banks and the credit card companies.) Military dictatorships combine two of these and occasionally all three in one stupendous accumulation of power, for example, Nazi Germany. Oh, you don't believe these thugs were religious. In Chapter 5 we will explore that possibility. But for now, recall Milgram's candidates were a cross-section of American society and for that reason at least somewhat religious.

WONDERFUL LIFE

In his splendid book *Wonderful Life: The Burgess Shale and the Nature of History*, Stephen Jay Gould fully develops the concept of contingent history with numerous detailed examples from the Burgess Shale. The book's title comes from Frank Capra's Christmas movie *It's a Wonderful Life*—Hollywood's unsurpassed example of this idea, and rightly so. Previously we spoke of it as the Butterfly Effect.

What has been said about the Butterfly Effect on human history over the last few thousand years applies with equal force back to the period when life first began—about 3.6 billion years ago. In the final chapter of *Wonderful Life* Gould imagines seven possible worlds as life might have been. Yet the combinations stirred by the butterfly's wing are such that he could just as easily have imagined seven million.

Let Gould speak for himself on the species closest to his heart and ours. The metaphor is a movie theater running a film called *On the Evolution of Life*:

> Run the tape [on life] again, and let the tiny twig [on the bush] of *Homo sapiens* expire in Africa. Other hominids may have stood on the threshold of what we know as human possibilities, but many sensible scenarios would never generate our level of mentality. Run the tape again, and this time Neanderthal perishes in Europe and *Homo erectus* in Asia (as they did in our world). The sole surviving stock, Homo erectus in Africa, stumbles along for a while, even prospers, but does not speciate and therefore remains stable. A mutated virus then wipes Homo erectus out, or a change in climate reconverts Africa into inhospitable forest. One little twig on the mammalian branch, a lineage with interesting possibilities that were never realized, joins the vast majority of species in extinction. So what? Most possibilities are never realized, and who will ever know the difference?

> Arguments of this form lead me to the conclusion that biology's most profound insight into human nature, status, and potential lies in the simple phrase, the embodiment of contingency: *Homo sapiens* is an entity, not a tendency. [2]

How are we to deal with this view of life and history emotionally? No design; no slime to man; no ultimate purpose; just endless, chance, choice, and change. Well, we begin by recalling that Bertrand Russell thought happiness depended more on good digestion than a view of life. And Gould wisely wrote that contingent history gives us *maximum freedom* to thrive, each in our own individualistic way. There are new things under the sun.

This definition of life implies no road map, and the preferred phrase is the one Darwin often used, "descent with modification." The notion that evolution has a direction—and worse an overriding purpose—is outmoded and foolish. Abrahamic religious *designs*, explaining phenomena by their ends or purposes, have events backwards. We have existed in a vast whirlwind of events over immense eras, forever adapting to the here and now or perishing. This is the condition of all organisms; it's the human condition, and we must deal with it.

Opposed to the soft yearning for directed evolution is the tough concept of contingent history: the idea that *no particular path* is inevitable. All outcomes are contingent on a multitude of quirks and accidents. It's possible, for example, that one early vertebrate worm was responsible for the evolution of all later vertebrates. Had some misfortune such as climatic change, a predator, a virus, and so on eliminated that worm, human beings would never have existed. So much for a divine plan!

ONLY FOLLOWING ORDERS

Let's return to our main themes armed with the knowledge that history is not destined to repeat.

All religious, military, and political organizations live according to two great rules:

- Keep everything secret.
- Cover your ass.

Therefore, when the Nazis protested that they were only following orders, this was a way to cover their asses by blaming somebody else. As Zimbardo would say, they were rotten apples, in a rotten barrel, constructed by rotten barrel makers—the Nazi hierarchy. Psychology now makes clear—contrary to what all religions preach—evil is not a fixed line in the sand separating the good from the bad. The line moves and is permeable in both directions. The right barrels can redeem criminals and the wrong ones can cause the mighty to fall. When Cassius said to Brutus, "The fault, dear Brutus, is not in our stars, but in ourselves, that we are underlings" he was only partially correct. Much of ethics is situational!

Milgram and Zimbardo's results were so startling and consistent that no one could hope to explain human behavior and not consider them. (For those among us who love coincidences consider the following: Milgram and Zimbardo were both born in the Bronx in 1933; they attended the same high school; they even sat beside each other in class. And incredibly, after leaving school, they studied identical aspects of human behavior, arriving at identical conclusions.)

If Lord Acton is the powerful right hand, then Milgram is the obsequious left. For example, Adolf Hitler was Acton's prime apprentice, and the German people were Milgram's compliant sheep. We are not to believe that everyone succumbed to power's temptations or that all the sheep ran off the cliff. Always there are heroes: Milgram's one-third, the black sheep, the goats.

Two of Milgram's nineteen variations on his basic experiment demonstrated how important heroes are as examples, as are wimps for the opposite reason. We admire heroes whether it be the biblical David fighting Goliath, Odysseus struggling to get home, Spartacus for his freedom, Galileo for the scientific method, Bertrand Russell for reason, or Ayaan Hirsi Ali for freedom from religion. Their honesty and bravery generally terrifies the authorities. Religions deal with heroes as heretics, apostates, and a danger to the natural order of things. In the past, before secularism and science defanged the Christian Church, they dealt with dissenters by drowning, the rack, or burning at the stake. The preferred practice of Islam has always been—and still is—amputation, whipping, and stoning to death.

Consider an extreme example of these two great rules, mentioned above, that all religious, military, and political organizations live by. Embedded in the tragedy we call the Iraq War are a thousand smaller tragedies no less horrific. The first among these equals was the hell pit called Abu Ghraib documented with photographs by the smiling perpetrators. These pictures would have remained secret except they fell into the right hands—those of MP Joe Darby, the whistleblower. For safety, the military put Darby and his wife into protective custody. It's possible they will never be able to safely return to their home in Appalachia. This is the price paid for making our world a better place. He says he would do it again—such is the bravery of ordinary heroes.

Now that this dirty big secret was out, the Bush administration went into full ass-covering mode. As a result, they immediately dispatched Donald Rumsfeld to Abu Ghraib to find the rotten apples responsible for these atrocities. Naturally, they only looked in select places at the bottom of the military hierarchy or barrel if you will. Translated, that means if caught blame others beneath you.

Undoubtedly, much of the cause of this rottenness was situational, but not all. These were not trained prison guards; they were weekend soldiers—military reservists. They had no expertise for their positions; they even had to sleep in empty prison cells. They worked weeks without a day off. They shot these photographs while on the night shift in the prison's basement. Furthermore, strong evidence exists that the interrogators pressured these overworked, undertrained reservists to "soften up" the prisoners for future questioning. Unbelievably, the army never charged anyone higher than Staff Sergeant Ivan "Chip" Frederick. And even Frederick admitted he deserved to be punished.

Certainly, there was some rottenness in the "apples," but the greater putrid decay was in the barrel itself: the prison, the prison warden (General Janis Karpinski), and the war. The greatest pu-

Karpinski and Rumsfeld at Abu Ghraib

trefaction, however, was in the rotten barrel makers: Bush, Cheney, and Rumsfeld. These three wise guys fought the wrong war in the wrong country against the wrong enemy for the wrong reasons. These men set their lawyers loose to find ways to circumvent the letter and the spirit of the Geneva Convention on prisoner abuse. These are the Christian gentlemen answerable for waterboarding. What makes this even more outrageous is that the United States *hanged* Japanese soldiers for waterboarding American prisoners in World War II. Astonishing isn't it, that at one time America executed those who practiced waterboarding yet a few decades later she practices it herself. Basic logic tells us one of these administrations was living in moral turpitude. You be the judge, which one it was!

Waterboarding is a type of torture that has existed in various forms dating back at least to the time of the Inquisition.

An immobilized captive has water poured over his face causing him to have the sensation (?) of drowning. The effects are devastating and long lasting. While a guest at Guantanamo Bay, Khalid Sheikh Mohammed—according to reports—was waterboarded an incredible 183 times.

When the "decision points" came down for George W. Bush and his administration, wars increased, the number of troops went up, the number of prisons went up, prisoners increased, wiretaps blossomed, civil rights fell, and casualties and death touched homes across America. All this occurred with the general blessing of the Christian churches and, sadly, the press. Once again, force attempted to solve every problem, and it left us in "Shock and Awe." The President was so close to being an Oriental despot, so near to being a god.

Christopher Hitchens moments after being waterboarded

Bush apologists and sycophants opined that waterboarding was not torture, but merely a form of advanced interrogation. In a feat of daring—dancing on the edge of foolishness—Christopher Hitchens, journalist and gadfly, had himself waterboarded to test their hypothesis. Although this was done only once and under "controlled" conditions, it was dangerous for a man of fifty-nine years with a quart of Johnny Walker Black Label whiskey coursing through his veins. Interested readers will find Hitchens' complete article in *Vanity Fair* magazine[*]; others need merely glance at the photograph above. Hitchens himself asserted:

> I apply the Abraham Lincoln test for moral casuistry: "If slavery is not wrong, nothing is wrong." Well, then, if waterboarding does not constitute torture, then there is no such thing as torture.

Well, Mr. Hitchens, this was a tough way to get material for a column! Would that Bush, Cheney, Rumsfeld, and for good measure Wolfowitz, had the bravery and honesty of this famous atheist.

---

[*] *Google* "Hitchens *Vanity Fair* waterboarding."

As the Christmas carol says, "God rest you merry, Gentlemen, let nothing you dismay."

HUMANS AS HEROES

To challenge alleged truths and cultural trends, we need men and women who see things as they might be rather than how they are—people like Joe Darby and Christopher Hitchens. This can be exceptionally difficult. Perhaps we are not, as the cliché says, speaking truth to power, but we are at least holding a candle up to dark places. All humans come from a heroic ancestry. Just to have survived and reproduced over millions of years testifies to this. Heroism is not foreign to us; it is part of who we are; it is contagious. Sometime in life, perhaps frequently, maybe over an extended period of time, each of us will be tested. A moment when we must stand and deliver. This is often called a "*Spartacus moment*," from the movie starring Kirk Douglas. Imagine yourself in a dangerous or challenging situation—one that requires either physical or moral courage. Imagine further that you successfully deal with this situation. Now do it again!

We need not hide under the stairs afraid of sky or earthly bullies. We leave such fear to those who would fall on their knees. People can be—if not wholly, at least in part—masters of their own destiny.

Change requires imagination, but action is needed to make it happen. The imaginations of the young are more fertile than the barren acres of old age. Achievement comes from that rare and happy marriage of dreamer and doer. But the dreamer always comes first. As the minstrel, John Lennon sang:

Imagine there's no Heaven
It's easy if you try
No hell below us
Above us only sky
Imagine all the people

Living for today
Imagine there's no countries
It isn't hard to do
Nothing to kill or die for
And no religion too
Imagine all the people
Living life in peace

Salman Rushdie contributed a short letter, in 1997, to a UN-sponsored anthology, addressed to the six-billionth child expected to be born that year. What follows is an excerpt from that letter on our theme of imagination and action:

> Intellectual freedom, in European history, has mostly meant freedom from the restraints of the Church and not the state. This is the battle Voltaire was fighting, and it's also what all six billion of us could do for ourselves, the revolution in which each of us could play our small, six-billionth part; once and for all we could refuse to allow priests, and the fictions on whose behalf they claim to speak, to be the policemen of our liberties and behavior. Once and for all we could put the stories back into the books, put the books back on the shelves, and see the world undogmatized and plain.
>
> *Imagine there's no heaven*, my dear Six-Billionth, and at once the sky's the limit. [3]

Some religious apologists believe freedom and individuality have their birthplace in Christian theology. For "proof" they point to the creation myth in Genesis. We are told that God created Adam and Eve as intelligent, curious beings with *free will* and gave them a choice between obedience (good) and disobedience (bad). These can be redefined as obeying God's commands or defying them. But having free will and possessing the ability to exercise that free will—i.e., freedom—are different ideas.

Consider human destiny had we not eaten from the tree of knowledge of good and evil. We would have forever remained as children under God's boring and capricious commands, unable to progress, change, or mature. There would have been no human adventure; instead we would have had "heaven" on earth.

Endless halleluiahs and hosannas in brain-dead praise of a universal dictator, a la Kim Jong-Il. It's no wonder hell is a much more interesting place than heaven. Do many people recall that Dante, as well as his famous *Inferno*, wrote a companion poem on the "good place," called *Paradiso*? I think not.

Adam and Eve made the right choice by eating from the tree of knowledge. We are an ever-curious species with unlimited potential for intellectual growth and adventure, and we will pull the bear's tail. Cursing the ground to be unfruitful, the serpent to be legless, Adam to hard labor, and Eve with great childbirth agony, the "gentle" deity sent the pair East of Eden lest they also eat of the tree of life and become immortal.

All religions praise servitude and deplore freedom—the very word *Islam* means submission to God. Think for yourself! Who always sides with earthly dictators? Who opposes birth control and women's reproductive freedom? Who bans books, movies, and plays? Who predictably supports the death penalty? Who opposes gay rights? Who opposes every piece of advanced social legislation? Who devises the most horrible punishments for the disobedient? Had Adam and Eve not eaten from the tree of knowledge it would have always been midnight in the Garden of Eden

Most ages have had defining historical events: Rome had the Goths; Christianity had the Dark Ages; Napoleon, the old royal order; Europe, the Fascism of Hitler, and Mussolini; the West, the communism of Marx and Mao. We are now afloat on a tidal wave of conflict between Islam and the West: between faith and reason, between anti-science and science, between submission and freedom. And like Brutus, we must take the current when it serves or lose our ventures.

In this book, we will look behind the curtain of Judaism, Christianity, and Islam to view the moral and intellectual damage these Abrahamic religions have done to our civilization. Individual liberty is the overriding value of Western society and the *sine qua non* of art and science. We must be vigorous in its defense or *our civilization* will perish. Freedom isn't free! Every tired dog loses its supper. Every fat pig goes to market. As Thomas Jefferson well understood, "The price of freedom is eternal vigilance."

CHAPTER—3

IN THE BEGINNING

Looking up at the stars, I know quite well
That, for all they care, I can go to hell.
W.H. Auden, "The More Loving One"

In the beginning was the Big Bang. Now the universe had perfect symmetry; neither was it void, but darkness was everywhere. And time said, "Let there be light," and there was light—after millions and millions of years. Before the Big Bang, there was no time because there were no events to record. No matter, no space, no time. Nothing—perhaps not even that!

In every society, on every continent, and in every age, humankind has concerned itself with finding the instant of creation—as if to answer *when did we come to be*? These creation chronologies come in two varieties: the theological and the scientific. Not all these attempts have been equally successful.

James Ussher

The theological hero was James Ussher (1581–1656), Anglican Archbishop of Armagh and Primate of All Ireland. By counting back through the "begats" of Genesis and using some numerology, he arrived at the exact date of all creation as 4004 BCE. If the reader doesn't find this date sufficiently accurate, the good Archbishop further refined the date through diligent research to October 23, 4004 BCE, a Sunday.

Ussher wasn't alone in his arithmetic. One John Lightfoot (1602-75), Vice-Chancellor of Cambridge University, was a contemporary. Lightfoot published his calculations on the date of creation in 1644, some six years before Ussher. And with an eye for exactitude that even the Archbishop couldn't match, Sir John found the hour of creation to be precisely 9:00 a.m. (but his year was different).

My gentle readers are no doubt impressed by this precision. We have journeyed from utter confusion to 4004 BCE to Sunday, 23 October, at 9:00 a.m.—a year *to* month *to* day *to* hour progression. But perhaps some readers feel a sense of disappointment with all this exactness since neither Ussher nor Lightfoot tells us the *time zone*. Granted these marks on maps didn't exist in their day, but for a spherical Earth, the different times certainly did. So this must have been 9:00 a.m. in the Garden of Eden. Unless? Unless these learned clerics thought the world was flat. In that case, it would be 9:00 a.m. everywhere on earth—even in England and Ireland.

Lightfoot remarks obliquely on this in the first and third pages of his *A few and new Observations upon the Book of Genesis* (1642) when he writes, "Heaven and Earth, center and circumference, were created all together, in the same instant, and clouds full of water..." Now this "center" and "circumference" relate more appropriately to a pancake than a sphere. So which was it?

The Old and New Testaments imply throughout their text that the Earth was a pancake or a square. Here are a few supporting quotations. And without a doubt, Lightfoot knew these passages—probably verbatim.

- Job 38:13 (KJV)
  That it might take hold of the ends of the earth, that the wicked might be shaken out of it?
- Isaiah 11:12 (KJV)
  And he shall set up an ensign for the nations, and shall assemble the outcasts of Israel, and gather together the dispersed of Judah from the four corners of the earth.
- Matthew 4:8 (KJV)
  Again, the devil taketh him [Jesus] up into an exceeding high mountain, and sheweth him all the kingdoms of the world, and the glory of them.

As the average fifth grader will inform you, spheres don't have "ends" or "corners," and it's impossible to see "all the kingdoms of the world" even from the summit of Mount Everest—unless the Earth is flat.

Whether Ussher or Lightfoot entertained a belief in a flat Earth is unclear. But since they were prone to a literal interpretation of Genesis, why be restrained in the Bible's remaining 65 books.

The idea of a spherical Earth is anti-intuitive—after all, the world looks everywhere flat. The thinker who first conceived such a revolutionary idea was Pythagoras (c. 570-495 BCE)—the same Greek whose theorem we had to memorize in high school and the first intellectual to look beyond the obvious. He based his conclusion on two pieces of empirical evidence. First, ships at sea disappear from the hull upward; second, during a lunar eclipse, the Earth's shadow on the moon is *always* curved. All this was two millennia before Columbus.

But I digress. Perhaps I have been too harsh on Ussher and Lightfoot? They are such easy targets—the butt of jokes in all geology textbooks. That's how we see them from our time, but in their own, they were prominent scholars [1] working within the zeitgeist of their age. In five centuries, the verdict on our age may be equally unsympathetic.

Consider Johannes Kepler, a genius out of nowhere, and Sir Isaac Newton, one of the most influential men in history. Kepler fixed the creation at 3992 BCE and Newton at c. 4000 BCE. This forcefully shows the enormous cultural influence we all trek through. We move like runners in quicksand and despite our most valiant struggles, we are submerged. Even though Kepler and Newton were revolutionaries in the most profound way in understanding the physical world, today we would judge them as religious fundamentalists. We must forgive all these men—they were victims not perpetrators. Remember their best and bury the rest.

THE CREATIONISTS

Yet, there are some we cannot forgive. Why? Because they have abandoned humankind's most outstanding attribute: the ability to reason. Who are they? Whom am I referring to? Richard Dawkins calls them the history-deniers or the 40 percenters.

William Jennings Bryan, (1860-1925) was a three-time Democratic Party nominee for President of the United States, and the 41st Secretary of State under Woodrow Wilson. Today we remember him as the ignorant prosecutor in the Scopes Monkey Trial—made infamous in the movie *Inherit the Wild*. The film portrays him as an ardent supporter of Archbishop Ussher's 4004 BCE creation date. Whether Bryan actually was or not is problematic, but the damage was done, and he will be forever remembered as a denier of Earth's natural history—one of the 40 percenters.

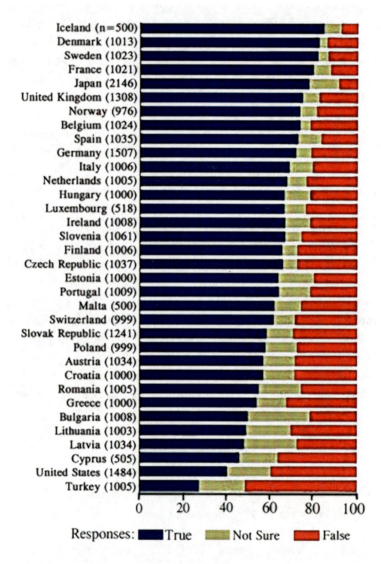

Public Acceptance of Evolution in 34 Countries, 2005

Mark Twain noted, "There are lies, damned lies, and statistics." At the risk of annoying the shade of America's greatest wit, I'm going to quote one such statistic. The survey above reveals at least 40 percent of the adult US population believe that evolution is false, and another 20 percent are confused on the issue. Look at the chart above (published in the August 11, 2006, issue of the journal *Science*). See for yourself! In a plunge for the bottom of the dunce pile, the US beats out Turkey, the single Muslim country on the chart. Among these 40 percenters is a subculture of hardcore XXX creationists—the Young Earthers—who delude themselves that the world is 6,000 to 10,000 years old. Ussher would be proud of them. However, as the women who know me will attest, I have shoes older than that.

Cynics and fanatics are opposites, yet strangely similar. Cynics doubt everything; fanatics believe everything that favors their position. Neither has to think or evaluate a new idea or piece of information. As for the rest of us, somewhere in the middle of these two extremes, life is not so easy. We have to behave as adults, examine a new idea, and try to decide whether it's true or false on its merits. At least that's the ideal.

I will leave the word "belief" to the extremists—the cynics and fanatics. For instance, it's not wise to say you *believe* in evolution and an ancient earth; rather affirm you know of *evidence* for both. You wouldn't want a doctor who believes in his almond extract to cure your cancer. Yet you would trust a specialist with a drug for which there was clinical evidence for its effectiveness. I wish to put forward the radical proposition that *belief* be directly proportional to the *evidence* for its veracity as Bertrand Russell wrote in the following famous passage:

> I wish to propose for the reader's favourable consideration a doctrine which may, I fear, appear wildly paradoxical and subversive. The doctrine in question is this: that it is undesirable to believe a proposition when there is no ground whatever for supposing it true. [2]

Young Earth Creationists (YEC) do not subscribe to this proposition. They know only what lies near their system of beliefs. No metaphorical interpretation of the Book of Genesis for them—they believe it literally. It's a six-day workweek for God and one day of rest. But the chief characteristic of fanatics is the total inability of anyone to argue against them—rational discussion based on evidence will not change their world view.

YEC (Young Earth Creationists) not only oppose evolution but all its supporting sciences: physics and chemistry (especially absolute dating methods), astronomy, cosmology, geology, molecular biology, genomics, linguistics, anthropology, and archaeology. Their defining characteristic is irrationality. They do no research; they publish no papers—except the odd bit of propaganda. Knowing this, it's necessary to conclude that it's futile to debate with them. Laughter may be your only resort. As someone once said, a good belly laugh is worth a thousand reasoned arguments. And then walk away. Better yet, walk away laughing. Remember, biblical literalists are literally wrong.

EVIDENCE-BASED DATING

Theologians have declared their answer as to when the creation took place. And make no mistake, every imam, priest, and pastor would still be clinging to Ussher's date, or something similar to it, were it not for the discoveries of modern astronomers—I exempt the YEC. If you would like some idea of church astronomy, read Dante's *Divine Comedy*: glory at his art, weep at his science.

In the beginning—the true beginning—the world was without form (pattern) but had perfect symmetry. This implies the universe was smooth like the surface of a sphere, appearing everywhere the

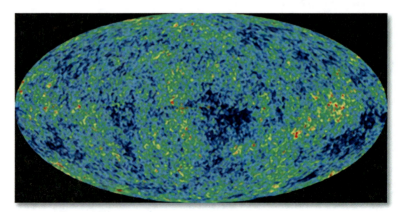

Cosmic Fingerprint: Echo of the Big Bang

same. As far as we know, symmetry was born alone with time in the Big Bang. Before this, there was nothing—like you before conception. The early universe—the first second[*]—was incredibly hot and had the utmost simplicity in addition to its symmetry. As it expanded, it cooled. And here's the point: *it cooled at varying rates,* as shown so clearly in the above picture of the Big Bang's background microwave radiation.

The red spots are hot, blue are cold. Be aware that the heat mirrors the density distribution: the red spots are denser as well as hotter. We have this wonderful picture of instability thanks to the satellite known as the Wilkinson Microwave Anisotropy Probe (WMAP). Launched in July 2001 on a five-year mission to go where no one has ever gone before. This picture captures the oldest light in the universe! It's from 379,000 years after the Big Bang—more than 13.7 billion years ago. This is equivalent to taking a photograph of an 80-year-old person on the day of their birth.

How did the astronomers arrive at the primordial instant for the Big Bang? It was conceptually easy, but technically difficult. Consider, if you had to drive 200 miles at 50 mph, you know it would take 4 hours—this is the simple conceptual framework. You divide the distance by your speed to equal the time:

$$\frac{Distance\ (200)}{Speed\ (50)} = time\ (4).$$

You might well object that instead of having to find only one unknown (time), now we must find two—distance and speed. Yes, except these two are easier to determine.

Humankind has always been fascinated with *how fast* and *how far.* Consider the latter. Look at a lamp post and notice what's in its background. Now walk thirty or forty paces and look at the same lamp post noting how the background has changed. Scientists call this shift in the backdrop *parallax.* The further you walk, the more shifting or parallax you get against the background for some object in the foreground—in our case a lamp post. Astronomers use this simple idea to find the distance to the *closest* stars.

---

[*] See *The First Three Minutes* by Steven Weinberg.

Friedrich Bessel (1784-1846) was a German astronomer and the first man to find the distance to a star by parallax other than our sun. Realizing the distance between his eyes was a bit too small to show any parallax for a star, Bessel took a cosmic step. He used the diameter of the Earth's orbit for the distance between his eyes—like our walking thirty paces. Now, he also had the genius to pick a very close star, 61 cygni—a subtle speck of light in the star-field of Cygnus, the Swan.

Scientists measure parallax in degrees of a whole circle ($360°$). The full moon takes up two degrees of the sky, while Bessel's parallax for Cygni 61 took only a tiny fraction of that. However, knowing this and the diameter of the Earth's orbit plus a little high school trigonometry (the sine law), he computed the distance to be 10.4 light-years—very close to the actual value of about 11.4 light-years. (Recall that a "light-year" is a measurement of *distance* not time.) His was a momentous discovery and a cause for great wonder.

Now 11.4 light-years equals 67,014,897,900,000 miles, that's 67 trillion plus a few odd paces—even computer help isn't that far away. Quoting large numbers for the "awe effect" is, however, ineffectual if not useless. On this point, consider the following story.

A famous astronomer was lecturing on the birth and death of the sun when he noticed a hand waving frantically at the back of the auditorium.

"Yes, young man, what is your question?"

"When did you say the sun would explode and become a red giant destroying the Earth?"

"*In 10 billion years.*"

"Thank heaven! At first, I thought you said one billion," declared the young man sitting down in relief.

Astronomy inevitably involves large numbers—astronomically large numbers. A billion (1,000,000,000) is a huge quantity; so huge we have no direct experience of its true size. Consider our smallest unit of time, the "second." How old must a person be to have lived a billion seconds? I ask the reader to estimate the answer—use your intuition before reading further.

. . . .

Surprisingly, it takes almost 32 years of seconds to equal just one billion; an unusual human might live three billion seconds. Numbers like this transcend our ability to know through direct experience. They're just mathematical symbols on paper, and we will treat them as such.

We need to swim much further out into the cosmic ocean to get anywhere beyond our galaxy. Parallax is possible for "close" celestial objects. For greater distances, astronomers use special stars—very special stars.

We call these unique objects Cepheid variables, and they are 5-20 times as massive as the sun. And this mass produces a high luminosity visible over millions of light-years. Beyond this, there is something very curious about these stars that provide astronomers with a virtual yardstick to measure the universe. To wit, their real brightness is precisely related to their pulsation period which is simply counted (the period-luminosity relation). Now it's straightforward to determine how far they must be away for such *real* brightness, found from their period, to appear as a diminished *apparent* brightness, found by observation.

Art and science have a long past dating back to prehistoric times. Unlike the history of religion and politics, it is not one repetitive, dreary sequence of wars, pogroms, and genocides. Yet many heroes of art and science lived and died in obscurity, receiving no visits from those benefitting from their genius. One such was Henrietta Swan Leavitt (1868-1921), an American astronomer and a graduate of Radcliffe College. Leavitt worked at the Harvard Observatory in the lowly capacity of a "human computer," assigned to count images on photographic plates. Studying these plates

Henrietta Swan Leavitt

led Leavitt to put forward a groundbreaking idea—discovered while she labored as a $10.50-a-week assistant—that was the basis for the work of all later astronomers. Leavitt's discovery of the period-luminosity relation of Cepheid variables radically changed the theory of modern astronomy, an accomplishment for which she received no recognition during her lifetime. So important was her achievement that astronomers call Cepheid variables the *standard candle* of the cosmos. She gave astronomers a reed like a measuring rod and told them, "Go and measure the universe and count the galaxies and the distances thereof."

Since Leavitt's time, astronomers have discovered several additional methods of finding interstellar and extragalactic distances. And the wonderful thing is they wholly agree with each other, lending a ring of truth to them all.

Far from city lights and a full moon, in the quiet coolness of a summer evening, the vaulted band of the Milky Way across the night sky is a glorious sight, free to every man and mouse. A set of binoculars at once reveals further richness and immensity. Everyone understands it takes time for light to travel from the stars to us. If *our* star went suddenly black, we won't know it for 499 seconds (8 minutes and 19 seconds). And light travels at 186,287 miles in each of these seconds. So a glimpse at our sun is a 499-second backward glance into the past. Consider the constellation Cygnus, the Swan, flying right down the Milky Way. It holds two magnificent stellar sights. Deneb, the tail of the swan, is a bright, blue supergiant star approximately 1,550 light-years from Earth. Albireo, the beak of the swan, is actually two stars, which exhibit a spectacular amber and blue contrast at approximately 380 light-years away. So this wondrous evening vision is a picture of history—a different history for each dot. Always holding each other close, space and time do an ancient dance as they move further and further away, all the way to the moment of creation 13.7 billion years ago. Or at least that is what I wish to show.

Cepheid variables provided the means for many significant discoveries. They allowed astronomers to show that the universe *was not* synonymous with the Milky Way galaxy but just one such among billions. These special stars continued to light the way and measure the path back to the beginning of time—even though they themselves were "born" billions of years after the Big Bang. To understand this we needed a new discovery, a new metric. It was a task for many hands and a few minds, and the main player was Edwin Hubble (1889–1953).

Edwin Hubble

Now that we know two methods (parallax and Cepheid variables) whereby astronomers find distances in the universe, let's investigate how they determine the speed of stars and galaxies. And rather than the word "speed," we will use the more precise term "velocity" which means *speed plus direction.*

THE CENTER OF THE UNIVERSE

In Greek mythology, Zeus charged two eagles with finding the exact center of the Earth. He released one to the east and one to the west. They met at Delphi, thus pointing out the center of the world. The priests placed a cone-shaped stone, called the omphalos, in front of Delphi's Temple as a marker for the navel of the Earth. Not only was man at the center of things, but also the Greeks imagined they lived at the center of the entire universe.

From the earliest times, all peoples have believed they are at the center of creation, perchance fashioned even in the image of God. The Eskimos still call themselves *Inuit* and the Chcycnne Indians of the Great Plains called themselves *Tsistsistas,* both meaning *The People.* Of course, the Jews refer to themselves as *The Chosen People.* Science has paved a broad path of withdrawal from this human centrism, and the retreat has much disturbed the equilibrium of the faithful. With heliocentrism, Copernicus laid the scientific bedrock for an objective view of man's true place in the solar system. But we have traveled far since then, and astronomers, not religious scholars, have been our guides.

Harlow Shapely used Cepheid variables to map the shape of the Milky Way and locate the Earth's position within it—30,000 light-years from the galactic center in a minor spiral arm named Orion. Edwin Hubble found Cepheids in the Andromeda galaxy. And this settled the Island Universe debate concerning the question of whether the Milky Way *was* the entire Universe, or merely one in an overabundance of galaxies that constituted the cosmos. This was a long retreat from geocentrism, but far from over.

Vesto Slipher (1875–1969), a forgotten American astronomer, ushered in the new metric alluded to above. He spent his career at Lowell Observatory in Flagstaff, Arizona. In 1912, he was the first to

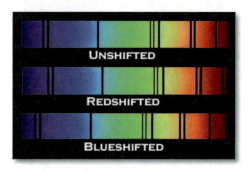

observe the galactic redshift* of spectral lines (*see* figure above), and he correctly related this to the galaxy's "recessional velocity." That is, the further away a galaxy is the faster it is moving away—a bizarre property. Even stranger, this was so in every direction from the Earth implying *we are at the Universe's very center*. Roll over Copernicans!

It may seem that we have wandered far from our task of finding the instant of the Big Bang—the moment of creation. But that prize is close at hand. And astronomy will award this prize for explaining *why* the more distant a galaxy is, the more its light is redshifted.

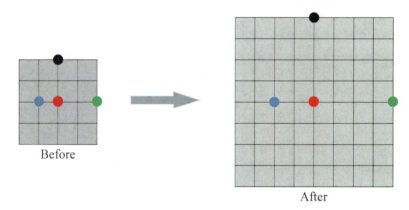

Before

After

The E-x-p-a-n-d-i-n-g Universe

Consider the Big Bang. In *no sense* was it an ordinary explosion with a center and every element radiating outward from that

---

* A shift in the spectral lines of very distant galaxies toward longer wavelengths, that is toward the red end.

center. Rather, we should call it the "expanding" not the "exploding" universe. The classical analogy is that of the surface (only) of a balloon with a collection of random dots on it. Blow air into the balloon and every dot runs away from every other dot. That is, the space between the dots expands. Do not imagine the balloon's center is any part of the analogy. It might be better to think of a rising loaf of raisin bread where all the space between the raisins (galaxies) is expanding.

Using the above diagram, let's consider the balloon analogy in more detail; the pale blue dot represents the Earth. As the universe expands—moving left to right—the blue dot sees the red, green, and black dots as moving away. But from red's point of view, the blue, green, and black dots are moving away. And so every dot sees every other dot as traveling away—having recessional velocity as astronomers say. No, we are not the center of our solar system; no, we are not the center of our galaxy; no, we are not the center of the Big Bang. Humanity's long journey from childhood to full maturity is over—the cosmos has no center. Rest easy Copernicus!

Edwin Powell Hubble was born in the small town of Marshfield, Missouri; he went on to change our views of the universe. Even Einstein thanked him for correcting what he said was the greatest blunder he ever made. What was Einstein's blunder? The great physicist thought we lived in a steady state universe— Hubble proved we don't. Today the public remembers Hubble only for the space telescope named after him, but he took the last step in finding the age of the universe. Let's see how he did it.

Science is a giant jigsaw puzzle; you can only fit in a new piece here or there because others put their pieces in before you. In Hubble's case, Leavitt and Slipher placed two important pieces. Hubble had the good fortune to work at the largest telescope of his day: the 100 inch on Mount Wilson. By finding hundreds of Cepheid variables so far away, that they had to be outside our galaxy, Hubble gave us the modern concept of island galaxies in an immense cosmos. And by using Slipher's results on redshifts, plus his own meticulously measured distances, Hubble was able *to quantify* galactic recession, meaning galaxies are moving away.

Consider again the diagram of The E-x-p-a-n-d-i-n-g Universe on the previous page. Now put yourself on the red dot in the

"BEFORE" figure with the blue dot one light-year away (say) and the green and black dots two light-years distant. With the expansion seen in the "After" figure all distances have been doubled— showing the green is four light-years while the blue dot is only two light-years away.

So, not only are *all* the dots traveling away from each other, as previously noted, but also the further away a dot, the faster it is moving away. In this case twice as fast. As a result, the galaxy's recessional velocity is directly related to its distance from you. Hubble expressed this in a marvelously simple way as follows:

$$Velocity = (Hubble\ constant)\ x\ (Distance)$$

or

$$V = H_o\,D.$$

Scientists call H_0 the Hubble constant of proportionality for the *present* time hence the subscript *zero*. This formula is very similar to our earlier one:

$$\frac{Distance\ (D)}{Speed\ (S\ or\ V)} = time.$$

With a little high school mathematics, you can write the first equation as

$$\frac{D}{V} = \frac{1}{H_0} = time.$$

Now here is our prize: the reciprocal of the Hubble constant is the time since the Big Bang. The physical interpretation of the Hubble time ($\frac{1}{H_0}$) is that it gives the time for the Universe to run backwards to the Big Bang. And this turns out to be an incredible 13.7 billion plus or minus 200,000 years. End of story!

RELIGION VS. SCIENCE

There are two roads in the human dilemma: religion and science. And we have just seen an example of each working on the identical problem: the age of the universe. Religion says creation took place on Sunday October 23, 4004 BCE, at 9:00 am; science says it happened 13.7 billion years ago give or take 200,000 years. One claims divine authority for its revelations based on "holy" writings and finds consolation; the other takes the world as it is and finds beauty and wonder.

The reader has a right to protest that I've staged a kind of perverse anachronism. I'm comparing the results of present-day scientists with religious erudition of the 1600s. And the reader would be correct except for millions of Young Earth Creationists.

Every religion, usually soon after its founding, tolerates no change to its "sacred" writings—meeting any such change with the threat of death or a fatwa. Islam claims the Qur'an is the *unalterable and final word* of God, in their case, Allah. Christians, especially in America, are still fighting over which version of the Bible to use. Most claim the King James Version (KJV) is God's holy word—because that's what Jesus spoke—everything else is the devil's work. Ultimately, religious leaders wish to preserve things as they are, they're conservative, and have few creative instincts. This conservative impulse is so glacial in its pace that centuries pass without visible change.

Consider the following famous example. Galileo Galilei was an irritant to the Catholic hierarchy; he looked for truth in the real world outside the bounds of God's "holy" writings. Moreover, he expressed his ideas in well-written and original books. Pope Urban VIII, whom Galileo thought was his friend, personally delivered him into the hands of the Supreme Sacred Congregation of the Roman and Universal Inquisition. Like all secret police, they had been keeping records on his activities for some time—22 years in fact. Twice he was taken and shown the instruments of torture—the last resort in bestial cruelty. He wasn't tortured, however, but put under house arrest for the rest of his life for holding, some say advocating, a forbidden idea.

This is a sketch of what the church calls Codex 1181, *Proceedings Against Galileo Galilei*, now jump ahead 359 years. The Vatican, after this very long time, establishes a commission, a conclave of clerics no less, to determine if the scientist really was correct. Following a thirteen-year investigation, they arrived at a decision. In the battle between religion and science, the former always gives way to the latter but only after centuries if it can. So following much "study" and reflection on November 4, 1992, Pope John Paul II forgave Galileo for being correct:

yes, the Earth really does rotate around the sun with a double motion.

You would think that would be the end of this affair, and all church hierarchy would accept John Paul's verdict, but you would be wrong. Mounting a preemptive rearguard action—two years before John Paul's announcement—was Cardinal Ratzinger, now Pope Benedict XVI. At La Sapienza University in Rome, Ratzinger cited the views of philosopher Paul Feyerabend, [3] whom he quoted as saying:

> The Church at the time of Galileo kept much more closely to reason than did Galileo himself, and she took into consideration the ethical and social consequences of Galileo's teaching too. Her verdict against Galileo was rational and just, and the revision of this verdict can be justified only on the grounds of what is politically opportune.

I guess Professor Feyerabend forgot about the 22-year police-state investigation and the threats of torture. He couldn't recall that Galileo had no copy of the charges or of the evidence against him, so the scientist had no advocate to defend him. Incredibly, the Inquisition stooped to use a forged, unsigned accusatory document followed by a lifetime sentence of house arrest. After all this, Feyerabend concluded the Catholic Church had been "rational and just." Thank goodness we have "philosophers" to make all this clear to us.

Ratzinger did not indicate whether he agreed or disagreed with Feyerabend's assertions, but the reader can draw his or her own conclusions. Furthermore, we shouldn't forget that Ratzinger was chief of the Holy Office of the Inquisition from 1981 to 2005. (It's noteworthy that the Catholic hierarchy, with a view to wider approval, has rendered the Supreme Sacred Congregation of the Roman and Universal Inquisition *politically correct* with a new name. The modern defrocked label is the Congregation for the Doctrine of the Faith.)

Back to the point at hand: religions—all of them—are conservative; they resist change, possibly for centuries. Churches and mosques condemn questioning; they punish unbelievers by methods most horrific. Galileo's book, *Dialogue on the Two*

Chief World Systems, was on the Prohibited Index for 200 years. To this day, the sermon is the only public discourse where no questions are allowed.

But you may protest again that religion clearly *has changed* in the last few centuries if ever so slowly. You might correctly point out no scientist today would repeat Newton or Kepler's claims on the age of the universe. And poets, artists, and writers were well aware of the retreat of faith and the loosening of religious control. Matthew Arnold expressed this in his immortal poem *Dover Beach* published in 1867:

The Sea of Faith
Was once, too, at the full, and round earth's shore
Lay like the folds of a bright girdle furled.
But now I only hear
Its melancholy, long, withdrawing roar,
Retreating, to the breath
Of the night-wind, down the vast edges drear
And naked shingles of the world.

In the enduring struggle between science and religion—between freedom and dogma—the clerics must give ground. Religion does no research; their position does not evolve in any important sense. After all, they have the *eternal word* of God written in their "holy" books. Questioning is anathema to the spirit of religion, conservatism is their creed. In contrast, the bottom line of the *scientific method* and every working scientist and researcher is "I may be wrong, let's reconsider." Or as Oliver Cromwell dramatically said it in a letter to the general assembly of the Church of Scotland, "I beseech you in the bowels of Christ think it possible you may be mistaken." But of course, they wouldn't. In the example of the date of creation, instead of Sunday October 23, 4004 BCE, it's 13.7 billion years plus or minus 200,000 years and certainly not exactly at 9:00 a.m. This plus or minus 200,000 allowance for inaccuracy is an admission of possible error. It's not a weakness, but strength and a mark of profound honesty. If you are young and searching for a career where you *never admit* you are wrong, try politics or religion.

Since Ussher's time science has demonstrated through geology, the fossil record, genetics, and evolution that an ancient Earth is eminently reasonable. Science and secularism have compelled religion to give ground or be laughed at. In the modern world, the Roman Catholic Church cannot espouse the mindset of the Dark Ages without causing censure from the sentient. So with great reluctance and a *melancholy, long, withdrawing roar*, they make an accommodation.

> *Religion changes when forced to.*
> *Science changes when it needs to.*

Some citizens find the habit of scientists changing their minds more than a little annoying. Yes, coffee is good for you. No, coffee causes cancer. Take your vitamin E. No, don't take your vitamin E it causes coronaries. Regrettably, the science reported in our newspapers is often filtered through scientifically illiterate reporters. Nevertheless, the habit of changing your mind on the presentation of new and compelling evidence is a powerful one. So powerful it's the crowning jewel of the scientific method and humanity's greatest hope. Richard Dawkins makes this point:

I have previously told the story of a respected elder statesman of the Zoology Department at Oxford when I was an undergraduate. For years he had passionately believed, and taught, that the Golgi Apparatus (a microscopic feature of the interior of cells) was not real: an artifact, an illusion. Every Monday afternoon it was the custom for the whole department to listen to a research talk by a visiting lecturer. One Monday, the visitor was an American cell biologist who presented completely convincing evidence that the Golgi Apparatus was real. At the end of the lecture, the old man strode to the front of the hall, shook the American by the hand and said—with passion—"My dear fellow, I wish to thank you. I have been wrong these fifteen years." We clapped our hands red. No fundamentalist would ever say that. In practice, not all scientists would. But all scientists pay lip service to it as an ideal—unlike, say, politicians who would probably condemn it as flip-flopping. The memory of the incident I have described still brings a lump to my throat. [4]

THE DENIERS

Many people deny religion and science are in an enduring struggle—the real ultimate fighting championship. True, there have been periods of relative peace between the combatants. Yet these détentes, however long, are just time outs between rounds while the opponents rest and regroup. They must resist each other because their world views are irreconcilable. Each side may repose decades before the next encounter, but unquestionably, it will come. *This is the conflicting-worlds model.* History past and present is the witness to its truth.

Some battles have far-reaching results—with supporters of the losing side fleeing the arena. So it was after the trial and life imprisonment of Galileo. Scientists and their traditions fled north from the hostile Catholic countries to the friendlier Protestant nations—Rene Descartes went to Sweden. It's one of those interesting coincidences of history that when Galileo died in 1642, Isaac Newton was born in England the same year on Christmas day.

Besides those who deny religion and science are combatants, there are those who *deny they can be* combatants about their core beliefs—maintaining they fight in different arenas and weight classes. *This is the separate-worlds model.* Stephen Jay Gould grandly named these the non-overlapping magisteria (NOMA) which would have science and religion stay within separate spheres, or realms of knowledge, and give each other mutual respect. Ay, there's the rub! Where are the boundaries? Is it possible to have non-interference? Seemingly, there are no statements of fact that religion can claim are its own, off-limits to science. Is science to have the whole of the empirical world—the world of sense? Does that leave religion with only the world of non-sense? NOMA would appear to highlight the problems between magisteria rather than dim them down.

Let's consider NOMA from both perspectives—the religious first. Whether Jesus had a father or not is a scientific question and could be determined by evidence if any were available. DNA might do. If NOMA religious advocates were sincere, they would dismiss this as the wrong magisteria. They might trumpet that scientific evidence has no effect on theological questions. How could it—all you really need is *faith*. But, of course, they say none of this.

Now it just so happens, an Israel antiquities dealer, Oded Golan, "found" something close to Jesus' DNA. I'm writing about the *Ossuary of James*. An ossuary is a limestone box containing human bones: they were common in ancient Israel until Titus Flavius destroyed the third temple in 70 CE. So common that in present-day Jerusalem they often serve as planter boxes for geraniums. Its inscription was intriguing: *James, son of Joseph, brother of Jesus* (Ya'akov bar Yosef akhui d'Yeshua, *note* arrow). This discovery was front-page news around the world—the first archaeological evidence for the existence of Jesus. Think

Ossuary of James, brother of Jesus

of it! The Royal Ontario Museum (ROM) in Toronto considered itself very fortunate to be the first institution to display this priceless relic in a blockbuster exhibition. The presentation was an immense success, with the ROM drawing 95,000 visitors during the show's six-week run. People lingered in reverence around the stone box, which sat inside a Plexiglas case. Many stood, some kneeled, in silent prayer. These are the gifts that *faith* can bring when you let the science slide. And slide it did.

Oded Galen, the Israeli antiquities dealer who owned the ossuary, is an intriguing character. The relics he acquires mysteriously increase in value for various reasons. His bone-box is original; the first part of the inscription, *Jacob son of Joseph*, is authentic. The second part, *brother of Jesus,* is a poorly executed fake and a recent addition. Some of its letters were the wrong height, some the wrong style, and some just the wrong letter, period. The Israel Antiquities Authority has declared it a forgery. Superintendent Jonathan Pagis, head of the Jerusalem fraud squad, summed it up best. "Oded Golan played with our beliefs. The beliefs of Jews and Christians. This is why it's the fraud of the century."

Whither NOMA in this morass of fraud fertilized by faith? The average human has the intelligence but not the tools to confront a fraud of this magnitude. We wish to believe, therefore we *do* believe. Skeptics use science to uncover frauds. Yet skepticism is anathema to faith, and science is unknown. Every religious person quickly abandons any pretentions to NOMA when they can replace their faith with evidence, and who can blame them. After all what is faith except that which remains when the evidence has run out and reason has left the building. Gould's proposal will never find a permanent or friendly home with religion.

Now consider NOMA from the scientist's perspective. Their standards for truth are extraordinarily high. A gazillion confirmations do not make a statement true. Yet a single false one effectively destroys it. Consider the Goldbach conjecture: every even number greater than 2 can be expressed as the sum of two primes[*]. For example, 8=5+3 and 20=17+3 and so on. Using high-speed computers, mathematicians have proven this conjecture true for the first one quintillion numbers (1,000,000,000,000,000,000). But that's not enough: a single false result would demolish it.

As a result, by scientific standards, we need only show a single type of NOMA transgression into the real world. The greatest of all trespassers is the miracle—a breaking of nature's laws. Or as clerics would grandly proclaim, God stepping out of eternity into time to do His will. Who hasn't desired a miracle in an impossible situation? Poets and minstrels have written and rhapsodized over their desire for one. Consider a famous quatrain from the *Rubáiyát* of Omar Khayyám on this very point:

> *Ah, Love! could you and I with Him conspire*
> *To grasp this sorry Scheme of Things entire,*
> *   Would not we shatter it to bits—and then*
> *Re-mould it nearer to the Heart's Desire*

In his *An Enquiry Concerning Human Understanding*, the great Scottish philosopher David Hume (1711-76) stated everything reasonable concerning miracles. In the first quotation below, Hume provides a direct challenge to Stephen Jay Gould's NOMA hypothesis. As I've said, no greater overlap between magisteria can be imagined than a miracle:

---

[*] A prime number can only be divided by itself and one.

The Christian religion not only was at first attended with miracles, but even at this day cannot be believed by any reasonable person without one. [5]

The second quotation is the most famous and remarkable rebuttal in world literature to the possibility of miracles:

When anyone tells me, that he saw a dead man restored to life, I immediately consider with myself, whether it be more probable, that this person should either deceive or be deceived, or that the fact, which he relates, should really have happened. I weigh the one miracle against the other; and according to the superiority, which I discover, I pronounce my decision, and always reject the greater miracle. *If the falsehood of his testimony would be more miraculous, than the event which he relates; then, and not till then, can he pretend to command my belief or opinion* [emphasis added]. [6]

If fundamentalist Christian or Muslim wishes to argue the above quotations don't falsify a single miracle, we reply that's not our work. You make incredible claims contrary to all the laws of nature. Now *you* must provide great evidence for your claims, otherwise exit stage left.

The age of great miracles has passed millennia ago—the parting of the seas, the raising of the dead, and the healing of the blind. At the present, we are left with the *tastelessness* of Jesus in a pancake or of his mother in a milkshake. Of course miracles are amazing events in themselves, but their acceptance or rejection by different groups is equally interesting. Hume also noted that *a wise man proportions his belief to the evidence.* However, that's an occasion almost as rare as a miracle itself. Instead of following Hume's wise maxim, acceptance is directly related to the distance between the miracle and your belief system. For example we see little, or rather no movement, on the part of the Roman Catholic hierarchy to beatify the prophet Muhammad for his miraculous "night flight" to Jerusalem aboard the white steed Borak. A hoof print of this mighty horse is apparently still visible on the site of the "holy" Al-Aqsa Mosque. From here Borak leaped to the seventh heaven with Muhammad still aboard, and while in these "heavens" the Prophet met Abraham, Moses, and

Jesus who ceded authority to him. Some say it was this heavenly meeting that ultimately prevented Muhammad from making the Holy See's short list for beatification. Conclusion: the Catholic religion and Islam are *too far* apart; so there will be no acceptance of this or any Muslim "miracles."

Entertain a second example closer to the Papal seat. There was a Catholic nun, Agnesë Gonxhe Bojaxhiu, being considered for beatification, a necessary step before canonization. The Holy See—in an unusual attempt at objectivity—asked the notorious anti-theist Christopher Hitchens to act as the devil's advocate in this case, and he did. To be beatified a single "miracle" must be certified; to be canonized a second is required. Any further "miracles" are gratuitous and considered as showing off. What follows is the account of the nun Bojaxhiu's "miracle." Astoundingly it took place a year after her death.

Once upon a time, there was a sick woman suffering from tuberculosis and an ovarian cyst. Her name was Monica and she lived in Bengal where three doctors treated and cured her in the local hospital. But according to Monica, her cure was entirely due to a metal locket strapped to her abdomen that belonged to the nun Bojaxhiu. She said a beam of light emanated from the amulet, curing the "cancerous" tumor. Her husband said she was cured by regular medical procedures; her doctors said the same. One of the doctors, Ranjan Mustafi, complained of being pressured by Bojaxhiu's Catholic order to declare the cure a miracle. But the doctor insisted it was not a miracle, nor was the cyst cancerous: she took medicines for nine months to one year and was cured.

Obviously, the Roman Catholic hierarchy hadn't read or didn't understand Hume on miracles. So they went ahead, and on October 19, 2003, in St. Peter's Basilica, Agnesë Gonxhe Bojaxhiu was beatified by Pope John Paul II. This was a scandalous case for beatification considering the rational alternative explanation for Monica's cure and Christopher Hitchens evidence—both dismissed. And the reader may be certain that another paltry "miracle" will be found and full canonization to sainthood will follow. This miracle-mongering keeps people from considering evidence-based medicine and is certain to cause needless deaths.

It keeps us in the dream world of our infancy. Incidentally, this nun Agnesë Gonxhe Bojaxhiu is also known as Mother Teresa.

When magisteria overlap, they become of interest to both religion and science. Dubious archaeological evidence, such as the Ossuary of James, must be scientifically verified; otherwise, it's just another religious fraud—the millionth piece of the cross. It seems unlikely that Christians or Muslims would have any interest in the miracles of Alexander the oracle-monger (c. 150 CE). He was famous throughout the eastern Roman Empire—Marcus Aurelius sought his counsel through the oracle Glycon. And this snake-god, a.k.a. the sweet one, with the Paris Hilton hair, was actually a hand puppet for the head of a large, live serpent. Lucian, the Greek satirist, wrote about Alexander, "By now he healed the sick, and in some cases had actually raised the dead." [7] But there will be no papal "investigation" of their verisimilitude nor will Alexander take even the smallest step on the path to saint-

Glycon

hood. No, no, his miracles will be dismissed as tricks and frauds—oh how easily our religious ethnocentrism allows this certainty. Some of these dismissive hand waves should be directed at their own less than absolute miracles: the image of Jesus in a pizza, Mary Mother of God in a subway's wall stain, or blood oozing from the eyes of religious statues.

NOMA finds no home in either the church or the laboratory. Religion and science, supernatural and natural, have been at war for millennia and this conflict mirrors the dual nature of humanity. This is part of our long childhood. There is always the prospect that religion will totally win as it did after Suleiman the Magnificent in the Muslim world or after the Emperor Constantine in Europe. Recall that when the church had things all to itself, historians called it the Dark Ages. It is possible science and secularism could triumph although we have no earthly example of this. But we do have an extraterrestrial model in the fictional television series *Star Trek*, especially the later versions. What are we left with in real time, since neither side has won, and NOMA is a mistaken scholar's fantasy? We are left with the *conflicting-worlds model*, and I will attempt to explore their titanic struggles in the past and present. It's the biggest show in town with the most far reaching outcomes. I maintain that much of history may be viewed through the lens of this conflict. As noted previously, Karl Marx proposed that all history is an economic struggle. In his eyes, the Trojan War was not an adventure to recover the wayward Helen, but a Bronze-Age clash to have free access into the Black Sea and avoid taxes. But power and control are deeper and more primal motivators than ever money could be.

MURDER IN THE NAME OF GOD

When I am in discussions with Muslims and Christians, I feel they always miss the point. Perhaps my presentation is poor or lacking in clarity. But to paraphrase Dr. Johnson, I have given you the explanation; I am not obliged to give you the understanding. My position is two-pronged. It is not enough to just be a *freethinker* insisting gods and demons do not exist. This is necessary, but not sufficient. It is not enough to just be an *anti-theist* and maintain that the concept of gods and demons is pernicious. This is necessary, but not sufficient. You need both! It is not just that the concepts of religion, all religions, are wrong; it is that they are immoral—and that's the point. The exact ground they insist is theirs—morality—is often a front for privilege and pedophilia. The church and mosque have fought every progressive step in human affairs from the abolition of slavery in the past to women's rights and birth control today. This is the true *conflicting-worlds model* at work.

In Christian countries, the majority of churchgoers are women, but they hold almost no positions of authority. In the Catholic Church, the situation is far worse than in the Protestant; it's unspeakable in Islam. Religion gains a powerful victory when the most oppressed are also its greatest supporters. Plato said he was glad to be born man and not woman. Yet we know the names of more ancient Athenian women than all the females of the Dark Ages combined. Socrates lamented that he was hen-pecked by his wife Xantippe; Pericles complained his wife Aspasia ruled him and their son ruled her. Unquestionably, there are degrees of freedom.

From Late Greek times came a woman of great intellectual ability and status: Hypatia of Alexandria (370-415 CE). She was the first noteworthy woman in mathematics as well as philosophy and astronomy. Playwrights, authors, and artists have written and woven plays, books, and paintings around the few surviving facts of her life. Carl Sagan mentions about her in his famous *Cosmos* television series, and Judy Chicago gives Hypatia a place-setting at her extraordinary sculpture *The Dinner Party*. A lunar crater and even a genus of moth bear her name. But the most extraordinary speculative depiction of her is in Raphael's Renaissance masterpiece *The School of Athens*.

The School of Athens by Raphael 1510-11

It is a part of the Apostolic Palace in the Vatican. She isn't at the center, or vanishing point of the painting—that honor was reserved for Plato and Aristotle. And the artist has painted her younger and more vulnerable than we might have expected. Yet she is the only woman among more than fifty men, and the only subject looking directly at the viewer. Raphael wraps her in white robes as a sign of her legendary chastity and the Catholic Church's unease with everything sexual. Contrast this ethic with Judy Chicago's vaginal sculptures in *The Dinner Party*. Conduct the church can't control it condemns. Unlike the others in the fresco above, who are all doing their own thing, she speaks directly to us. Who was this woman?

We know more about her spectacular death than her life. And I cannot do better than to quote Carl Sagan on this subject:

> The last scientist who worked in the Library was a mathematician, astronomer, physicist and the head of the NeoPlatonism school of philosophy—an extraordinary range of accomplishments for any individual in any age. Her name was Hypatia. She was born in Alexandria in 370. At a time when women had few options and were treated as property, Hypatia moved freely and unselfconsciously through traditional male domains. By all accounts she was a great beauty. She had many suitors but rejected all offers of marriage. The Alexandria of Hypatia's time —by then long under Roman rule—was a city under grave strain. Slavery had sapped classical civilization of its vitality. . . . Cyril, the Archbishop of Alexandria, despised her because of her close friendship with the Roman governor, and because she was a symbol of learning and science, which were largely identified by the early Church with paganism. In great personal danger, she continued to teach and publish, until, in the year 415, on her way to work she was set upon by a fanatical mob of Cyril's parishioners. They dragged her from her chariot, tore off her clothes, and armed with abalone shells, flayed her flesh from her bones. Her remains were burned, her works obliterated, her name forgotten. Cyril was made a saint. [8]

Hypatia
detail from
The School of Athens

Well, as you have read, her name is far from forgotten. I suppose we must assume St. Cyril had the requisite tawdry two miracles to become a saint. This man had other "reasons" to despise Hypatia. The most famous quotation attributed to her makes this clear: "All formal dogmatic religions are fallacious and must never be accepted by self-respecting persons as final." Cyril trusted neither science nor free thought; Hypatia was emblematic of both.

Most historians believe that Dark Ages began on September 4, 476 CE, when a Germanic chieftain deposed Romulus Augustus, the last Emperor of the Western Roman Empire. But the seeds, of course, were planted earlier. One large kernel was the slaughter of Hypatia—a symbol of science and learning—by a Christian mob with the blessing of a saint. Leading this multitude to do evil was a brute named Peter the Reader, Cyril's assistant. Religion had won this round and ruled with unchallenged power and corruption for a thousand years of unparalleled ignorance and filth. Voltaire said, "If God did not exist, it would be necessary to invent him." As a postscript to that we should say, "In the beginning, God was humanity's cruelest invention."

CHAPTER—4

OF HUMAN BONDAGE

If slavery is not wrong, nothing is wrong.
Abraham Lincoln

*My principal objections to orthodox religion are two
—slavery here and hell hereafter.*
Robert Green Ingersoll

There was a paradox at Marathon. Every soldier bravely fighting for his *personal* freedom was a slave owner. Herodotus tells of a Greek slave boy killed by a volley of Persian arrows while bringing water to a parched warrior. Contrasted with the fallen Greek warriors interned in the burial mound, their dead slaves were buried in a separate small hill, now unknown and unhonored. The glorious victory at Marathon did not free Athenian slaves—that would have been unthinkable.

Therein lies an abyss between the modern and ancient worlds: they were blind to the evil of slavery while we find it abominable. But in a hundred or a thousand years what will our descendants say about us? Will killing a great ape be tantamount to murder? Will there be any great apes left? Will they look favorably on our species chauvinism? Will our cavalier attitude toward extinguishing life forms be intolerable when another universe must pass away before such creatures come again? Many are already critical of such attitudes and activities.

Let's look more closely at slavery because its ethic is the antithesis of today's. By contrast, the clarification of one sheds light on the other—when the moon eclipses the sun, we learn something about both. Egypt, Mesopotamia, and India throughout their long histories never whispered a word against slavery, the most debasing of all human institutions.

All but the poorest Athenian citizens had slaves—lots of slaves. At the time of his death, Plato owned five. Athens probably had as many as 80,000 slaves during the 5th and 6th centuries BCE. Sparta had a collective group of slaves, called helots.

This was to be expected of an authoritarian society, and none were more authoritarian than the Spartans. At the "sacred" Greek sites of Delphi and Dodona, priests owned even more slaves. Some historians consider the ancient Greeks too enlightened a culture to commit human sacrifice. Yet the Greeks did commit these monstrous acts as a major component of their religious beliefs and female slaves were always good candidates. The Greek belief in Dionysus, the god of crop fertility, was a major element in these sacrifices. Dionysus symbolized flesh and blood as bread and wine. (Sound familiar?) Early on, however, the Hellenes, the Greeks, gave up this bloody barbarism. All but—you guessed it—the conservative priesthood at Delphi and Dodona.

Psychology tells us that it's more likely for an authoritarian society to have slaves than a democratic. History speaks this truth. Any highly stratified culture or group has already taken strides down the road toward slavery. Religion and the military know this structure well; they would never question it. It's always "Yes, your Eminence" and "Yes Sir, Captain."

From their mythology, the Greeks had the perfect archetype for slavery by totalitarianism. The unfortunate victim was the Titan Prometheus (meaning fore-thought), a challenger to the omnipotence and omniscience of Zeus. In Western society, the overriding archetypes for rebellion are Lucifer and Prometheus. The great English poet John Milton understood this and the hierarchical nature of religion when in *Paradise Lost* he has Lucifer declare, "Better to reign in Hell than serve in Heaven." Prometheus was the brother of Atlas and Epimetheus (meaning after-thought), and a more sympathetic character than Satan. The Titan stole fire from Zeus and gave it to humankind to light the world. And fire is the symbol for life and transformation; it brings light to darkness and by extension understanding to chaos. He was the champion that Shelley celebrated in the opening lines of his masterpiece *Prometheus Unbound*.

Monarch of Gods and Demons, and all Spirits
But One, who throng those bright and rolling worlds
Which Thou and I alone of living things
Behold with sleepless eyes! regard this Earth
Made multitudinous with thy slaves, whom thou

Requitest for knee-worship, prayer, and praise,
And toil, and hecatombs of broken hearts,
With fear and self-contempt and barren hope.

Paul Manship, the Rockefeller Center, New York

The Athenians had a law forbidding any citizen striking a slave. This wasn't pure altruism, but to prevent social unrest since it was often impossible, by dress, to distinguish citizen from slave. The Romans had no such discernment difficulties—the classes were easily discriminated by their cloth and their clothes.

The glistening white marble of the Pantheon and the magnificence of the public baths plus the grandeur of the Coliseum and many more came at an enormous cost. A hidden, beaten, and often butchered slave class supported all these. This is what men descend to when they aspire to the luxury of gods without science. This is what happens when you have slave-power instead of horse-power.

Under the Republic and Empire, Roman governance was sternly totalitarian. Of course, the pagan church was in bed with consul and emperor. Whether the early Christians were lion fodder or not in the Coliseum is uncertain, but Jupiter and Mars treated them mercilessly—no ecumenical spirit here! After 300 CE, pagan religion and philosophy began to fade, and in 312, Emperor Galerius legalized Christianity. Shortly after Galerius' death, Constantine switched his allegiance from Jupiter to Christ, but the state still tolerated paganism for a time. Finally in 390 CE, Theodosius I outlawed it. No ecumenical spirit here either!

Not only was the church in bed with Caesar, the church was Caesar.

Our point of interest here is the attitude of this church, the Catholic Church, toward the slavery all around them. Indeed many of the early Christians themselves were slaves. To understand this you must look at the Bible's attitude on the same subject. (By "Bible," I mean the King James Version [KJV] or the New International Version [NIV], not one of those awful "Good News" varieties. On occasion, I use my own rewriting of famous lines and label them the New Updated Bible [NUB].)

What the Bible declares on slavery, both Old Testament and New, has always been controversial and unsettling. Both advocates and abolitionists have made differing interpretations of it. But as Shakespeare says, "The devil can cite scripture for his purpose." And it's up to the reader to decide who the real devil is here. We must let the Bible speak for itself, and it has much to say on this topic. Leviticus 25:44-46 (NIV) proclaims:

> *Your male and female slaves are to come from the nations around you; from them you may buy slaves. You may also buy some of the temporary residents living among you and members of their clans born in your country, and they will become your property. You can will them to your children as inherited property and can make them slaves for life, but you must not rule over your fellow Israelites ruthlessly.*

In other words, don't enslave fellow Israelites, but do whatever you can get away with to foreigners. And do it down through the generations of your family to theirs.

Consider the "civilized" attitude of Exodus 21:20-21 (KJV):

> *And if a man smite his servant [slave], or his maid [slave], with a rod, and he die under his hand; he shall be surely punished. Notwithstanding, if he continue a day or two, he shall not be punished: for he is his money.*

Meaning, don't beat your slaves so brutally that they die—at least not for a day or two. Remember they're like your oxen and plow—property.

The next quotation is surely one of the low points ever recorded (Numbers 31:17-18). The Israelite commanders had killed all the men of Midian but spared the women and children. This "merciful" action greatly displeased *Generalissimo Moses*, so he sent them back to make things "right" ordering:

Now kill all the boys. And kill every woman who has slept with a man, but save for yourselves every girl who has never slept with a man.

Thomas Paine, one of the Founding Fathers of the United States, notably commented on this in his *Age of Reason*:

Among the detestable villains that in any period of the world have disgraced the name of man, it is impossible to find a greater than Moses, if this account be true. Here is an order to butcher the boys, to massacre the mothers, and debauch the daughters. [1]

Numbers 31:35, by its own count, says this was 32,000 virgins. Let's be clear about the situation of the virginal daughters. The very men who slaughtered their fathers, mothers, brothers, and sisters are now keeping these as sex slaves. All this under the order of the "divine" Moses—the same man our teachers

Moses with the
Ten Commandments
Rembrandt (1659)

directed us to admire. (What were they thinking? Apparently nothing at all!) However, we shouldn't find any of this surprising. After all, these Israelites were Bronze Age brutes wandering around the desert killing whomever they could and without the honor of wolves.

Modern readers have no point of moral contact with the atrocities listed above. And these crimes came from the Pentateuch (Torah), whose second book, Exodus, gave us the Ten Commandments. Accordingly, we should have a closer look at these commandments. The initial four are the ravings of an Oriental despot demanding exclusive and endless worship and praise.

The despots of Asia are, of course, the very model for Yahweh requiring no script rewriting. As for a text that is meant to be the founding document of monotheism, there is an awful lot of handwringing over *other* gods. If perchance you diverge from his strict curriculum to worship another god by way of an idol, then neither you nor your descendants will be for-given unto the third and fourth generation. This second Commandment is chilling in its anger and ferocity. Consider the exact wording in the KJV:

> *Thou shalt not bow down thyself to them, nor serve them: for I the LORD thy God am a jealous God, visiting the iniquity of the fathers upon the children unto the third and fourth generation of them that hate me.*

Well that seems about right! Let me see if I understand this. God is cursing me for all eternity for something my great grand-father did. No court on earth would deliver such an outrageous verdict today. Either God is morally inferior to our courts or morality has evolved. Make your choice!

After the Oriental despot scene, we get into the classic "Thou shalt not" parts—standard stuff found in every civilization and primitive tribe. I found the following extensive list at Wikipedia "ancient legal codes".

- Assyrian laws/Code of the Assura (ca.1075 BCE)
- Babylonian laws
- Code of Hammurabi (ca. 1790 BCE)
- Code of the Nesilim (ca. 1650-1500 BCE)
- Code of Urukagina (2,380-2,360 BCE)
- Code of Ur-Nammu, king of Ur (ca. 2050 BCE)
- Codex of Lipit-Ishtar of Isin (ca. 1870 BCE).
- Cuneiform law (2,350-1,400 BCE)
- The Gentoo Code
- Gortyn code (5th century BCE)
- The Draconian constitution (7th Century BCE)
- Hittite laws (ca. 1650-1100 BCE).
- Mosaic Law/Hebraic law—Ten Commandments.
- Traditional Chinese law
- Twelve Tables of Roman Law (451 BCE)

The tenth Commandment, "Thou shall not covet," seems to be original, and the first recorded attempt at *thought control*. Yet it's crucial to note there is not a single word against slavery in the entire Ten Commandments. "Thou shalt not bring a man, a woman, or a child into bondage" is *missing*.

After these commandments, we have all manner of injunctions, laws, and prohibitions about ox goring. Yes, you read that correctly. Perhaps this is not so important in your life right now. And shortly after this, without warning or fanfare, we read in Exodus 22:18 (KJV), "Thou shall not suffer a witch to live." This is probably the single most pernicious sentence in all of literature. For the next three millennia, this will be Europe's *Final Solution* for all older women who stray from the norm.

Those of you who believe we should get our morality from these Bronze Age brutes are themselves committing an immoral act. Morals evolve! We have to grow out of the infancy of these early times. We cannot do that by holding inflexible beliefs about a book we barely know. Today a man like Moses would be facing the International War Crimes Tribunal in The Hague on charges of genocide and crimes against humanity.

Something else is very curious about these Ten Commandments. Something so peculiar that at first you cannot believe it's true. In Exodus, Moses/God gives these edicts at least *twice*, and for an encore, he enumerates them again in Deuteronomy. Now as unusual as that is, here's the truly strange part—they're *all different*. Either Moses or god had a dreadful memory or their Xerox machine was broken. But you say this can't possibly be true—well, let me count the ways.

Moses was on Mount Sinai when Yahweh first *spoke* the Ten Commandments to him. God then instructed him to go down and tell his people to shape up. Moses does exactly this in Exodus 20:2-17—this is the familiar list noted previously. Later, Moses goes back to the Mount where Yahweh gives him two stone tablets listing these laws. Like any good teacher, God realized that just telling the sheep the Ten Commandments wasn't enough; they needed a written copy as well. But as Moses goes down the mountain lugging the tablets, he sees the people dancing and worshipping a statue of a golden calf and generally having a good time. This causes him to have a temper tantrum and to smash the priceless tablets to the ground (Exodus 32:19). Note that we never actually see this second version of the Ten Commandments.

Fortunately, Moses had a total replacement guarantee from god on the stone tablets. So back up the mountain he goes where Yahweh says to him in Exodus 34:1 (NIV):

> *Chisel out two stone tablets like the first ones, and I will write on them the words that were on the first tablets, which you broke.*

These Ten Commandments (I actually count 15) are given in Exodus 34:11-27—and regardless of what Yahweh just said—they are stunningly different from the ones we know. Well, let me show you the ways:

> *The first offspring of every womb belongs to me, including all the firstborn males of your livestock, whether from herd or flock. Redeem the firstborn donkey with a lamb, but if you do not redeem it, break its neck. Redeem all your firstborn sons. No one is to appear before me empty-handed.* (NIV)

> *Bring the best of the first fruits of your soil to the house of the LORD your God.*
> *Do not cook a young goat in its mother's milk.* (NIV)

The first quote is Exodus 34:19, the second 34:26—both from the latter list of Ten Commandments. The casual reader could interpret these edicts as just Yahweh's attempt to micromanage the daily lives of the Israelites But—oh, no!—because for the *first time*, Exodus 37:27 refers to these directly as the Ten Commandments. But they're not the ones I learned, and they're certainly not the ones on the 5,000-pound granite behemoth that was once inside the Alabama State Judicial Building. And still there is no prohibition against slavery anywhere.

In his old age—Moses is supposed to have lived 120 years—he repeated the "Ten Commandments" once again (Deuteronomy 5:6-21). By now, like many old men, he was becoming grumpy and demanding attention. These laws are very close to those of Exodus 20. The major difference is the fourth: keeping the Sabbath as a day of rest. The original reason was because God created the universe in six days, and he rested on the seventh. In Deuteronomy, the cause is entirely different, and we're tempted to think it's the garrulous Moses again drawing attention to himself. The reason given here is laid out in Deuteronomy 5:14 (NIV). And the second sentence is one of the great non-sequiturs of the Pentateuch.

> *Remember that you were slaves in Egypt and that the LORD your God brought you out of there with a mighty hand and an outstretched arm. Therefore the LORD your God has commanded you to observe the Sabbath day.*

Of course, the glorious leader on this epic journey was none other than Moses. Applause please! Personally, I've always thought this commandment was two words short: Six days shalt thou labor and do all thy work and on the seventh, thou shall do the rest *of it.*

ISLAMIC COMMANDMENTS

Islam claims descent through Abraham and his concubine Hagar by way of their son Ishmael. The Qur'an also recognizes Moses (Musa) and Jesus (Isa) as prophets. So it's hardly surprising they have their version of the Ten Commandments. Although never explicitly mentioned as such in the Qur'an, these are essentially the same as Exodus 20. Muhammad was illiterate (?), but excellent at copying, as were the writers of the Qur'an who came after him. Their version of "Thou shalt not steal" comes from Surah/ Chapter 5:38 and has a new twist.

> *As for the thief, both the male and female, cut off their hands. It is the reward of their own deeds, an exemplary punishment from Allah. Allah is Mighty, Wise.*

As with the Pentateuch, the Qur'an nowhere has a prohibition against slavery. And little wonder because Muhammad himself owned, bought, captured, and sold slaves. Yet apparently, he freed many; the Qur'an looks favorably on manumission as a way to expiate sin. Incredibly, the African countries of Chad,

Mali, Mauritania, and Sudan still practice slavery professing divine approval from the Qur'an. Claiming sanction for slavery and other odious acts from "holy" books is an ancient and cruel tradition, one in which Christianity is also well versed.

Under Islam, the condition of slaves generally improved, certainly over earlier Roman times and medieval Christian practices. The Muslim laws governing all aspects of slaves were complex and highly legalized. For example, Islam allowed for sexual intercourse between a *male* master and a *female* slave—the kind of action Solomon was expert at with his 700 wives and 300 concubines. The Qur'an refers to this as *ma malakat aymanukum* or "what your right hand possesses." However the "deprived" master must not have sex with his wives' slaves. Muhammad had sex with at least two of his female slaves, one of whom he later married. Consider the following revealing passage from Surah 33, verse 50, of the Qur'an:

> *O Prophet! Lo! We have made lawful unto thee thy wives unto whom thou hast paid their dowries, and those whom thy right hand possesseth of those whom Allah hath given thee as spoils of war [female slaves] . . . and a believing woman if she give herself unto the Prophet and the Prophet desire to ask her in marriage—a privilege for thee only, not for the (rest of) believers—We are aware of that which We enjoined upon them concerning their wives and those whom their right hands possess— that thou mayst be free from blame, for Allah is Forgiving, Merciful.*

The Slave Market
by
Jean-Leon Gérôme

Ah, how perfect for the Prophet: a special commandment Muhammad handed down by himself for himself, allowing him unlimited sex and wives. Others arc restricted to four wives, but may also have sex with any number of slaves.

Surely multiple mistresses/wives must elicit memories of religious groups with virtual harems of worshippers. *Warren Jeffs* is the former leader of the Fundamentalist Church of Jesus Christ of Latter Day Saints

(FLDS Church) and a convicted pedophile. *Jim Jones*, of Jonestown infamy, banned sex among Temple members outside of marriage, yet he himself rapaciously had sexual relations with both male and female cult members. *David Koresh* was the leader of the Branch Davidian religious sect. Koresh had sexual intercourse with girls as young as 12, fathering at least a dozen of the compound's children. *Winston Blackmore* is the Bishop of "Bountiful," British Columbia. Regrettably, for Winston, the Royal Canadian Mounted Police arrested him in January 2009 on charges of polygamy. At the last count, Blackmore has 25 wives and 101 children.

Like any baboon troop, the top male gets his pick of the females. In wild animal groups, this makes for good genetics. In religious cults and congregations, it makes for headlines and new standards for horniness.

The difference between a cult and a religion is apparent: cults have few members religions have many. All the peculiar aspects of cults are also found in religions. It's just that time and geography acculturate the followers to one and not the other. "Normal," no matter how bizarre, is what's around you. Consider the easy acceptance of slavery in our past.

THE MISSING COMMANDMENTS

The Ten Commandments comprise some excellent prohibitions— ones found in all legal codes. Nevertheless, the introductory throat clearing by the deity saying, "I am the Big I am" is childish and smacks rightly of Oriental despotism. And this continual worrying about other gods, who might steal his worshippers, is ludicrous for the bedrock book on monotheism. Lastly, the Tenth Commandment is a slap at free enterprise and the universal drive to acquire. Moreover, from a modern perspective, these foundational moral laws for Judaism, Christianity, and Islam are astonishing for what they omit:

- An edict declaring the equality of woman—the Old Testament grouped them with the ox and the ass.
- A law prohibiting slavery of all kinds.

Of course, these two missing commandments are related—the sword in the scabbard so to speak. Religions have always treated women as second, or lower class objects. "Cover yourselves, and get thee to the rear of the bus and be silent" has forever been the unspoken commandment. Listen carefully, you can hear it still among certain groups.

Thus far, in this chapter, I have been mostly critical of God's commandments, edicts, and laws. The challenge arises: could you or I do any better? I think the answer to that is yes—a lot better. I would ask the reader to also think of five moral laws before I list my attempt. We'll stop at five as if to have half a Decalogue or a Pentalogue if you like.

My first is a universal law found in every culture and civilization. We call it the Golden Rule. Some call it the ethic of reciprocity. The modern concept of human rights is based on this principle. Anyone attempting to live by this rule must see the whole world as their village and not just his or her family, friends, neighbors, and fellow citizens. It seems quite evident that the occurrence everywhere of the Golden Rule implies an earthy evolutionary, not a divine celestial origin.

The following is a chronological list of the Golden Rule compiled from the world's religions and cultures:

Ancient Egyptian: *Do for one who may do for you, that you may cause him thus to do.* (ca. 1800 BC)

Zoroastrianism: *Whatever is disagreeable to yourself do not do unto others.* Shayast-na-Shayast 13:29

Judaism: *Do not seek revenge or bear a grudge against one of your people, but love your neighbor as yourself.* Leviticus 19:18 (NIV)

Buddhism: *Hurt not others in ways that you yourself would find hurtful.* Udana-Varga 5:18

Taoism: *Regard your neighbor's gain as your own gain, and your neighbor's loss as your own loss.* T'ai Shang Kan Ying P'ien.

Confucianism: *Do not do to others what you do not want them to do to you.* Analects of Confucius 15:23

Jainism: *In happiness and suffering, in joy and grief, we should regard all creatures as we regard our own self.* Lord Mahavira, 24th Tirthankara

Greek Philosophy: *One should never do wrong in return, nor mistreat any man, no matter how one has been mistreated by him.* Socrates (*Crito*)

Hinduism: *This is the sum of duty: do not do to others what would cause pain if done to you.* Mahabharata 5:1517

Roman Paganism: *The law imprinted on the hearts of all men is to love the members of society as themselves.*

Christianity: *And as ye would that men should do to you, do ye also to them likewise.* Luke 6:31 (KJV)

Islam: *Hurt no one so that no may hurt you.* Muhammad, The Farewell Sermon

Baha'i Faith: *Blessed is he who preferreth his brother before himself.* Bahá'u'lláh

Humanism: *Don't do things you wouldn't want to have done to you.* British Humanist Society

Unitarianism: *We affirm and promote respect for the interdependent web of all existence of which we are a part.* Unitarian Principles

Phenomenal, isn't it? Over thousands of years and immense stretches of geography, all these cultures, religions, and philosophies arrived at the identical moral law. The inference is apparent: none can claim priority or uniqueness. It also seems evident that the Golden Rule arrived by natural selection because it preserves life. How else can you reasonably account for its ubiquity? To paraphrase Rousseau, "Man was born good, but everywhere institutions make him evil." What institutions? Fascism, Marxism, Maoism, Christianity, Islam, and other totalitarian disciplines—all those with a fixed, unyielding ideology to which humankind is forced to genuflect and ultimately kneel. An American bumper sticker says, "And Every Knee Shall Bow." Or what? Or they will be broken! As many have observed, all great crimes are committed in the name of a "higher" good.

The biblical parable of the Good Samaritan superbly illustrates the law of reciprocity. A Jew was traveling from Jerusalem to Jericho when bandits attacked him. They left him naked and near dead at the side of the road. By chance, a priest saw him lying there but passed on by. A Levite saw him there but also passed on by. Both refused to help. Then a hated Samaritan came by, saw the Jew's condition, and felt compassion. He attended to his wounds, put him on his own donkey, and took him to an inn to take care of him. "Which of these three do you think was a neighbor to the man who fell into the hands of robbers?" Jesus asked. We are, of course, all neighbors, and a full realization of this would solve many world problems.

Vincent van Gogh dramatically depicted all of this in his painting *The Good Samaritan*. In the background, you can see the Levite and further back still the priest walking on by. Nothing in this painting is static, even the air is alive and moving, reflecting the drama of the moment. The culture, time, and place of this scene are foreign to us. By analogy, it would be similar to an American or Canadian soldier coming to the aid of a wounded Taliban fighter. We should expect nothing less. In the present world, we are all neighbors.

The Good Samaritan
by
Vincent van Gogh (1890)

I have heard it said that the world's religions have failed because they didn't teach the Golden Rule with sufficient sincerity and vigor. But that's false! We have all failed! When we allow governments to dehumanize our enemies by labeling them Huns, Japs, Dagos, and Ragheads, then they are no longer our fellow humans but vermin to be exterminated. This is one way we allow governments and institutions to divert us from our natural goodness to do evil. Men and women aren't born evil; no child comes from its mother's birth canal evil. The Christian concept of original sin is a sickness shaped by sociopaths.

After this extended exposition of the Golden Rule, I'll just list all the commandments of my Pentalogue:

1. The Golden Rule.
2. Thou shalt not follow a multitude to do evil.
3. All peoples of whatever gender or sexual orientation will be equal under the law.
4. Our beliefs and actions will be based on evidence rather than fear and faith.
5. Slavery in all its many forms and morphs must be abolished.

Rule 2 is from Exodus 23:2 and was Bertrand Russell's favorite Old Testament injunction. It is worth noting that my Pentalogue is totally distinct from the biblical Decalogue. On the other hand, I'm confident that *your* Pentalogue will overlap in at least one or more cases with mine. Did you duplicate any from the ten in Exodus? Naturally the Golden Rule in its fullest interpretation would wholly subsume my remaining four. But edicts and laws should be spelled out and pointed out lest malefactors creep through the cracks.

None of my rules detracts from the moral power of Commandments 6 and 8: Thou shalt not. . . . Yet for those recovering from Christian ethnocentrism, they will find it remarkable that certain concepts other than the Golden Rule are also universal, for example, "Thou shalt not kill" and "Thou shalt not steal."

To illustrate this point, consider the following true account of some Inuit (Eskimos) on the Canadian tundra. The following comes from a marvelous little book called *Glimpses of the Barren Lands* by Thierry Mallet, privately published in New York in 1930. For many years, Mallet was a fur trader among the Inuit people in their unforgiving land. He eloquently wrote about what he knew. He lived it.

With his exploring instinct, Mallet climbed a *pingo*, a dome-shaped mound of earth standing alone in the immense flat tundra. After a long struggle through coulees and huge boulders, he ultimately reached its summit only to be startled by an Inuit grave. I'll let Mallet speak for himself; he's describing this burial site:

At the head of it, a few feet away, a spear stood erect, stuck deep in the ground and solidly wedged in at the base between heavy rocks. The point was of native copper. From it fluttered, in rags, the remains of a deerskin coat.

At the foot lay, side by side, a kayak with its paddle and a harpoon and a twenty-foot sleigh with its set of dog harness and a snow knife. Both kayak and sleigh were held down by stones carefully placed along their entire length.

On the grave itself I found a rifle, a small kettle with a handful of tea leaves inside, a little wooden box containing ten cartridges, a pipe, a plug of tobacco, matches, a knife, a small telescope, and a neatly coiled rawhide belt. One could see that everything had been lying there a few weeks only. No inscription of any sort. But the weapons showed that it was a man who had been buried in that lonely spot.

As I leaned against the grave, my eyes wandered around. I tried to picture to myself the faithful companions of the deceased hunter struggling up that hill, bearing on their shoulders the rigid body of their dead; their search for hundreds of rocks, and the work of piling them, one by one, for hours and hours, until the mound was able to defy the efforts of the wild animals and the incessant pressure of the years to come; finally the long descent to the camp, to bring up again, one by one, the precious belongings of the deceased.

To me, there alone, leaning on that grave on the top of that immense hill, the whole undertaking seemed incredible. The more I thought, the more I marveled, searching for the motive which had prompted those native, not only to choose that almost inaccessible spot to lay their dead at rest, but to abandon unhesitatingly on his grave that wealth of articles which I knew represented an immense value to them, in their constant bitter struggle for mere existence.

Pagans they were—pagans they still remain. Although they have a certain code to which they are faithful.

And that code included "Thou shalt not steal." No pharaoh was more lovingly laid to rest or with items more precious. Here among the destitute, unlike ancient Egypt, there were no grave robbers. The English philosopher Thomas Hobbes argued that people were naturally wicked and not fit to govern themselves. He famously said, "life in the state of nature is solitary, poor, nasty, brutish, and short." Sometimes, Mr. Hobbes, it's solitary, poor, honorable, brave, and short.

WORLD'S GREATEST?

If someone asked you to name the world's greatest writer, you might reply Shakespeare, Tolstoy, or Homer. If you were asked to name the world's greatest painter, you might answer Michelangelo, da Vinci, or Rembrandt. If you were further asked to name history's greatest scientist, you could say Einstein, Newton, or Archimedes. Continuing with this if you were finally questioned for the name of history's greatest social hero, you might have reason to pause awhile. Karl Marx gave one answer: Spartacus. In a letter to Engels, he described Spartacus as "the most splendid fellow in the whole of ancient history." Americans are more likely to remember him from Stanley Kubrick's 1960 movie *Spartacus* starring almost everyone in Hollywood, and adapted from Howard Fast's novel of the same name.

Who was Spartacus? He was a Thracian slave trained as a gladiator at Capua for the amusement of Roman citizens. Along with seventy companions, using kitchen implements as weapons, he escaped and hid on the slopes of Mount Vesuvius. When the news of this spread throughout the countryside, thousands of others, including children, joined Spartacus.

The Oath of Spartacus
by
Louis-Ernest Barrias (1869)

Romans, at first believing this was a minor problem, sent a minor force to suppress these upstart slaves as a lesson to anyone else. But this army was soundly beaten, as was the next, and the next, and the one after that. At its peak, Spartacus and his "extended family" comprised some 120,000 free slaves from numerous countries speaking many languages.

This revolt—officially called the Third Servile War—*was not* an attempt to reform Roman society and abolish slavery as Kubrick implied in his epic film. Yet it was a vast uprising of oppressed people against a slave-owning aristocracy.

By now, the Roman Senate was paying full attention and fearful that Rome itself might be in danger. Pompey the Great was in Spain to the west with his army, and other legions were to the east in what is now Turkey. So the Senate appointed the experienced Marcus Crassus to take command and crush this rebellion.

Marcus Crassus
The Louvre

I can say with complete certainty that the reader has never met anyone like Crassus. He was the third man in the First Triumvirate along with Pompey and Caesar, and quite likely the richest person in antiquity. Notorious for *rapaciousness* and *brutality*, he acquired his fortune through "legal" murder and theft—the Romans called it the Proscription List. Most shameful was his acquisition of burning homes. Upon receiving word of a house on fire, he would arrive and purchase the property for a modest sum, and then employ his army of firefighters to put out the flames. (You must appreciate that ancient Rome didn't have socialized services like fire departments.) Furthermore, as with any good Roman aristocrat, he dealt in slaves. Crassus held every high office in Rome except *Pontifex Maximus*, high priest of Jupiter, but he bought and bribed others to give this position to Julius Caesar.

With the backing of the Senate and his bottomless purse, he acquired and outfitted ten legions. That's as many as 45,000 or more elite troops. To instill iron discipline—always a favorite virtue with authoritarians—he had his troops *decimated*: an ancient Roman practice whereby every tenth man was killed (by lot) for a perceived breach of order. Now, on to discipline Spartacus.

Crassus versus Spartacus—there could be no deeper contrast in personalities. The Roman system had eaten the young Crassus and spat out a monster. His code was a perversion of the Golden Rule: do to others before they do it to you. The Roman system had tried to devour Spartacus, but spat out one of history's greatest heroes—the ultimate underdog refusing to kneel to power and privilege. Plutarch, the biographer of the ancient world, described him as:

> *[A] Thracian of one of the nomadic tribes, and a man not only of high spirit and valiant, but in understanding, also, and in gentleness superior to his condition, and more of a Grecian than the people of his country usually are.* [2]

The outcome of the assault by Crassus' legions on Spartacus' "extended family" was predictable. When the general's centurions finally overran their encampment, they unexpectedly found 3,000 captive Romans—all of whom were unharmed. Yet when the beast had the rebel army in his fangs, he crucified all those still alive along the road from Rome to Capua—some 6,000. The rotting corpses hung there for years.

There are many stories concerning Spartacus' death. Since the slaves had no uniforms to distinguish rank, and Spartacus gave up his horse to fight this ultimate battle on foot, he was just one among thousands. In the life of "Crassus," Plutarch recounts his death:

> *And so making directly towards Crassus himself, through the midst of arms and wounds, he missed him, but slew two centurions that fell upon him together. At last being deserted by those that were about him, he himself stood his ground, and surrounded by the enemy, bravely defending himself, was cut to pieces.* [3]

According to Kubrick, Crassus demanded of the 6,000 ragtag survivors, "Which one of you is Spartacus?" And in a point of high drama, first one, then another, then all 6,000 were on their feet saying with single voice "I'm Spartacus." This is not historical although it is true to the spirit of the rebel gladiator. In some sense, we are all Spartacus searching for freedom within the social order of responsibility: freedom from danger, freedom from multinational and corporate greed, freedom from pollution, freedom from indoctrination, and freedom *of* and freedom *from* religion.

The separate fates of the First Triumvirate of Caesar, Pompey, and Crassus were surprisingly similar. Caesar, as we all remember, was stabbed to death on the Ides of March. Pompey was beheaded in Egypt, and Crassus lost his head in Syria while fighting the Parthians. Apparently, these warriors were well aware of his legendary avarice, and to commemorate this they filled his gaping maw with molten gold: *sic transit gloria mundi.*

NEW TESTAMENT SLAVES

Mark Twain wilily observed, "Man is the only slave. And he is the only animal who enslaves." He later added, "Man is the only animal that blushes. Or needs to."

We have affirmed Twain's first observation throughout the ancient and modern worlds. All peoples practiced slavery with greater or lesser degrees of cruelty: the Hebrews of the Old Testament, the Greeks at Marathon, the Romans everywhere, and the Arabs to the present day. During all this time, however, we have seen nothing of Twain's second observation.

But some of those still not fully manumitted protest that surely the New Testament speaks out loud and clear against all forms of slavery. No it does not! Not a sentence, not a phrase, not even a whispered word. Oh, slaves are mentioned, and the New Testament tells us to treat them as we would our ox, ass, or dog. People as property. The garrulous Apostle Paul puts it directly to slaves in the following passages:

> *Slaves, obey your earthly masters with respect and fear, and with sincerity of heart, just as you would obey Christ.*
> Ephesians 6:5 (NIV)

> *Slaves, obey your earthly masters in everything . . . since you know that you will receive an inheritance from the Lord as a reward.*
> Colossians 3:22, 24 (NIV)

All who are under the yoke of slavery should consider their masters worthy of full respect . . . Those who have believing masters are not to show less respect for them because they are brothers.
1 Timothy 6:1-2 (NIV)

Teach slaves to be subject to their masters in everything, to try to please them, not to talk back to them, and not to steal from them, but to show that they can be fully trusted.
Titus 2:9-10 (NIV)

In all this, the Apostle wasn't saintly, kind, or unduly wise. (It's important to note that the early Christian church was the largest slave owner in the Roman Empire.) Let's summarize Paul's "job description" for chattel slaves.

— SLAVES WANTED —

Must show real fear and trembling in the presence of their masters. Must obey their masters in everything. Have to respect their masters whether they are Pagans or Christians. Even though you will be under the yoke of slavery, you have to consider your masters worthy of respect in all matters. And, oh yes, you will be paid after you die. Wimps need not apply.

Reply to Saint Paul (a.k.a. Saul): Slave Booster

As pointed out previously, neither Jesus, Paul, nor any biblical character in the whole of the Gospels spoke a single word of condemnation against slavery—unbelievable. In the time of Jesus, Palestine had several slave revolts. Everyone of consequence owned slaves: the high priests, the middle classes, even the temple in Jerusalem owned slaves. During Jesus' arrest, Simon Peter cut off the ear of Malchus, a slave of Caiaphas, the high priest. Considering all this, Jesus *had to know* about slavery. He truly did render unto Caesar the things which are Caesar's—in this the Son of God was not unduly wise or kind.

Let's return to the Apostle Paul, the New Testament's expositor of the Christian position on slavery and one that pro-slavery advocates would cite for almost two millennia. Paul's short

Epistle to Philemon deals explicitly with masters and men, slave owners and slaves. The Apostle admonishes the masters to treat their slaves well. This enjoinment for fair treatment of slaves was not new, however. At that time, the Stoics were also arguing for fair treatment—like the laws the Athenians had written four centuries earlier. But texts such as "*Slaves, obey your earthly masters with respect and fear . . .*" doubtless made beatings and brutality more common.

The letter to Philemon unfolds as follows: Paul befriends and converts a fugitive slave named Onesimus to Christianity. However, the slave's master, Philemon, is also a friend of the Apostle and a Christian "gentleman." (Take note again, Christians were slave owners.) Furthermore, Onesimus is rumored to have stolen money from Philemon to aid in his escape. (No thought is given to the master's theft of Onesimus' "Life, liberty, and the pursuit of happiness.") Paul, with the runaway in his care so to speak, chooses to send him back to his master—an historic decision. The contrast with the behavior of Spartacus is striking. Poor Onesimus, Paul *enslaved him twice*: once to Christ and again to Philemon. Oh, I forgot to add that Onesimus would get his reward in heaven . . . just wait. Then the Epistle continues with Byzantine circumlocutions: Paul entreats Philemon to care for his captured slave mercifully and as a Christian brother. Nevertheless, returning the runaway to his master gave a solid religious underpinning to slavery—something history's long memory would never forget. This was the ultimate rendering unto Caesar by the perfect company man, Paul of Tarsus.

The biblical translators of the word *slave* have judiciously considered our modern sensibilities. Although a cynic might infer certain words have been translated in such a manner as to conceal what is now socially unacceptable. For example, when you read "servant, manservant, or bondman" think "male slave." When you read "maid, maidservant, or bondmaid" think "female slave."

With modern computers, it's possible to do a detailed word analysis of the Bible. This study reveals how infrequently the word *slave* actually occurs in the New Testament. Some small historical investigation indicates the Pagan zeitgeist of the first centuries was slave manumission. The Christians were, as they say, "a called out group," an ecclesia in its root meaning, and the infrequency of the word *slave* reflects this isolation. A large percentage of the early converts—looking for a better life—were slaves or recently manumitted slaves, which makes this avoidance doubly puzzling. They had their eyes on the next world and the *imminent return* of Jesus Christ in the clouds. We are still waiting!

The whole of the New Testament comprises 138,020 Greek words[*]. Of these only 178 are from the slave word group: *slave, female slave, enslave, slavery,* and *a slave to god*. Of course, the phrase *a slave to god* is not what we're looking for.

As an aside, the Greeks would never have referred to themselves in this manner; they loved freedom too much. With respect to Zeus and his dysfunctional extended family, they would have labeled themselves his companions or friends. The actual Greek word for slave is δουλοσ (doulos). Yet there are six Greek words for servant, and δουλοσ isn't one of them. So every mistranslation from slave to servant is a signal of the modern scholars' deception—even though, as we have seen, all the authors of the New Testament used it and never blushed.

ABRAHAM AND BRAHMA

It is customary to refer to Judaism, Christianity, and Islam collectively as the *Abrahamic religions*. Myth and legend tell us the patriarch had a hand in founding all three. An analysis of this trio is at the heart of this book. Yet old Abraham may also have gone to India or perhaps originated there assuming such a person actually existed. There are striking similarities between the Hindu god Brahma and his consort Saraisvati, and the Jewish Abraham and his wife Sarai, that seem more than just coincidences. Possibly it's Abraham for Jews and Christians, Ibrahim for Muslims, and Brahma for Hindus. This gives the adjective "Abrahamic" an even larger scope, and for this reason, we'll have a look at Hinduism and slavery.

---

[*] These count numbers depend on the different so-called canonical texts used, and these change with the times and sects—Catholic, Protestant, Greek Orthodox, and so on.

Hinduism proudly legalizes slavery in its caste system. The only religion with a documented concept of the untouchables—the outcastes. It's a religion spreading slavery by scripture. Originating in the doctrine that all people are born unequal, Untouchables are the most pitiful victims of organized religion.

Sage Manu, the "greatest" advocate of the caste system, laid down all its laws, rules, and codes in his Manu-Smriti (written about 200 BCE). Traditionally there were four castes:

Brahmins—Priests and teachers
Kshatriyas—Rulers and warriors
Vaisyas—Businessmen
Shudras—Laborers.

But the untouchables were beneath even the laborers, outside the caste system so to speak. The reader will recognize this system is just the *priest, potentate, peasant* model mentioned earlier (pages 14-15) with the peasant class divided into businessman, laborer, and untouchable.

The atrocities committed against Untouchables, known as Dalits, are legion. These crimes are so outrageous that comfortable Westerners, drinking coffee in their easy chairs, cannot, I repeat cannot, comprehend them. Here's a random sample of headlines from India's major newspapers: "Dalit boy beaten to death for picking flowers," "Dalit witch paraded naked in Bihar," and "7 Dalits burnt alive in a caste clash." Furthermore, to be born Untouchable and a woman is a double curse. Yet these poor creatures don't seem to be untouchable when it comes to rape by higher caste members.

The Indian constitution officially prohibits untouchability—but laws without enforcement are just black marks on white paper. In 1989, the government passed The Prevention of Atrocities Act. This legislation made it illegal to parade people naked through the streets, force them to eat feces, take away their land, foul their water, and burn down their homes. Since then things have gotten worse. As I said, laws without enforcement are just black marks on white paper.

This is what life descends to when religion ascends to govern everything. Men and woman are born good, but everywhere stratified society deforms them to do evil.

PRIESTLY PEDOPHILIA

As Bertrand Russell observed, if you open a crate of oranges and the top layer is rotten, then the prospects for the next layers are dismal indeed. Consider the Holy Roman Catholic Church and its current sodomy and pedophilia outrages as the top layer. If we dig back into its past, the lower levels of fruits so to speak, we can expect more of the same—rotten level after rotten level— ever worse as we dig deeper into the putrefaction.

Grass root protests have occurred all across North America by parents and concerned citizens against allowing known child molesters moving into a neighborhood. The outrage is doubly strong when the police move in a molester without *first* telling the residents. Incredibly, these same parents, willingly and with enthusiasm, conduct their children directly into the molester's lair: the church. For two millennia, Catholics have claimed the Apostle Peter and his successors in Rome to be the temporal head of Christ's Church. This same church has a two millennia history of sexual abuse and cover up. Let history speak:

309 CE: The earliest known written record of priestly sexual abuse comes from Elvira, Spain. This church council prescribed up to ten years of fasting and excommunication for molestation, with no hope of forgiveness even at the point of death. For bishops, the council laid out harsher punishments.

330-379 CE: "A cleric or monk who seduces youth or young boys . . . is to be publicly flogged. For six months he will languish in prison-like confinement . . . and he shall never again associate with youths in private conversation nor in counseling them," wrote theologian Saint Basil.

1049 CE: Cardinal Damian's *Book of Gomorrah* on the depravity of the priesthood, derisively rebuked priests who sexually defiled men or boys. He was particularly hard on superiors who stomached offenders. He pleaded with the pope to clean house. Pope Leo IX ignored Damian's emphasis on the suffering of victims. All this reads like today's headlines.

1140 CE: The *Decretum Gratiani* is a collection of Canon law, including a specific reference to "sexual violation of boys." It proposed that priests guilty of pederasty should suffer the same penalties as laypersons. Oh, that it were so!

1568 CE: Pope Pius V's edict *Horrendum Est* declared priests who sexually abuse boys, men, and girls were to be deprived of all monies, degraded, or evicted from the clergy, and turned over to secular authorities.

The 1074 Decree of the Council at Rome made celibacy mandatory for the priesthood although earlier edicts said much the same. But as we can see from the above crime sheet, priestly wickedness existed both before and after this date. Hence, whether priests marry or not is irrelevant to child molestation. This inference is clear!

It appears the scourge of abuse in the Catholic Church is less an anomaly than a tradition. Look around you. Read your newspapers, computers, and iPods; see for yourself the tradition still lives. To see this as a new and isolated crime is to not know history. To comprehend why the Catholic hierarchy is incapable of stopping it—both then and now—requires deeper digging. Like a mythical monster, the crime is double-headed: the act itself and the secret cover up.

When authority yokes children under a privileged priesthood, to whom the laity gives all deference and respect, the child is as surely a slave as any poor wretch born on the mud floor of an ancient Roman chattel house. The priesthood and the laity have done a centuries-old dance—one leads, the other averts its eyes. When a novice priest is about to enter the inner sanctum, he must speak three shibboleths: secrecy, secrecy, secrecy! Moreover, he must teach these to the monks and nuns. But beyond all this, the priests, bishops, cardinals, and even popes must inculcate them into the minds of the abused and violated children. If this indoctrination is not enough, then they are paid "hush money" and forced to sign non-disclosure documents. These are the same little boys and girls—the innocents—the ones whose parents joyfully ushered them into the pedophile's lair. Although overlooked by Dante, hell should have a unique circle for child abusers and their secret enablers. Even Dante kept their secret.

This culture of secrecy reached an apotheosis when Ratzinger was Prefect of the Congregation for the Doctrine of the Faith (read Inquisition). On May 18, 2001, the then-Cardinal Ratzinger sent a letter to every bishop in the Catholic Church. The epistle reminded them of the severe penalties facing any clergy who revealed or turned over to the secular authorities allegations against priests involving sexual abuse. These enquiries are, he said, the sole prerogative of the Congregation and all such allegations are to be sent directly to his office—they continue to accumulate. We have no idea how many there are or how deep their depravity. But you can be certain these are not tales of Peter Rabbit. This letter so frightened the bishops and those beneath them that police investigations are routinely blocked or obstructed. Instead, they transfer the pedophile from diocese to diocese, parish to parish, even to different countries. When this no longer works, the hierarchy in Rome transfer the molester directly to the Vatican apartments. Now he is safe and secure in the arms of the church forever and ever. Amen.

The consequences of this obfuscating secrecy are many. The victims—the terrified children, the tormented adults—*never see justice*; the crimes go unpunished. Between 1950 and 2002, in America alone, at least 10,667 [4] charges of child sexual abuse were made against priests. And certainly, that's only a small percentage of the actual abuse cases. By transferring child abusers from parish to parish, the church leads molesters to fresh pastures to foul, and foul again. All medical authorities assure us pedophiles are ultimately incurable; the best you can do is to keep them away from children and adolescents. But none of this is important to the imperious men in flowing robes and high hats. Their only concern is for the welfare of themselves and the interests of the church. So this is the place the vaunted high morality of the Catholic Church has led us: a dung heap. Figuratively they cover their asses so literally the children cannot cover theirs. These bishops and cardinals—the ones doing the transferring—are the enablers Dante forgot.

EMPERORS, POPES, AND SLAVERY

Slaves have always been convenient sex objects whether they were willing or not. Nonetheless, over time their condition improved in the Roman Empire. Yet the Empire's largest slave owner, the Christian church, had little hand in this amelioration, although they rewrote history to give themselves the biggest white hats. We shouldn't be surprised at this because with dictatorial groups the end always justifies the means.

Most historians credit this improvement to the Stoics—Emperor Marcus Aurelius was a Stoic. In his *Meditations* he wrote, "We should not say 'I am an Athenian' or 'I am a Roman' but 'I am a citizen of the Universe.'" They believed in the brotherhood and sisterhood of humankind and the equality of all, master with man. Evidence suggests the Stoics denounced slavery itself—their leader Epictetus had been a slave.

Marcus Aurelius
Emperor: 161–180 CE

Even slavery they thought didn't preclude an individual from practicing an ideal of inner self-mastery. Stoic philosophers like Seneca championed the rights of the oppressed; he managed to persuade the young Nero to grant slaves the right to appeal against cruelty to the Roman courts. And a famous Stoic lawyer Ulpian made it illegal for parents to sell their children into slavery. Unbelievably Constantine, the first Christian emperor, annulled most of the beneficial work of his pagan predecessors and again allowed parents to sell their children.

Constantine
Emperor: 306–337 CE

Thomas Aquinas
1225–74 CE

Many thinkers have observed that all great crimes are done in the name of a higher good. They might also have added that many small crimes are committed to the same ideology. Evil men do evil acts; good men do good acts, but to get a good man to do evil requires religion.

Fortunately for the famous Catholic philosopher Augustine of Hippo (354–430 CE), he had an abundance of religion and a head packed with god stuffing. With Byzantine locutions, he ended up *justifying* slavery as the result of sin and not a natural condition. Augustine also opined that the Jewish custom of freeing slaves after six years didn't apply to Christian slaves because of St. Paul's admonition. Incidentally, Paul's rough advice was analogous to that of Colonel Saito's to the prisoners in the film *The Bridge on the River Kwai*, "Be happy in your work."

It's interesting that a little taste of slavery, up close and personal, can nullify the most "profound" religious musings. St. Patrick (415–493 CE) was a former slave, and he argued vehemently against this practice. Reality is a great philosopher.

The Scholastic philosopher St. Thomas Aquinas (c. 1225–1274)—in a flight of classification and dissection that required little originality or compassion—arrived at the same conclusion as Augustine: slavery is God's punishment for sin. Punishment now, punishment later. And he further concluded, with no premise and less inference, that a child of a slave—even though it had committed no sin—was rightly enslaved for life. Also, being one not to miss any detail, he further noted that anyone who helps a slave to escape is guilty of theft because a slave is just property.

None of my remarks are meant to imply Augustine and Aquinas didn't want slaves to be treated properly with the right to food and rest. These renowned Catholic theologians were following the Old Testament and the New, the laws of Moses and the teachings of St. Paul. To deviate from these revealed truths would be heresy. Their writings, their every thought, had to harmonize with God's holy word. That left little room for novelty and originality. Augustine and Aquinas were good men who followed a multitude to do evil: the justification of slavery.

In the 13th century, Christians were amazed and stimulated by Latin translations of Jewish and Arabic versions of Aristotle's works. Scholastics like Aquinas realized this new universe of understanding had to be harmonized with the "word" from Jerusalem. It's simplistic to say religion has faith without reason; science has reason without faith—yet this is the root difference between them. Aquinas wanted both, so reason and faith had to be reconciled. The good scholar spun such a cobweb of erudition attempting to do this that many are still stuck on its sticky strands after 800 years.

So with the black light cast by Augustine and Aquinas illuminating the way, the papacy continued on its barbarous path supporting slavery. In 1488, King Ferdinand II (the one who bankrolled Columbus) gave Pope Innocent VIII a gift of 100 slaves. The pope distributed these to his cardinals and the Roman

Alexander VI
1492–1503

nobility. Perhaps he had enough of his own.

The next pope, Alexander VI, a.k.a. the Borgia Pope, issued the papal bull *Dum Diversas* proclaiming:

We grant you [Kings of Spain and Portugal] by these present documents, with our Apostolic Authority, full and free permission to invade, search out, capture, and subjugate the Saracens and pagans and any other unbelievers and enemies of Christ wherever they may be, as well as their kingdoms, duchies, counties, principalities, and other property [...] and to reduce their persons into perpetual slavery.

Incredible, isn't it? Just as the Old World was discovering the New with its limitless possibilities and wondrous civilizations of Mayans, Aztecs, and Incas, this pope had a Bronze Age moment.

Perhaps he was too busy with his mistress and their four children to give the matter much thought. After all, he had already missed the earlier edict on celibacy. And his extravagant nepotism took up the rest of his time. Oh, and I forgot to mention the wild orgies—yes, the wild sex orgies; they were time-consuming as well as exhausting. While the parties rolled on in the papal palaces, everyday life in the streets of Rome was abominable. The city crawled with assassins and informers; robberies and murders were committed without fear of punishment.

It would take more than amazing grace to save wretches like these, both papal and public! So let's pass on by and move closer to our own time.

THE CRUELEST CUT

In the springtime of my life, when I was a boy on my uncle's farm, there came a time for the castration of the piglets. My uncle would duly equip himself with his straight razor for the surgery and turpentine for the antiseptic. My cousin and I *never* went into the barn to witness this ghastly business. The ear-piercing squeals from the diminished piglets plus our wild imaginations were sufficient reality for us. Occasionally a calf would be castrated, and one time an unmanageable bull had a tight elastic band put around the top of his scrotum until his testes and his temper both atrophied. Geldings, capons, oxen, and so on are all castrati—done for taste and obedience.

Castration is such a permanent condition. Not only is the sexual drive greatly weakened, but also the genetic line is virtually extinguished. By selective breeding—unnatural selection—we subdue the wild element in animals and make them placid and pliable to our wishes. We dehorn, debud, and declaw. We use gelding, spaying, neutering, fixing, orchiectomy, or any other action, surgical, chemical, or otherwise to emasculate, to castrate. We will be masters of the beasts. Man will have dominion over the other animals!

On more occasions than you might imagine, humans have castrated each other. The overwhelming majority of these were done before anesthetics and antiseptics. The pain inflicted must have been unimaginably deep and the death rate sky-high.

It seems inconceivable that Jesus, God's son for the Christian world, would recommend castration to his followers, but he did exactly that in Matthew 19:12 (KJV):

> *For there are some eunuchs, which were so born from their mother's womb: and there are some eunuchs, which were made eunuchs of men: and there be eunuchs, which have made themselves eunuchs for the kingdom of heaven's sake. He that is able to receive it, let him receive it.*

Are we to believe that anyone followed this monstrous advice? History answers yes, and more often than you might expect. The famed Christian scholar Origen (c. 185–254 CE) is widely reported to have castrated himself in strict obedience to Matthew 19:12. Perhaps such fanaticism shouldn't surprise us. After all, we almost daily read or hear of Muslim suicide bombers blowing up themselves and bystanders in the name of Allah. We have our own lunatics in the Christian world. Church Father Tertullian refers to St. Paul as being *castrated—the entire genitalia.* Paul would say he made himself a slave for the kingdom of heaven. *Sic transit sanitas.*

The thrust to castrate originates in an unnatural and unhealthy attitude toward sex that has persisted in Christians for two millennia. Paul of Tarsus was its biggest cheerleader. The present pope Ratzinger pontificates through Africa from the comfort of his popemobile that condoms cause AIDS, and he thereby condemns untold millions to a terrible death leaving parentless children. Why is his life more valuable than theirs, yours, or mine? This is gross stupidity yoked with soaring immorality. Remember Ratzinger is a disciple of Paul's.

The proof that Paul was castrated is circumstantial, but we execute people based on less. His antipathy toward women was legendary even for a misogynist. He considered women dirty, unclean, filthy, and sinful and the cause of the fall of man. Paul wasn't the only misogynist in antiquity, just its Godfather. He makes all this clear in one of the most mean-spirited paragraphs in the entire New Testament: I Timothy 2:11-15 (NIV):

A woman should learn in quietness and full submission. I do not permit a woman to teach or to have authority over a man; she must be silent. For Adam was formed first, then Eve. And Adam was not the one deceived; it was the woman who was deceived and became a sinner. But women will be saved through childbearing—if they continue in faith, love and holiness with propriety.

What greater crime could a woman commit than to bring "Death into the World, and all our woe" as Milton wrote in the opening line of *Paradise Lost*? With this spurious justification, religion became one vast commandment for woman-hating. Plus, as we shall soon learn, Paul's admonition commanding women to keep quiet in church had bizarre consequences.

Protestants shouldn't get too smug and comfortable because I've been concentrating on Catholics. Martin Luther's (1483–1546) misogyny could make Paul blush. Here are a few intellectual gems from the reformer's *Works* or *Table Talk*:

- God created Adam master and lord of living creatures, but Eve spoilt all, when she persuaded him to set himself above God's will. 'Tis you women, with your tricks and artifices, that lead men into error.
- The word and works of God is [sic] quite clear, that women were made either to be wives or prostitutes.
- We may well lie with what seems to be a woman of flesh and blood, and yet all the time it is only a devil in the shape of a woman.
- Even though they grow weary and wear themselves out with childbearing, it does not matter; let them go on bearing children till they die, that is what they are there for.

Luther did take northern Europeans from the darkness of Catholicism, but he merely found another cave to hide in.

Legions of women have labored for centuries cleaning halls, homes, and churches for their male religious leaders. They make the pews comfortable. Of course, they prepared the food and did the cleanup, mended the clothes, scrubbed the floors, and myriad other menial jobs to ease the path for pastor and priest. For their endless labors, they receive little or nothing in return, except the greedy outstretched hands of the church reaching into their purses for money or into their wombs for children to indoctrinate. From birth to death, women have been obedient slaves—church chattel. Women in 1972, compared to men, went to church roughly 10 times more a year. By 2006, that gap had shrunk to six more times a year. Why should those most poorly treated go to the house of misogyny at all? Why would a woman want to belong to an organization that neither respects nor rewards her? This oppression of women is the world's most all pervasive real-life example of the Stanley Milgram effect with the church as the captain, women as the corporals and the victims.

Many brave women from the past have had no illusions about the woman-hating nature of Christianity. Any short list of heroes must include Mary Wollstonecraft, Elizabeth Caddy Stanton, and Margaret Sanger. Wollstonecraft considered the Romish clergy to be "idle vermin." Stanton, with the help of a committee, re-wrote the Old and New Testaments taking out all the sexist and patriarchal parts to create a *slim* volume called *The Women's Bible*. And Sanger, the founder of Planned Parenthood, had the slogan "No God! No Master!" on the masthead of her newspaper *The Woman Rebel.*

In a classic chiasmus, Genesis 1:27 (NIV) tells us:

So God created man in his own image,
in the image of God he created him;
male and female he created them.

So the master of the universe created man and woman *perfect and in his image.* Consequently this religious obsession with the genitalia of both genders, and the seeming need to rework, re-shape, cut, slice, mutilate, or otherwise alter God's perfect image is most curious. Nevertheless, finding paradoxes and con-tradictions in "Holy Books" is good sport but of no consequence to the non-rational. Apparently all the blood, suffering, and dis-ease pleases god. It's a symbolic sacrifice of virility to him, a substitute for castration. The Islamic mania to excise the clitoris of prepubescent girls and stitch up the vulva like a piece of raw meat is well known. Here we'll stick with the Judeo-Christian tradition of circumcision.

It all starts with Abraham. In Genesis 17:9-12, God commanded Abraham to circumcise every male in his household, and to do this to every newborn on its eighth day of life. (Jesus was circumcised on the eighth day.) Not just Jews but many in Western society still follow this mandate. I was circumcised. Were you? America has one of the highest circumcision rates anywhere, running at 79 percent. In most other Western countries, the rate is dropping and a few European states are considering outlawing it completely. The more religious a society is, the higher the rate of circumcision, and conversely.

So Abraham created a mighty river of bloody foreskins—including his own—that has flowed out of the past to this present day. What should we do with all these? Apparently, God wanted them as a covenant between him and the victim, but unfortunately, he never took them. Well, the biblical character David had a novel idea. I Samuel 18:27 (NIV):

> *David and his men went out and killed two hundred Philistines. He brought their foreskins and presented the full number to the king so that he might become the king's son-in-law. Then Saul gave him his daughter Michal in marriage.*

Obviously, Saul was duly impressed. He thought, "What a guy David is, he buys a wife with foreskins."

I write in a jocular fashion to mask my revulsion at this act inflicting horrific pain, crippling disease, and too often, death. Let me explain. You will find the following difficult to comprehend or perhaps even believe. Among the vast array of bizarre acts that *Homo sapiens* is prone to, taking a baby's cut and bleeding penis into your mouth and sucking off the severed foreskin and then spitting it, plus blood and saliva, into a ready bowl must rank near the very top. But the ultra-Orthodox Jewish circumcision ritual known as the *metzitzah be'peh* does just that. A mohel—a rabbi trained in these "techniques"—infected three babies with genital herpes in 2004 in New York City. In November of the same year, one of the infants died and the other two will have a lifetime of affliction. The health department later discovered that the same mohel had infected another infant in 2003 and two more cases were discovered in 2005. One of these infants suffered permanent brain damage.

The city attempted to stop this mohel, but the Jewish community maintained this was a religious covenant formed with God. Out came the lawyers and the First Amendment claims while common sense and human decency were put away. Even as the lawyers and the rabbis argue, the mohel still plies his craft of sucking the penises of babies with his diseased mouth. *Sic transit sanitas!*

The rabbis maintain problems of this type i.e., death, are extremely rare. But we don't really know. Most of these ultra-Orthodox Jews, like the Catholic Church, never freely volunteer such information; they seek to deceive the public. To them, their religion is more important than life itself—even the life of an eight-day-old baby.

Are there any infections or complications concerning circumcision in the hygienic operating rooms of America and not the dining rooms of Jewish homes during a bris (ritual circumcision)? Unfortunately, our statistics may be too unreliable to give an *exact* answer. Neither the American medical community nor any agency of the U.S. government keeps complete and accurate records of the number of circumcisions performed, or the number of circumcision-induced morbidities or deaths. Using medical terms I have never seen before, they list 28 possible complications that can arise—even in a hospital setting—the last being death. This list is in the Chapter Notes.

The 10 percent complication rate generally cited applies only to hospital circumcisions. Since the majority of male circumcisions in the world are *not* done in a medical setting, but in unsanitary conditions with rudimentary and unsterilized cutting tools (used razor blades, glass shards, pocketknives, swords, even machetes, etc.), it is certain the actual complication rate greatly exceeds 10 percent.

In fact, the fubar rate from circumcision is 100 percent because, deprived of its normal, functioning foreskin, the circumcised penis is necessarily stripped and desensitized of its natural physiological functions, regardless of other morbidities that may accompany the amputation. All down the sides of Abraham's river of bloody foreskins, they wander—too inhibited to speak, too kept down by religion to protest, and too emotionally injured to know where to turn for help. So on the banks of the river, they sit and silently weep.

For those who look carefully, all along this river's banks—like the highways of America—there are small memorials to the infants who died from circumcision. Unlike the highway memorials, all these are unnecessary and hence preventable. How many tiny graves are there? For the world's circumcised male population in 1994, they range from a low estimate of 1,295 to a high of 26,987 (*see* Chapter Notes). The actual number is probably nearest their average of 14,141—almost five times as many as were murdered in the 9/11 terrorist attacks. And unlike the victims in the twin towers, these infants had only days of life. Perhaps we should all sit on the banks of Abraham's river and weep.

The Castrato

"Sandro, Sandro, finish your music lesson, and then come to supper . . . bring Maria," shouted his mother.

Sandro had quickly completed his music; now he was doing his mathematics. Two years ago, he had finished his entire arithmetic—the stuff accountants do—so now he was thinking with numbers, exploring their patterns, and learning new ones. Yes, he was doing mathematics. The young schoolmaster, Mario Umberto, who had arrived from Milan two years ago, was a marvel at teaching mathematics and science—full of stories about famous men: Galileo, Leonardo, Gauss, Cardano, and Fibonacci. All the children in the school loved his stories and his easygoing manner.

Alessandro Moreschi
1858–1922

Professor Umberto soon realized that Alessandro Moreschi was no ordinary student. The boy had a phenomenal talent for mathematics with the singing voice of an angel. There are three great mathematicians of all time; Einstein is not one of them. They are Archimedes, Carl Gauss, and Isaac Newton. When Gauss was a boy of ten, just six months older than Sandro, his teacher gave him the following legendary problem. Add up all the numbers from one to a hundred: i.e., $1+2+3+\ldots+98+99+100$. Some actually start adding—all this without calculators—and they never get the right answer. Prodigies like Gauss and Moreschi think in number patterns and quickly realize $1+100=101$ and $2+99=101$ and again $3+98=101$ and so on. How many 101s are there? Exactly 50. So the sum of all these is 50×101 or 5,050—all done in the head. Both Gauss and Moreschi almost instantly had the answer. Signore Umberto was quiet, almost stunned, at first. If a teacher is exceedingly fortunate, he will find one such student in his lifetime. Professore Umberto had found his!

Sandro Moreschi lived in the village of Monte Compatri, some 20 km southeast of Rome. His build was medium, his jaw solid, and his hair wavy black. People came from the neighboring villages, even from Rome, to hear his angelic voice when he sang in the local church. But Sandro's other even greater talent was recognized only by his new teacher Signore Marco Umberto. Southern European children are often precocious in many ways unknown further north.

Mama and Papa were wonderful parents to their large family of eleven children. Papa was a field worker in the nearby vineyards, and at home, he did subsistence farming with a few pigs and chickens plus a huge garden. Life was extremely hard for this poor Catholic family, but they did their best to shield their children from its harsh realities.

At supper, Mama *always* asked Sandro about his music. He loved the singing with all the adulation, even applause, for his talent. The actual musical notes and clefts were easy for him. Like mathematics the whole notes were as numbers and the sharps and flats were the fractions all wrapped up in groups of eight. Mama never asked him about his mathematics—it formed no part of her world. He often told her he wished to be a teacher, maybe even at the university. She just nodded and smiled.

Tonight's supper was different. Tonight Mama had a wonderful surprise for Sandro and the rest of the family. In a few days Father Luca, their local priest who had never been in their humble home, was coming to join them at supper. And of even greater importance, as if that were possible, he was bringing a famous member of the Sistine Chapel choir, a Signore Nazareno Rosati. Past his singing prime, this man was now a Vatican scout for new choir talent. The children were amazed and excited. For this occasion Sandro was getting new pants and a jacket; he had never had a jacket before. Everyone else was getting plenty of soap. Alessandro got his new clothes, and all the family waited for the "great people" to arrive.

21 ccw and 34 cw spirals

Meanwhile at school, Umberto was showing his star pupil the numbers of Leonardo Pisano, also called Fibonacci. These are 0, 1, 1, 2, 3, 5, 8, 13, 21, 34, 55, 89, 144 . . . Almost instantly Sandro saw that each number was the sum of the previous two. How simple he thought: 2+3=5 and 34+55=89. In private lessons at lunch and after school, Umberto showed him where these numbers occur in nature and in our culture. The piano octave has 5 black, 8 white for a total of 13 notes, all consecutive Fibonacci numbers. The teacher took the pupil for walks and pointed out how the faces of daisies and sunflowers have two sets of spirals, one each way, but always with adjacent Fibonacci numbers. Sandro was

enchanted—he was determined to learn as much mathematics as possible, perhaps as much as Cardano whom the great da Vinci would contact to solve his difficult problems. In all this Umberto encouraged Alessandro. Many mathematical prodigies also have great insight and ability in music. The opposite isn't true.

The day arrived, the "great people" came, Mama dusted their chairs every time before they sat down, and Papa slaughtered a pig for a grand supper. Maria and the other children were aware that Sandro and his voice were the center of attention. Signore Rosati seemed fixated on Sandro—he even had him sing several songs a cappella, and after each he nodded approvingly. After the grand meal, Mama put *all* the children in another room so that the adults could talk in private. So they did. Then the "great people" left without fanfare, and life went back to normal.

In the following days, Mama was very solicitous; Sandro twice caught her crying. He felt vaguely uneasy, but everything seemed usual. Except, except, Papa had sent all the other children away for a few days to his relatives.

The next afternoon, when Sandro came home from school, two strange men and Signore Rosati were in the kitchen. Papa was nowhere to be seen. Mama had just filled their communal bathtub with warm water and abruptly left. Suddenly the two strangers grabbed Sandro; one removed his pants and immersed his lower body in the warm water while the other pressed hard on his carotid arteries. He wiggled and squirmed, but the four rough unyielding hands held him firm. The helpless Sandro cried out, "Mama, Mama, help me!" All this time Rosati was between his legs, and suddenly he felt a pain so incredibly intense, so unbearably powerful, that thankfully he lost consciousness. The knife sliced open his scrotum as if it were an apple and the "surgeon" deftly excised each testicle and wrapped it in a dirty cloth. His practiced hand did all this as if Sandro were a piglet. The bathtub had turned bright red as the strong rough hands lifted his limp body. Rosati liberally poured acidic red wine over his mutilated genitals and then placed him in a waiting bed with his mother *now* in attendance.

When he awoke late the following day, the whole of his lower body felt dead. He was aware of his castration. Both his parents were now present plus his brothers and sisters. Maria held his hand and wiped the beads of sweat from his face. No one talked about it. His mother invented some story about him being gored by a wild boar—but no one believed her except possibly herself. As the numbness slowly left, the dreadful pain grew in proportion and persisted for almost two months. After this, Alessandro returned to school and his regular life. Some of the boys teased him about being a girl—but that also passed. Everyone knew the truth.

During Sandro's convalescence, Professore Umberto visited him at least twice a week to continue his lessons. Mama had never heard of such a thing before, and she did not approve.

"Let him rest" she would say. "There'll be time enough for school later."

One Sunday morning a few months later, when Sandro was preparing to sing in the chapel of the Madonna del Castagno, just outside his native town, his Mama had another surprising announcement. Sandro would soon be going to Rome—to the Vatican choirs. He would be a rich and powerful man! When Sandro asked how he could continue his mathematical studies in Rome, Mama was astonished and annoyed. "You don't need that because now you're going to be rich and famous," she declared.

Meanwhile school continued. Sandro unexpectedly grew several inches. Mama prepared for his going to Rome. Umberto somehow obtained two intermediate-level mathematical texts for the young scholar to take with him and study in his spare time. The teacher said they could write and exchange ideas and problems—Sandro thought all would be well.

Fortunately, when the day came to depart, the Vatican *did not* send Nazareno Rosati, his abuser. Sandro liked Rome, the Vatican, even his small room. He had never dreamed of such wealth and splendor. "Only the gods deserve such opulence," he thought. But he completely misjudged the level of dedication demanded. Singing, practicing trills and ornament passages, exercises before the teacher and a mirror, literary study of librettos—all this before lunch. After lunch was much worse. Completely worn out when he reached his small room after supper, he could think only of rest. Six days they labored and did all their work, and on the seventh, they performed—he had no spare time.

Umberto often wrote to Sandro, but he never received the letters, nor did the teacher receive his. After a few months, the teacher went to the Vatican to visit his former student and solve this mystery. He found the atmosphere stiff and formal—even unfriendly. The unctuous officials implied Umberto's interest in Sandro was unnecessary and unwelcome. From this, the teacher inferred these same officials had confiscated his letters after reading them. Unexpectedly they presented him with a package, which he later found contained the textbooks he had given his former student. Yet he found Sandro relatively unchanged—still as friendly as ever—a live bird in an abattoir of conformity.

Among geniuses, there is often a certain naiveté as when Richard Wagner wrote a libretto originally titled "The Mountain of Venus" but later renamed *Tannhäuser* to avoid lascivious comments and titillating laughter. Sandro also had this "gift." One afternoon he innocently asked a priest why there were no girls or women in the Vatican choirs. After a long withering gaze, the cleric informed him of the Pauline dictum that women should never speak in church, least of all sing. The priest was referring to Paul's speech in I Corinthians 14:34 (NIV):

[W]omen should remain silent in the churches. They are not allowed to speak, but must be in submission, as the Law says. If they want to inquire about something, they should ask their own husbands at home; for it is disgraceful for a woman to speak in the church.

When Umberto returned to Compatri, he fully realized Sandro's life was on a new trajectory—one he had not chosen but one he would adapt to. In 1873, at only fifteen, Moreschi was appointed First Soprano in the choir of the Papal basilica of St. John Lateran, an unheard-of position for one so young. He also sang in the salons of Roman high society where he made an immense impression. At twenty-five, he became First Soprano of the Sistine Chapel Choir, a post he held for the next thirty years.

There is a tide in the affairs of young mathematicians, and they must take the current when it serves or lose their ventures. Their creative period is somewhere between fifteen and thirty. All else they do in later life is mere commentary on their earlier original work. Sandro had missed this tide but had been swept away to other seas.

Umberto had found new seas of his own to explore. He married Sandro's older sister Maria whom he had met during his tutoring visits. They had children whom Uncle Sandro showered with gifts on his infrequent visits. The teacher noticed personality changes as the former pupil progressed through his teenage into his "adult" years. He no longer had the cocky arrogance of the young genius who believes he can solve any problem no matter if all previous geniuses had floundered on its difficulties. I'll trisect angles in the morning and square circles in the afternoon. But the ultimate characteristic of all mathematicians is the ability to put up with frustration—sometimes for decades. Sandro, however, became frustrated after a few minutes and had childish temper tantrums both onstage and off.

Curiously, Paul's dictum prohibiting women from speaking in church prevented all castrati from following the sage of Tarsus in I Corinthians 13:11 (NIV):

When I was a child, I talked like a child, I thought like a child, I reasoned like a child. When I became a man, I put childish ways behind me.

Paul's misogyny had stolen so much from all these prepubescent boys. What did one more thing matter? He took their childhood, their manhood, possible other careers, their family, their descendants, and ultimately their adulthood. In an important way, he left them with childish ways forever.

Alessandro Moreschi was the last of the great castrati singers and the only one for whom we have recordings of his voice. (*See* the Chapter Notes for a link to his singing of the Bach/Gounod *Ave Maria*.) At the height of the craze for castrati, upwards of some 4,000 young boys had their genitals mutilated each year. Frequently they died from the experience: most often from an overdose of opium to dull the pain or prolonged pressure on the carotid arteries to induce unconsciousness. The Vatican was a tacit partner in all this cruelty. Only a handful of castrati became famous. Some retained sexual prowess without fertility, but in another one of their many acts of kindness, the church forbade them from marrying. (The church wouldn't allow them to have sex without the possibility of 'having children—sounds familiar doesn't it?) In a sixty-year period, approximately a quarter of a million boys were castrated in Italy alone.

So great was the popularity of castrati in the salons and concert halls of Europe that women would swoon and shout, "Long live the knife." By Moreschi's time, however, they were no longer fashionable, and when he joined the Sistine Chapel there were only six others in the choir. Unlike truth, beauty can vary over time. Nonetheless, as the last great castrato singer, Moreschi had an illustrious career.

Sandro retired in 1913 at which date he qualified for his pension after thirty years of service. In retirement, he lived within walking distance of the Vatican at 19 Via Plinio. He died there in 1921 at age sixty-three probably of pneumonia. His funeral was a grand event in the church of San Lorenzo in Damaso. Although a public affair, the "great people" formed a barrier all around the casket. Despite being quite elderly, Umberto was in attendance, but Sandro's sister Maria had died the previous year. Not one to be intimidated by the clergy, the teacher pushed his way forward to touch the casket. Several priests infuriated by Umberto's impudence asked him who he thought he was. He shot back, "I have been and always will be a *true friend* of Alessandro Moreschi."

BIBLICAL JUSTIFICATION FOR SLAVERY

We have seen that the Bible—in both Testaments—nowhere condemns slavery. Oh, it gives regulations for the treatment of slaves, as you might for horses or oxen, But so did Hammurabi's Code written much earlier in c. 1790 BCE. Perhaps if a moral law is stagnant for three millennia it qualifies as one of God's eternal verities. You be the judge. In that context, consider the following peculiar story from Genesis 9:20-25 (NIV):

Noah, a man of the soil, proceeded to plant a vineyard. When he drank some of its wine, he became drunk and lay uncovered inside his tent. Ham, the father of Canaan, saw his father's nakedness and told his two brothers outside. But Shem and Japheth took a garment and laid it across their shoulders; then they walked in backward and covered their father's nakedness. Their faces were turned the other way so that they would not see their father's nakedness.

When Noah awoke from his wine and found out what his youngest son [Ham] had done to him, he said,
"Cursed be Canaan!
The lowest of slaves will he be to his brothers."

Why poor Canaan, Ham's son? For that matter why Ham? He only saw the old man naked. Remember Noah was 600 years old by this time, and had a terrific hangover. Biblical scholars will

Noah's Curse
by Ivan Stepanovitch
(1817-75)

tell you this cursing of Ham/Canaan was to justify the coming eradication (genocide) of the Canaanites from the Promised Land. If you can morally accept these *texts of terror*, perhaps you could also accept the Hutu's cleansing their land of the elitist Tutsi cockroaches. Or maybe even Hitler's grand dream of eradicating the world of Jewish vermin for the Arian Ubermensch. Just because a text is thousands of years old, it should not escape common moral standards be it the Torah, Bible, Qur'an, Plato, Aristotle, or whatever or whomever.

Nevertheless, a group of Protestant "intellectuals," without the pretext of Noah's hangover or senility, twisted the story in a new direction. Now the Canaanites became the world's black races, and this was the justification for their eternal enslavement. Noah's Curse and this interpretation is the general Abrahamic religious position. All this is very curious because Canaanites are Caucasoid not Negroid—I suppose these "intellectuals" skipped those high school classes.

If you think this idea is too absurd to be true, consider that none other than Jefferson Davis, President of the Confederacy, endorsed it. Speaking before the Mississippi Democratic State Convention on July 6, 1859, he defended chattel slavery and the foreign slave trade by alluding to the "importation of the race of Ham" as a fulfillment of its destiny to be a "servant of servants." In antebellum days, this kind of talk and sentiment were common throughout the South and the audience for Davis's fantasies was in perfect harmony.

Well, not everyone agreed. General Robert E. Lee was so morally opposed to slavery that he freed his slaves in the late 1840s, believing "slavery as an institution is a moral and political evil in any society, a greater evil to the white man than the black." His counterpart in the north, general Ulysses S. Grant, owned four slaves while fighting for the North (which opposed slavery) against the South (which was in favor of slavery). At the end of the war, he refused to free his slaves until forced to do so by law. This is how black slavery ended in America. Confusing isn't it? History is like that.

How it began in America is equally curious. We all had childhood heroes. Mine was the famous Elizabethan sea captain Sir Francis Drake. His exploits were the stuff of legends. Although vastly outnumbered, but with the help of his cousin John Hawkins, he defeated the Spanish Armada. With the blessing of the Queen Elizabeth I, he executed piratical raids all over the Americas—so terrified were the crews of the galleons and inhabitants of the Spanish colonies that they referred to him as Draco the Dragon. After Magellan, Drake was the second person to circumnavigate the world. The only difference being Drake lived, Magellan died. I even built a detailed model of Drake's famous ship the *Golden Hind*. Perhaps I had seen the movie *Sea Hawk* starring the swashbuckling Errol Flynn once too often. Then I learned Sir Francis' dirty little secret, the one our teachers never told us, he was a *slave trader*.

The English hero Sir John Hawkins captured, chained, and transported the *first black slaves* from Africa to the Caribbean and the Americas in 1565. His initial voyage was so profitable that Queen Elizabeth I collaborated with him by letting Hawkins rent the huge 700-ton *Jesus of Lubeck* for his next slave-trading voyage. His more famous cousin Sir Francis Drake, never one to ignore a profit, was in with him from the beginning. These two men set in motion a complicated and momentous train of events—a perfect example of the Butterfly Effect. This is how slavery started in America.

Let's jump ahead 444 years to Ghana on July 12, 2009. A handsome black man is speaking from the balcony of the Cape Coast Slave Castle, which he, his wife, and two daughters have just toured. These dark cells with their oppressive atmosphere reminded him of the Nazi death camp Buchenwald that he had recently visited. Incredibly, these slave cells in Ghana still reek of the feces and urine that the wretched inmates had to sleep in. The tall speaker puts his arm around his daughter's shoulders as if to protect her from what she has just seen. If the occupants left these cells still living, they passed through the Door of No

Return to descend into the hull of a slave-trading ship. Some twelve million made this journey in what we should call the African Holocaust. No one can sufficiently describe the terror these poor wretches must have felt. The man on the balcony remarked how bizarre it was to have a church built directly on top of the slave cells and for the congregation never to hear or imagine the cries beneath them. He couldn't comprehend that Christians could do such bestial acts. Perhaps someone should have told him the Nazis at Buchenwald were not atheists—they were Lutherans. As Adolf Hitler said, "We need believing people." And he had them. It always takes "believing people" to commit genocide.

The tall, handsome black man on the balcony is, of course, Barack Obama, as President of the United States, arguably most powerful person in the world. His wife Michelle descends from slaves and her genes may very well have passed through the Door of No Return. It seems appropriate that the President should stand on the balcony above these slave dungeons as a symbol of the extremes that humanity is capable of. Ecclesiastes 1:9 (KJV) says, "There is no new thing under the sun." But clearly, the author of this quotation didn't anticipate the day Barack Obama spoke at the Cape Coast Slave Castle.

THE GREATEST STORY EVER TOLD

The greatest true story ever told about slavery is fiction. It involves a big "nigger" named Jim and an ignorant white boy called Huck. But I'll let the author introduce his own book:

> You don't know about me without you have read a book by the name of *The Adventures of Tom Sawyer;* but that ain't no matter. That book was made by Mr. Mark Twain, and he told the truth, mainly. There was things which he stretched, but mainly he told the truth. That is nothing. I never seen anybody but lied one time or another, without it was Aunt Polly, or the widow, or maybe Mary. Aunt Polly—Tom's Aunt Polly, she is—and Mary, and the Widow

Huckleberry Finn

Douglas is all told about in that book, which is mostly a true book, with some stretchers, as I said before.

Thus begins what is possibly America's greatest novel, *The Adventures of Huckleberry Finn*, written, as Mark Twain says, in a number of local dialects. The style is deliciously comedic etched on deeply serious social issues, in particular the church's support of chattel slavery. The setting is timeless, but with an antebellum flavor as you might expect. An organizational object in the book is the Mississippi River, which serves as a timeline. Let's listen in as Huck describes his civilized life with the Widow Douglas:

After supper she got out her book and learned me about Moses and the Bulrushers, and I was in a sweat to find out all about him; but by and by she let it out that Moses had been dead a considerable long time; so then I didn't care no more about him, because I don't take no stock in dead people.

Pretty soon I wanted to smoke, and asked the widow to let me. But she wouldn't. She said it was a mean practice and wasn't clean, and I must try to not do it any more. That is just the way with some people. They get down on a thing when they don't know nothing about it. Here she was a-bothering about Moses, which was no kin to her, and no use to anybody, being gone, you see, yet finding a power of fault with me for doing a thing that had some good in it. And she took snuff, too; of course that was all right, because she done it herself.

Eventually Huck ran away from this "civilized" society. He joined up with Jim, Mrs. Watson's escaped slave—they were both searching for freedom. Huck's escape was mere foolishness compared with the seriousness of Jim's. The authorities took a dim view of runaway slaves and those who help them, so Jim and Huck slept during the day and rafted down the Mississippi at night.

The mighty river floated on out of the evening mist into the frosty starlight moving majestically on its never-ending voyage to the sea. It wiggled and rolled as if to make itself comfortable for the journey. The black and white life forms on the raft were now indistinguishable. Under the immense canopy of the stars and the stillness, Jim and Huck felt small and powerless. And the silky blackness of the water they floated on, broken occasionally by a fish slapping the surface with its tail, harbored huge denizens Huck had sometimes seen anglers pull out. Huck was in as much mental anguish as Jim because everything he had been taught—and it wasn't much—told him it was wrong to help a runaway slave escape to freedom. That's what he learned at school, when he went, and that's what the preachers taught, when he listened.

> I got to feeling so mean and so miserable I most wished I was dead. I fidgeted up and down the raft, abusing myself to myself, and Jim was fidgeting up and down past me. We neither of us could keep still. Every time he danced around and says, "Dah's Cairo!" it went through me like a shot, and I thought if it *was* Cairo I reckoned I would die of miserableness.
>
> Jim talked out loud all the time while I was talking to myself. He was saying how the first thing he would do when he got to a free state he would go to saving up money and never spend a single cent, and when he got enough he would buy his wife, which was owned on a farm close to where Miss Watson lived; and then they would both work to buy the two children, and if their master wouldn't sell them, they'd get an Ab'litionist to go and steal them.
>
> It most froze me to hear such talk. He wouldn't ever dared to talk such talk in his life before. Just see what a difference it made in him the minute he judged he was about free. It was according to the old saying, "Give a nigger an inch and he'll take an ell." Thinks I, this is what comes of my not thinking. Here was this nigger, which I had as good as helped to run away, coming right out flat-footed and saying he would steal his children—children that belonged to a man I didn't even know; a man that hadn't ever done me no harm.
>
> I was sorry to hear Jim say that, it was such a lowering of him. My conscience got to stirring me up hotter than ever, until at last I says to it, "Let up on me—it ain't too late yet—I'll paddle ashore at the first light and tell." I felt easy and happy and light as a feather right off. All my troubles was gone. I went to looking out sharp for a light, and sort of singing to myself. By and by one showed. Jim sings out:
>
> "We's safe, Huck, we's safe! Jump up and crack yo' heels! Dat's de good ole Cairo at las', I jis knows it!"

I says: "I'll take the canoe and go and see, Jim. It mightn't be, you know."

He jumped and got the canoe ready, and put his old coat in the bottom for me to set on, and give me the paddle; and as I shoved off, he says:

"Pooty soon I'll be a-shout'n' for joy, en I'll say, it's all on accounts o' Huck; I's a free man, en I couldn't ever ben free ef it hadn' ben for Huck; Huck done it. Jim won't ever forgit you, Huck; you's de bes' fren' Jim's ever had; en you's de *only* fren' ole Jim's got now."

I was paddling off, all in a sweat to tell on him; but when he says this, it seemed to kind of take the tuck all out of me. I went along slow then, and I warn't right down certain whether I was glad I started or whether I warn't. When I was fifty yards off, Jim says:

"Dah you goes, de ole true Huck; de on'y white genlman dat ever kep' his promise to ole Jim."

Well, I just felt sick. But I says, I *got* to do it—I can't get *out* of it. Right then along comes a skiff with two men in it with guns, and they stopped and I stopped. One of them says:

"What's that yonder?"

"A piece of a raft," I says.

"Do you belong on it?"

"Yes, sir."

"Any men on it?"

"Only one, sir."

"Well, there's five niggers run off to-night up yonder, above the head of the bend. Is your man white or black?"

I didn't answer up prompt. I tried to, but the words wouldn't come. I tried for a second or two to brace up and out with it, but I warn't man enough—hadn't the spunk of a rabbit. I see I was weakening; so I just give up trying, and up and says:

"He's white."

St. Paul could never have said those words. But the ignorant boy on the river had risen to a new enlightenment about blacks: they were human too. They had feelings. They loved their children. They weren't of the race of Ham or any other such nonsense, which comes from ignorance, glazed in biblical intellectualism but really a cloak for racism. Consider the following *revised* quotation from Paul's I Corinthians 13:1 (New Updated Bible or NUB).

If I speak in the tongues of men and of angels,
and know not the evils of slavery,
I am only a resounding gong or a clanging cymbal.

THE FIRST PROMETHEAN HERO

We began on the fields of Marathon with the slaves who fought and died for their Greek masters. We have seen the universality of the Golden Rule as well as the subjugation of women through various means. We have marveled at the heroism and nobility of Spartacus in his quest for freedom. Our wanderings through the ages have allowed us to witness the slavery condoned by St. Paul in the New Testament. We are appalled by the pedophilia of the priesthood as well as self-castration. We have witnessed the bizarre religious fascination with male circumcision and female mutilation. We have learned of the enslavement of young boys, the castrati, to be in line with Paul's prejudices against women speaking in church. Incredibly, we have seen the biblical "justification" from the Old Testament for black enslavement in the American Civil War. We ended on the happy fields and rivers with Mark Twain's fictional character Huckleberry Finn denying institutional slavery with the simple sentence, "He's white."

We have traveled far—yet we still need to know something more. Who was the first person to unequivocally denounce slavery as evil? Like so many things in Western culture, the first condemnation came from the Greeks. We have come full circle. Hecuba was the queen of Troy, wife of King Priam, taken as a slave at the war's end. Euripides, in 424 BCE, wrote a tragedy called *Hecuba* on slavery and other topics. In it, he has the leader of the chorus declare:

Alas! how cursed is slavery always in its nature, forced by the
might of the stronger to endure unseemly treatment.

I would nominate the Greek tragedian Euripides as the first Promethean hero. All those around him—and for millennia to come—were blind to the evils of slavery. Even the prophets of the Abrahamic religions closed their eyes to what he saw clearly. Euripides belongs in the hall of the immortals.

CHAPTER—5

THE PAGAN JESUS

We are in Rome in the early first century CE, and rumors of a new messiah are electrifying the city. The two elderly men we met earlier at the Battle of Marathon are conversing. Epios speaks first.

"At the Pantheon construction site today, some workers mentioned a new Asiatic prophet and his twelve disciples. Did you hear anything about him? You always seem to know these things before I do."

"I heard much the same," replied Phemios, "from two centurions who had just returned from the East. They said there will be a great celebration of his birthday next month on the winter solstice, December 25th."

"What else did you learn?"

"He is said to be a mediator between good and evil. Some identify him with the lamb, others with the lion. The centurions claim he can redeem the souls of the sinful to a higher life. According to them, this is done through baptism to remove sin and a sacred meal of bread and water—sometimes consecrated wine is used."

"I think I've heard this before," remarked Epios.

"There's more, much more," the poet said. "In the catacombs beneath Rome, there is a sculpture of the infant prophet lying on the lap of his virgin mother, while all around him were Persian Magi praying and offering gifts."

"I've heard about these caves too—apparently they're everywhere in the Empire," affirmed Epios.

"There is another connection with a cave," his friend added. "The centurions say the prophet was buried in a cave and after three days he rose from the dead. And that took place on the spring equinox. Since his birth and death are so closely connected with the movements of the sun, his holy day is appropriately Sun-day," concluded Phemios.

The engineer mentioned further that the workers at the Pantheon had spoken of an inscription from one of these caves, which read:

He who will not eat of my body and drink of my blood, so that he will be made one with me and I with him, the same shall not know salvation.

"Does this prophet have a name?" concluded Epios.

"Yes. His followers call him Mithras."

"Mithras? I was certain you were going to say Osiris. Everything you have said about Mithras, others have said about Osiris—but a thousand years earlier. The Egyptians still appeal to him for resurrection and eternal life."

PAGAN PARALLELISM

Tertullian [ca. 200 CE] states that the worshippers of Mithras practiced baptism by water, through which they were thought to be redeemed from sin, and that the priest made a sign upon the forehead of the person baptized; but as this was also a Christian rite.

I suspect most readers had another prophet in mind. The parallels between the above inscription and John 6:53-54 (NIV) are startling. The words may vary but their meaning is identical:

Jesus said to them, "I tell you the truth, unless you eat the flesh of the Son of Man and drink his blood; you have no life in you. Whoever eats my flesh and drinks my blood has eternal life, and I will raise him up at the last day."

Christians find this parallelism with Mithras, and to a lesser degree, with Adonis, Attis, Dionysus, Osiris, Tammuz, and Krishna, deeply troubling. Many choose to ignore it and so remain ignorant; others invent various strategies to explain away this similarity and so display ignorance. The early Church Fathers Tertullian and Justin Martyr made-up the first and most enduring tactic—called *Diabolical Mimicry*. The devil, old Satan himself, they say foresaw the coming of Jesus Christ and he created false religions with the same rituals to deceive us—plagiarism by anticipation. In modern times, the Christian apologist C. S. Lewis opined this nonsense from his easy chair. The whole argument distills to the platitude "The devil made me do it."

Sol Invictus Mithras—the unconquered sun Mithras—was his full name; he was the main religious force in the Roman Empire during the first three centuries of the Common Era. Manliness, fidelity, and bravery were important virtues for Mithraism, hence its popularity with the military. This religion was so male-oriented that women were not allowed to join—a recipe for limited growth. Furthermore, their rituals required *seven* levels of initiation spread over long periods—another recruitment problem.

The Vatican was built upon land formerly devoted to the worship of Mithras—so this settles the priority question. His followers were led by a *papa*, the Greek word for father, and the word *pope* derives from this. Incredibly, the early Church Fathers took all the elements of Orthodox Christian rituals from Mithraism: altar, wafer, miter, water baptism, doxology, and so on. The conclusion is so apparent, let us whisper the heresy so as not to awaken the faithful—Christianity is an offshoot of Mithraism. (Interested readers should see the Chapter Notes for a reference.)

Who masterminded this amalgam of Mithraism and Judaism to create Christianity? Enter one Paul of Tarsus, problem solver and troublemaker. Tarsus was a major Mithraic center and the capital of the province of Cilicia. Saul lived there until he was thirty, so he must have had detailed knowledge of the entire religion. Pompey's soldiers, after subjugating bordering Cappadocia in 63 BCE, brought Mithraism home to Rome. Paradoxical isn't it? What Darius, Xerxes, and Artaxerxes couldn't do against the Greeks at Marathon, Salamis, and Plataea, Pompey's soldiers accomplished at a leisurely pace: they brought a later variety of Zoroastrianism into Europe. The Mediterranean mystery cults had one major difference from Christianity: they were *not exclusive*. It was possible, and the usual case, to be a member of several cults simultaneously. For example, you could worship Isis and Jupiter while still being a follower of Mithras. Christianity allowed no such broad-mindedness. The first Commandment is startlingly clear on this point in Exodus 20:2-3 (KVJ):

I am the LORD thy God, which have brought thee out of the land of Egypt, out of the house of bondage. Thou shalt have no other gods before me.

This was a major reason Christianity won and the other religions became relics of the past.

Mithraism and Judaism combined to become Christianity. Jesus, son of the Hebrew sky-god (repackaged Yahweh), and Mithras, son of Ahura Mazda (also called Ormuzd) are the identical myth. The rituals of Christianity are the rituals of Mithraism, including the Eucharist and the Communion. The language of Mithraism was the language of Christians. Paul of Tarsus as the first "Christian" bears responsibility for merging the two by his preaching and teaching. By showing that Christianity was just new and *improved* Mithraism—for example, women were allowed membership even if they had to keep quiet—it was easier for him and others to make converts. This worked brilliantly because by the beginning of the fourth century CE, Mithraism was no more, at least by name.

Tauroctony: Mithras Slaying the Bull

The central icon for Christianity is the crucifixion, but for Mithraism it's something called the Tauroctony—sacrifice is the essence of each. As you can see in the picture above, it depicts a young man in a Phrygian cap symbolically slaying a bull. It's of interest to note the snake and the dog are both drinking the bull's blood as if it were the elixir of life. Since researchers have found this figure in every Mithraic cave, and in a position of prominence, so it must be central to their religion. Nevertheless, there is much controversy as to its purpose and meaning. Without a written context, what would someone completely unfamiliar* with Christianity make of the crucifixion? A puzzle no doubt—perhaps a method for executing criminals? That's precisely our modern position with respect to the Tauroctony. The facts are few; the theories are many—here's the common one.

The idea of a savior is Mithraic, so is the symbolism of bulls, rams, sheep, and the blood of a transformed savior washing away sins and granting eternal life. This is why the dog is lapping up the bull's blood in the Tauroctony. The seven sacraments (the number of completeness), the banishing of an evil host from heaven, the apocalyptic end of time when God/Ormuzd sends the wicked to hell and establishes peace are all Mithraic. Roman Emperors, who were Mithraist first and Christian later, mixed the rituals and laws of both religions into one. Constantine established December 25, the birthday of Mithras, to be the birthday of Jesus also. The Mithraic Sunday replaced the Jewish Saturday for Christianity. The Catholic Church, based in Rome and founded on top of the most venerated Mithraic temple, eradicated all competing son-of-god religions within the Roman Empire, giving us modern Christianity.

As mentioned previously, Christians must make a choice. Either ignore all the parallels with Mithras and remain ignorant, or attempt to explain them away by *Diabolical Mimicry* and display ignorance. There is a cliché for this position.

---

* Cicero, who was completely familiar with crucifixion, described it as "a most cruel and disgusting punishment."

ASTRAL BULL

In December 1989, David Ulansey, professor of Philosophy, wrote an article for *Scientific American* interpreting the Tauroctony in a different and entirely original manner. His version varies significantly from the previous one. I'll merely touch on its major points, but interested readers should see the Chapter Notes for a link to the complete article.

The earth *rotates* on its axis once every day—like a child's top. Its axis *wobbles* one complete revolution every 25,920 years—also like a child's top. Both these movements appear to move the heavens rather than the earth. And it moves the heavens in such a way that the time of spring gets earlier every year by 20 minutes. (Spring happens when the sun crosses the celestial equator making the days longer than the nights in the northern hemisphere.) These 20 minutes accumulate causing the sun to move *backward* through one zodiac sign every 2,160 years (25,920 ÷ 12 = 2,160). We call this changing of the sun's springtime position along the zodiac *precession of the equinoxes*. Hipparchus, the greatest astronomer in antiquity, made this brilliant discovery around 125 BCE.

Precession of the Equinoxes

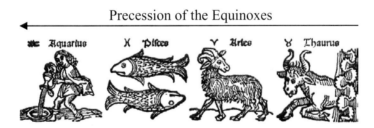

David Ulansey attributes this discovery to the rise of Mithraism. How is this possible? What's the connection? In his *Scientific American* article, he answers these questions:

From the geocentric perspective, the precession (a movement of the earth) appears to be a movement of the entire cosmic sphere. For people who held both a geocentric worldview and the belief that the movements of the stars influenced human fates, the discovery of the precession would have been literally world-shaking: the stable sphere of the fixed stars was being unseated by some force apparently larger than the cosmos itself. Ancient intellectuals, accustomed as they were to seeing the work of the gods reflected in the works of nature, could easily have taken this great movement as evidence for the existence of a powerful, hitherto unsuspected deity.

And that deity was Mithras. His followers invented a back-story from Persia for their newly created god to give him the stature of great antiquity. Fabricating in the name of religion is an ancient and polished art—the Book of Daniel is a prime example.

Back to the Tauroctony. When we see Mithras slaying the bull, we have an icon of the passage from the old age of Taurus to the new age of Ares sometime around 2,000 BCE. The entire scene is an ancient graphical representation of the precession of the equinoxes and part of the back-story for Mithras. In the days before artificial light, people knew the night sky and all their constellations.

Presently the spring equinox is in the constellation of Pisces the fish. The transit from Ares to Pisces occurred in the early 1st century, but Christians were likely unaware of it. Hebrew society at that time, unlike the Greek, had no interest or knowledge of science—a tradition Paul was happy to pass along. Remember Hipparchus was Greek. Hebrew curiosities were with things astrological, not astronomical.

It's interesting just how much of Jesus' life was associated with fish and fishing. Even the occasional Bible reader will recall such instances. For example, his ministry begins and ends at Galilee with a catch of fish. Also, an *acrostic* connection exists between Jesus and "the fish" which we'll explore later in this chapter.

COSMOLOGICAL BULL

In the beginning was the lie that we were the center of all creation. Every part of science leads us away from this kindergarten conception. Galileo, Darwin, and Einstein are a few who have helped us mature and leave this playground of solipsism. Even in the present day astrologers seem unaware of the precession of the equinoxes or that it invalidates their occult game. Why?

Briefly, had you been born at the same time on the same day 2,000 years earlier, you would have come into the world under a *different* zodiac sign. Horoscopes are really "horrorscopes." But the lie of astrology still has legions of followers.

Astrology is the twin brother of religion. They are alike in so many ways. Both place humankind at the center of the universe and so view the world in supernatural terms. Both belong to the childhood of our race. Cosmo and his New Age friends have been acting out for the last few decades with claims that we are transiting from Pisces to the Age of Aquarius. The promises of this new age are too abundant to list—we have all heard them in music and lyrics. Things too stupid to be spoken are sung.

All these passages from age to age have an aura of astrology and *other worldliness*. There is only a single kernel of truth in all this New Age sewage and that's the precession of the equinoxes discovered by the Greek genius Hipparchus. All else is gibberish. If you can believe the stars are so set in the universe as to determine or influence our individual lives on this small planet, then you will believe anything regardless of the evidence. And you have no knowledge of the size and the complexity of the universe revealed by modern cosmology (*Google* "NASA Astronomy Picture of the Day Archive". You have dehumanized yourself and destroyed your greatest gift, the ability to reason.

We may be puny creatures! We may be parasites devouring the third planet of an ordinary star, one of 300 billion, in a small arm of an out-of-the-way spiral galaxy, a minor part of the Local Group of Galaxies, a minute fraction of the Virgo Super-Cluster, one of innumerable such clusters—a mere mote in the eye of the universe. Yet, science has given us a vision of the cosmos built on evidence. And it's a world of such wonders as were never dreamed or deciphered by any astrologer. We are splendid creatures! You and I are rolled out of stardust, baked in the furnace of creation. "What a piece of work is a man, how noble in reason, how infinite in faculties, in form and moving how express and admirable, in action how like an angel, in apprehension how like a god!" (Hamlet, Act II, Scene 2.)

GNOSTICISM

The One, Holy, Roman Catholic, and Apostolic Church, having eradicated the enemies from without, turned inward, and didn't like what it saw. Elaine Pagels, in her marvelous book *The Gnostic Gospels* (Vintage Books, New York, 1981), lays the groundwork for the Orthodox anger toward their Gnostic neighbors:

> Unlike many of his contemporaries among the deities of the ancient Near East, the God of Israel shared his power with no female divinity, nor was he the divine Husband or Lover of any. He can scarcely be characterized in any but masculine epithets: king, lord, master, judge, and father. Indeed, the absence of feminine symbolism for God marks Judaism, Christianity, and Islam in striking contrast to the world's other religious traditions, whether in Egypt, Babylonia, Greece, and Rome, or in Africa, India, and North America, which abound in feminine symbolism. Jewish, Christian, and Islamic theologians today are quick to point out that God is not considered in sexual terms at all. Yet the actual language they use daily in worship and prayer conveys a different message: who growing up with Jewish or Christian tradition [and a fortiori Islamic], has escaped the distinct impression that God is *masculine*? And while Catholics revere Mary as the mother of Jesus, they never identify her as divine in her own right; if she is the "mother of God," she is not "God the Mother" on an equal footing with God the Father! [1]

The monotheistic Abrahamic religions were/are constructed on bedrock misogyny. From Paul's injunction that women must cover their heads in church to Islam's edict that women must hide their entire body, the motivation is always the same: keep women under male authority. These men are frightened of women's seductiveness and reproductive power; perhaps that's why they turn to children for recreation. Wherever Pope Benedict XVI, a.k.a. Ratzinger, tours in the world, thousands of demonstrators fill the streets protesting the church's stand on condoms, homosexuality, and most of all their position on priestly pedophilia and women's rights. After nearly two millennia, the situation is unchanged! Cover your head woman and get to the back of the church and out of sight, but leave your children here under our "protection."

Gnosticism was a religious movement advocating gnosis, meaning knowledge, enlightenment, or the occult, as a way to develop your spiritual self. Many Gnostic texts were written by (or attributed to) women. Mary Magdalene played an important role in Gnostic writings, second only to Jesus. In their theology, they used both female and male images for the Supreme God. For example, their female divinity was Sophia, the goddess of wisdom. Theologians speculate that they probably treated women members as equal to men in their communities. In some Gnostic sects women preached, prophesied, baptized, and even celebrated the Eucharist. The Orthodox Christian churches considered all these ideas and practices heretical—so they began banning and burning these books.

Forty-two years after the Council of Nicaea in 325 CE, the bishop of Alexandria issued an Easter edict to burn all Gnostic texts. Book burning and banning[*] is an ancient, nasty business by obscurantists seeking to maintain power by hiding the facts. It's rarely successful; nor was it in this case. Someone collected the books to be burned but instead he buried them in a six-foot jar near Nag Hammadi in Upper Egypt only to be rediscovered by two farmers in December 1945. These texts form the major part of what we now call the Gnostic gospels. Nevertheless, the Orthodox Church was victorious in suppressing, if not eradicating, Gnosticism. What they did for Mithraism, they did for all challengers.

Now that the One, Holy, Roman Catholic, and Apostolic Church was supreme master both within and without its domain, innovation, curiosity, and education ceased. Learning seemed more difficult and rare. The fifth proposition of Euclid's *Elements*, a.k.a. the pons asinorum, was as far as these "great church intellectuals" ever got. With complete obedience to authority, the church kept to well-worn paths of thought crossing the bridge of asses as they marched lockstep into the millennium called the Dark Ages when they had things all to themselves.

---

[*] The authors and works on the *Index Librorum Prohibitorum* of the Catholic Church is a list of the world's great books. Somehow, no one knows exactly how, these censors left off the list *The Tale of Peter Rabbit* by Beatrix Potter.

Gnosticism, like Orthodox Christianity, has deep roots in Judaism. Both branches picked up some unusual elements, but none can surpass what they adopted from the Jewish kabbalistic tradition—the latest religious fad of Hollywood movie stars. Biblical scholars and historians call this element "gematria." However, it's nothing but a peculiar form of numerology. Gnostics had a remarkable attachment to this form of the higher foolishness.

The Old Testament was in Hebrew and a little Aramaic, the New Testament, in Greek. These languages *did not have* number symbols; instead, they used letters of their alphabets for counting. The reader is already familiar with this practice: everyone has made a table of items and numbered/lettered them a, b, c, and so on. Simply stated, each character in the ancient Hebrew and Greek alphabets did double duty as both a letter and a number. *So, every word was also a number.* Clerics call the practice of summing up the numerical values of the letters in a name gematria. With our knowledge of Roman Numerals from public school, everyone can do this. The Romans, however, unlike the Hebrews and Greeks, used only the letters I, V, X, L, C, and D as numbers:

I = 1, V = 5, X = 10, L = 50, C = 100, D = 500

Quite late in the Roman Empire, scholars introduced M for 1000, probably to *complete* the list at seven symbols. However, DD or other variations were originally used. Consider the following two words and their gematria values:

CIVIC=100+1+5+1+100 = 207.
LEGION=50+1 = 51 (E, G, O, and N have no numerical value).

Since no part of the original Bible was written in Latin, we will consider only Greek gematria as practiced by the Gnostics.

Please look over the following table of Greek letters and their corresponding numerical values. Anyone familiar with the Greek alpha-beta will notice the three shaded letters in addition to the normal twenty-four. The numbered notes after the chart explain these and other unusual points.

UNITS	TENS	HUNDREDS
Alpha A α = 1	Iota I ι = 10	Rho P ρ = 100
Beta B β = 2	Kappa K κ = 20	Sigma Σ σ ς[3] = 200
Gamma Γ γ = 3	Lambda Λ λ = 30	Tau T τ = 300
Delta Λ δ = 4	Mu M μ = 40	Upsilon Y υ = 400
Epsilon E ε = 5	Nu N ν = 50	Phi Θ φ = 500
Stigma ς[1] = 6	Xi Ξ ξ = 60	Chi X χ = 600
Zeta Z ζ = 7	Omicron O o = 70	Psi Ψ ψ = 700
Eta H η = 8	Pi Π π = 80	Omega Ω ω = 800
Theta Θ θ = 9	Koppa ϙ[2] = 90	Sampsi ϡ[4] = 900

The Greek Alphabet and Numerals

[1] The letter ς (stigma) was not in the Greek alphabet. Why it's used for the number 6 is uncertain. If the numbering pattern had been orderly, then 6 would have been denoted by ζ (zeta).

[2] An obsolete letter used only as a number.

[3] The Greeks had two lower case forms with the same value: ς (sigma) used only at the end of a word and σ used elsewhere. The terminal letter sigma has the same form as stigma.

[4] This is another obsolete letter, used only as a number. Omega is the final letter in the Greek *writing* alphabet.

Let's do some Greek gematria. The New Testament has about 138,020[*] words, give or take a few depending on textual variations. That's a lot of choice, but consider this attractive example. In old Greek manuscripts, scholars often placed the number *99* at the end of a benediction or a prayer. For centuries, the meaning of this was a tiny mystery, until the 1900s. But consider, what could be more natural—the last word in the Bible is *Amen* with a gematria value of 99.

---

[*] *Google* "Catholic Bible Statistics".

A	m	e	n	
A	μ	η	ν	
1	40	8	50	= 99

The Bible mentions gematria. Where you might ask? I sus-pect many readers already know: Revelation 13:18 (NIV):

This calls for wisdom. If anyone has insight,
let him calculate the number of the beast,
for it is man's number. His number is 666.

N	e	r	o		C	a	e	s	a	r	
N	ε	ρ	ω	ν	K	α	ε	σ	α	ρ	
50	5	100	800	50 +	20	1	5	200	1	100	= 1332

Apparently the above sum is not the number we are seeking, but a moment's reflection reveals something else. As John says, "If anyone has insight . . ."

$$1332 = 666 \times 2$$
$$= 666 + 666$$

So Nero's gematria is twice 666.

With no Internet, DVDs, TV, iPods, and so on, the Kabbalists and Gnostics turned to their numerology for entertainment. They danced on the edge of the occult and often waltzed into numero-logical nonsense. Reader beware, there's danger here!

What follows is the Gnostics' sanctum sanctorum in this game of gematria. Recall pages 28-30, where I noted that in most cultures the number *seven* has a cultural context implying com-pleteness. Authors often put this number in the title of their books—I bet you have thought of one already.

If *seven* is the number of completeness, then *eight* begins a new list or cycle. Although not culturally significant today, in biblical times the number *eight* had symbolic value representing renewal and rebirth. Allow me to put on the *ill-fitting cloak* of a true believer to list a few biblical examples illustrating this. We should always recall, however, as Shakespeare wrote in *The Merchant of Venice*, "The devil can cite scripture for his own purpose!"

- All the Gospels say that Jesus rose from the dead "on the first day of the week." For Jews that was Sunday, the 8th day of their week.
- The Ark contained 8 souls: Noah, his wife, his three sons, and their wives. When these 8 stepped out of the Ark onto a new world, they had to start a new order and regenerate all life on earth.
- The Jewish ritual act of circumcision had to be done on the 8th day (Genesis 17:12). Concerning that, Luke 2:21 says: "On the 8th day, when it was time to circumcise him, he was named Jesus, the name the angel had given him before he was conceived."
- Aeneas, a paralytic, was healed in Jesus' name and rose out of his bed after 8 years (Acts 9:33-35).
- Jesus' brilliant Transfiguration took place 8 days after the first announcement of His future sufferings. Exactly three disciples witnessed this showing of the glory to be at the Second Coming.
- The entire Bible details 8 resurrections, distinct from Jesus and His saints:
  3 in the Old Testament (1 Kings 17, 2 Kings 4 and 13)
  3 in the Gospels (Matthew 9, Luke 7, John 11)
  2 in Acts (9 and 20).
- The Resurrection is the 8th "great sign" in John's Gospel.

The preceding list should be sufficient to make the point that *eight* is the number symbolizing rebirth and renewal and, as we shall see, resurrection.

But wait a minute! This bulleted list is not truly impressive considering the field of choice. The entire Bible contains over 35,000 verses; that's a lot of choice for such a paltry list. Gnostics would object and rebut that there are many more instances of 8 in the Scriptures—but most of these depend on gematria.

The most important word in the life of any Christian is *Jesus*. The most important word in the Bible is *Jesus*. In an heroic feat of sesquipedalianism, televangelists manage to stretch the pronunciation of J–E–S–U–S out to four or five syllables. Remarkably, Joseph and Mary did not even choose this name. In a scene commemorated by many artists, the archangel Gabriel announced to an astonished Mary in Luke 1:31 (NIV):

You will be with child and give birth to a son,
and you are to give him the name Jesus.

If gematria has any deep meaning at all, the Gnostic would say, it must begin with this name. Using the original Greek from the Gospels, let us find the *number value* of His name. Here is their strongest example—their sanctum sanctorum:

$$J \quad E \quad S \quad U \quad S$$
$$I \quad \eta \quad \sigma \quad o \quad \upsilon \quad \varsigma$$
$$10 \quad 8 \quad 200 \quad 70 \quad 400 \quad 200 \quad = \quad 888$$

Almost anticipating your disappointment, the Gnostic says it's not only 8 but 8 emphasized by three repetitions. And that's why this number symbolizes resurrection like Jesus Himself. (The word *Christ* is an adjective meaning the anointed one.) So there you have it, the jewels of gematria, or as some would say, the zircons of numerology.

OTHER BIBLICAL PATTERNS

The first of April is the day we remember
what we are the other 364 days of the year.
Mark Twain (1835–1910)

With the advent of modern high-speed computers capable of searching huge masses of data quickly and accurately, it's not surprising we have entirely new methods for uncovering "hidden messages" in the Bible.

In 1987, Michael Drosnin's *The Bible Code* made the best-seller list. Simon & Schuster launched this book with a full-page advertisement in the *New York Times* and an initial printing of a quarter million copies. Fundamentalist Christians and Orthodox Jews went wild with enthusiasm. You might ask how this code differs from biblical gematria.

Drosnin arranges the 304,805 or so Hebrew letters of the Torah (the first five books of the Old Testament) into a single, large array. Spaces and punctuation marks are omitted, so that the "wordsruntogether." A computer then searches this array for names and words by skipping to every 2nd, 5th, 66th, 351st, or nth letter.

You can do this by starting at the beginning or the end—this maneuver doubles your chances. Because of these skips, the series of letters found are called equidistant-letter sequences (ELS). If any group of these letters from the various skips is a word or a name, Drosnin screams "hit," otherwise he ignores it and moves on. His match for Yitzhak Rabin had a skip value of 4,772.

Consider a simple ELS example using only the single word *generalization*. It contains a skip three sequence spelling out *Nazi*—all this within a single word—who could have guessed.

I can almost hear some reader crying, "That's enough!" All this is nonsense. With billions of step sequences for every large array, the opportunities for "hits" are endless—you can find whatever you want. When you mine data, you may discover fool's gold. It's like buying all the tickets on a lottery—you have to win. This makes Drosnin's entire technique claptrap. It's doubtful if one can be too skeptical in these cases.

The pages of New Mexico physicist David Thomas' website and the Australian mathematician Brendan McKay's[*] are excellent for debunking ELS. McKay, while searching Moby Dick, found ELS assassination "predictions" for Indira Gandhi, Leon Trotsky, Rev. M. L. King, Abraham Lincoln, and John F. Kennedy—this beats Drosnin's meager list of one (Yitzhak Rabin). Melville would marvel at these findings in his masterpiece, since all the time he thought he was writing an epic about the struggle between man and nature, Ahab and the whale. Thomas discovered coincidences involving the number 19, not in the Qur'an (*see* pages 206-207), but in Ted Kaczynski's "Unabomber Manifesto." And the list goes on. As Thomas says on his site, "Any message can be derived from any text."

Why is it that Muslims never seriously consider the gematria or ELS patterns in the Bible, and on the other hand, Christians completely ignore similar "designs" in the Qur'an? Perhaps because the mind knows only that which lies near the heart.

---

[*] *Google* "David Thomas Bible Code" or "Brendan Mckay Moby Dick".

Drosnin published a sequel, *Bible Code II*, but this second tome didn't make the slash of the first. The minds of the millions may grind slowly, but I believe they move inexorably forward. The ad on the cover of his second book should read *Come, believe the unbelievable; be a fool with me.*

ACROSTICS AND PALINDROMES

Long before the ELS nonsense of Drosnin, there were other literary patterns in the Bible. These, however, were not "hidden codes" or secret knowledge, but merely wordplay. Consider the humble acrostic.

The Hebrew scribes of the Old Testament occasionally used acrostics as if to imply total coverage—as we would say from A to Z. Psalm 119 is an acrostic poem consisting of twenty-two stanzas of eight verses each. In many ways, it's the Bible's most unusual psalm: it's the longest chapter in the longest book. In the original Hebrew, the first eight verses begin with the letter *aleph*, the second eight with *beth*, the third with g*imel*, and so on. In this fashion, the psalmist plods through the entire Hebrew alephbeth.

The Old Testament has nine of these primitive abecedarian acrostics—those using the alphabet in order, as a beginner would do. These are hardly divinely inspired wordplay but more like the scribbled products of weary pedants.

The New Testament has a much more attractive acrostic. In Matthew 7:7, we have an unusual arrangement of words:

Ask, and it shall be given you;
Seek, and ye shall find;
Knock, and it shall be opened unto you:

For added emphasis, the first letters of the lines spell out the word *ASK*. Although the English translators certainly did this unknowingly, it's very appropriate.

The most important Christian example, however, cannot be found in Scripture. Yet it flourished in the early Church, and it lives today on car bumpers everywhere:

Ιησους Χριστος Θεου Υιος Σωτηρ
This translates as "Jesus Christ, Son of God, the Savior."
The initial letters of the five words spell out
ΙΧΘΥΣ (Ichthus), Greek for fish.

This is a striking symbol for an historic acrostic now known colloquially as the "sign of the fish" or the "Jesus fish." For early Christians it served a special purpose: secret symbols for your faith meant personal safety. Since many Roman emperors demanded worship as gods, they ruthlessly suppressed competition. To be a Christian in ancient Rome meant you were having a bad day—after Constantine became emperor, Christians reversed the situation.

As a memory aid, poets and scribes often employed a more interesting literary device. Poetry in English is a matter of meter and rhyme, but in Hebrew and Greek, it was a matter of parallelism and repetition. The author said it; then in different words, he/she said it again. Known as a chiasmus (also called a ring structure) this was a literary device employed in ancient literatures and oral traditions. The *Iliad* and the *Odyssey* used chiasmic structures of amazing virtuosity that performed both aesthetic and mnemonic functions hundreds of years before "Moses" wrote the Torah.

Where do we find these passages in the Bible? Consider the following examples. The first is from Genesis 1:27:

A—So God created man
　B—in his own image,
　B—in the image of God
A—he created him.

The pattern is AB=BA, expressing just two ideas: God created man, and man is in God's image. They were as common in the ancient world as limericks are in the modern.

Mark 5:3-5 has a longer example of this structure. These verses describe the well-known scene of the Gadarene swine and the demon-possessed man.

A—This man lived in the tombs,
    B—and no one could bind him any more,
        C—not even with a chain.
        C—For he had often been chained hand and foot.
    B—No one was strong enough to subdue him.
A—Night and day among the tombs.

The poetic form is ABC=CBA, expressing three ideas, not six. English teachers illustrate it with examples like "she went to Los Angeles; to New York went he."

The reader should not confuse a chiamus with a palindrome like "Madam, in Eden I'm Adam." A chiasmus is a "palindrome of ideas" not letters or words. Consider this famous first palindromic paragraph from the Garden of Eden by J. A. Lindon.

IN EDEN I
Madam, I'm Adam.
Eve. (She replies.)
Even in Eden, I win Eden in Eve.
Mad Adam! (Eve)
Tut tut. (Snake)

In the beginning, everything was beautiful, healthy, and symmetrical. Hence, Adam was uncertain whether he should speak left to right or right to left so he spoke in palindromic sentences; Eve and Snake responded in kind. And thus, the first humans "deified" this wordplay that we have been burdened with ever since. Some zealots of the craft extend this to words with reversible meanings, declaring that when Genesis 1:1 says "heaven and earth" we are meant to interpret this as a three-word list with "and" as "DNA." After all, they state, Hebrew does read right to left. (Perhaps I had best end this paragraph before my embarrassment makes my face even "redder.")

CHILD'S PLAY IN THE BIBLE

The Bible, as Alfred North Whitehead noted, is remarkably humorless. And it's equally devoid of serious wordplay. What does exist is of interest only to children and Kabbalists. Consider the Atbash code from Jeremiah. It's a very simple replacement cipher for the Hebrew or any alphabet. You substitute *aleph* (the first letter) for *tav* (the last), *beth* (the second) for *shin* (the second last), and so on, reversing the alphabet. This is far too simple a cipher to hide anything. So why was it used? No one truly knows. But I suspect that when the killing got chilling and the goring became boring the author of Jeremiah did this just for amusement. Entertain the following English examples:

Here is the Atbash cipher for the English alphabet.

a	b	c	d	e	f	g	h	i	j	k	l	m	n	o	p	q	r	s	t	u	v	w	x	y	z
z	y	x	w	v	u	t	s	r	q	p	o	n	m	l	k	j	i	h	g	f	e	d	c	b	a

Most words "Atbash" to a nonsensical series of letters.

God transforms to *Tlw* (indicated by shading above)
Jesus to *Qvhfh*

Some, however, are identifiable.

Holy transforms to *slob*
Glow to *told*

And that's the celebrated Atbash cipher of Hebrew scholars and mystics. Don't be disappointed—it's not worth it.

According to the historian Suetonius, Julius Caesar used a similar cipher with a shift of three to protect messages of military significance:

> If he had anything confidential to say, he wrote it in cipher, that is, by so changing the order of the letters of the alphabet, that not a word could be made out. If anyone wishes to decipher these, and get at their meaning, he must substitute the fourth letter of the alphabet, namely D, for A, and so with the others.
> Suetonius, *Life of Julius Caesar*

The Caesar shift allows you to encode in 25 different ways, by shifting each letter between 1 and 25 "steps" along the alphabet. So a shift of 1 would mean A becomes B, B becomes C, and Z goes to A when you arrange the letters on a circle. It's little better than the Atbash code, except since Caesar's opponents were illiterate it didn't matter, anyhow.

PALTRY PUZZLES

Let's summarize the literary patterns—true and false, serious and silly—that we have uncovered in the Bible.

Gematria, the sudoku of the Gnostics, is not entirely false or without merit. And it's not too much of a stretch to culturally interpret the number *8* as the quantity of renewal or rebirth. After all, look what we do even today with the number *7* representing completeness. Revelation 13:18 gives reference to the gematria of the beast whom we found to be Nero. Perhaps the gematria of *Jesus* as *888* was an accident, or perhaps the Gnostics made it that way.

However, if you wish to see the lunacy that gematria can run to, Google *Theomatics: God's Best Kept Secret* by Jerry Lucas and Del Washburn. And for a devastating review of this book, read "The Bible and God's Numerology" in *Order and Surprise* by the late Martin Gardner [2]. It's not so much that Lucas and Washburn have run off in all directions as taken a warp-speed rocket to the Pegasus galaxy.

Gematria may occasionally be in the sanity wards of the religious, but Michael Drosnin's ELS dwells permanently in its deepest padded cells. America's greatest debunker of pseudoscience, Martin Gardner, also commented on these equidistant letter sequences in his book *Did Adam and Eve Have Navels?*

As a simple experiment, I considered only the first fifteen words in Lincoln's Gettysburg Address and checked every *n*th letter for *n* equal to 2 through 10—that is, letters separated by one through nine letters. I found thirty-two three-letter words and the following four-letter words: *sort*, *soar*, *Nero*, *huts*, *hoot*, and *NATO*. Imagine how many longer words would turn up in books as long as Genesis or a play by Shakespeare, and allowing *n* to vary from 2 through 100. In ancient Hebrew there were no vowels. This results in considerable vagueness over what word was intended. I could have found much longer words in the first fifteen words of Lincoln's speech had I been allowed to insert vowels between consonants. [3]

Joseph Addison, English essayist, while referring to the acrostic and the anagram wrote, "The acrostic was probably invented about the same time with the anagram, though it is impossible to decide whether the inventor of the one or the other were the greater blockhead." And David, the same person who bartered for a bride with 200 foreskins, may well be that blockhead. Why? Because he is the reputed author of the Psalms and most of the acrostics occur there. All biblical acrostics are the simple alphabetical variety apart from the accidental one in Matthew 7:7.

The classic chiamus a.k.a. *ring* structure served a double course in the ancient world—poetic and mnemonic. When papyrus and parchment were rare and paper unknown, memorization of sacred books was a respected skill. History records that the average Athenian youth had committed to memory both the *Iliad* and the *Odyssey*. Possibly the Hebrews borrowed this device from the Greeks, but had neither their skill nor their aesthetic power to transform the Bible into the lord of the rings.

For comedic value, I mentioned palindromes. Although none occur *by design* in either Testament, and, of course, any such are lost in translation.

We have played with the seriously silly Atbash code from Jeremiah. And readers wishing to learn more on this subject should consult any beginner's guide to cryptography.

Is that it then? With 66 books, 31,071 verses, and 783,137[*] words to play with, and this is the best we have! Surely, there is more wordplay and structure in God's "holy" word. Some point to the often cited "pun" from Mathew 16:18 (NIV), "And I tell you that you are Peter, and on this rock I will build my church." Not laughing yet? Well *Peter* is *Petra*—Greek for rock. And it just so happens there is at least one more example of wordplay in

---

[*] The results depend on the religious division. This is for the Protestant NIV Bible. The Catholic Bible with its 73 books yields higher numbers.

the Bible that some people claim is accidental while others insist it's intentional.

Humans are pattern makers—this probably more than anything else defines us as a species. We will have patterns in both time and space. We will have patterns in our theology in both action and word. We will have patterns be they true or be they false. What follows is a famous if not fabulous biblical pattern. Give us enough data and enough time, and we will find anything you wish.

Let's begin with a question. Can the reader think of a single work of art—in any medium—created by a committee? Stumped? Even after my critique of religion, may I suggest the King James translation of the Bible? In large part, the KJV sounds and reads majestically while these modern "good news" translations are dreadful. This was the common appraisal of Christopher Hitchens, William Faulkner, George Orwell, John Updike, Vladimir Nabokov, and a host of other famous writers. But how was it possible for fifty or so *scholars* to construct some of the greatest lines and phrases of the English language? Remarkably, all this grandeur was done with a paltry 8,000 words. On the other hand, Shakespeare raided the entire English lexicon to pen his plays and poetry with an astonishing 30,000 words— some of which he invented. As well as words the Bard, as his plays attest, enjoyed wordplay for he used it regularly. Incredibly, he even employed it on his tombstone.

Shakespeare died of unknown causes at age 52 on April 23, 1616. In an almost prescient move, he had his gravestone and its obituary of sorts already completed:

Shakespeare's Tombstone Inscription

Good friend, for Jesus' sake, forbear,
To dig the dust enclosed here.
Blessed be the man that spares these stones,
And cursed be he that moves my bones.

From its curious content and carving make of this inscription what you will; many have interpreted it as a clue to the "Shakespeare question." That is, who was he and did he write the plays that bear his name. Whatever these answers may be, the Bard of Avon's final exit line affirms his love of wordplay, and that is my point.

In 1610, the fifty odd scholars completed the translation of the KJV. But as *The Story of English** relates, King James thought it needed some revisions so that "it would not only read better but sound better"—this polishing took nine months. Also significant is Shakespeare's success and favor with the court in the first years of the 17th century: "The young actor-playwright quickly caused a sensation with his plays," says *The Story of English*. I write this only to indicate it was just possible that the greatest master of the English language *may* have had a hand in this extended polishing to elevate a scholarly work to the Mount Parnassus of great art.

And then there is Psalm 46. The Psalms, which were originally intended to be "sung" to musical accompaniment, are generally considered the most beautiful parts of the Old Testament. Everyone, even non-theists, knows the 23rd Psalm. However, it's in Psalm 46 (that is, 23+23) that many believe Shakespeare did some of his most ingenious wordplay. From the beginning of this psalm, count down to the 46th word which is *Shake*. Now go to the end of this psalm and count up to the 46th word, which is *spear*—hence *Shakespeare*. Critics of this curio point out that we have omitted the word *selah* which may occur anywhere in a psalm. Yet scholars tell us *selah* is a musical term indicating a pause or instrumental interlude for reflection and not properly meant to be read. Also for parallelism, we have omitted the title of the psalm. So there you have it. The Bard put his name in the 46th psalm to indicate I have been here; I did this!

But why did he choose the 46th Psalm; why not the more famous 23rd? Shakespeare was born in 1564, so he was exactly 46 years old in 1610. This is the reason. And the unique placement

---

* *The Story of English* by Robert McCrum, William Cran, and Robert McNeil, New York: Penguin Books, 1993. And a PBS TV special.

of *shake* and *spear* does not occur in the NIV or the other modern translations of the Bible. Moreover, "William Shakespeare" is an anagram of "Here I was like a psalm."

I believe the Bard would be pleased by the discovery of his name in this psalm. I further imagine him on the Greek Happy Isles with Homer and Cervantes plus a multitude of other immortal writers reciting their works to appreciative audiences. This curio would have provoked him to laughter and reflect on what a teasing Hamlet said to a toadying Polonius in a gem of dialogue in Act III, mocking all those who would see only what they wish to see:

Hamlet: Do you see yonder cloud that's almost
         in shape of a camel?
Polonius: By the mass, and 'tis like a camel indeed.
Hamlet: Methinks it is like a weasel.
Polonius: It is back'd like a weasel.
Hamlet: Or like a whale?
Polonius: Very like a whale.

Previously I alluded to this human failing of false pattern making that can have grave or delightful consequences—henceforth let's call this the Shakespeare Syndrome. "Life," wrote G. K. Chesterton "is full of a ceaseless shower of small coincidences . . . . It is this that lends a frightful plausibility to all false doctrines and evil fads." And what are these small coincidences but a lumpiness in the cascade of a billion daily events—a trivial coming together in time and place.

Search history and you will find abundant examples to support almost anything. Someone claims economics is the single and pervasive motivator of all human actions. He cites the Trojan War as a battle by the Greeks to avoid paying a tax to trade into the Black Sea. So the great deeds of Achilles, Epios, and Odysseus were about money; Homer's poetry was a penny to their pocketbook. After he has finished gathering "evidence," he writes a book to tell the world. People call him Karl Marx; he changes history—millions die. Someone claims to have a cure for cancer. He collects anecdotal evidence to "prove" that apricot pits eliminate malignant tumors. He writes a book. People call him Everyman; he changes lives—hundreds die. The patterns of Marx and Everyman aren't true ideas in the whirlwind of events—just ghosts in the minds of true believers.

Fundamentalist Catholics and Christians scour the Bible for passages on the End of Days, Armageddon, and the "coming" Apocalypse. Sites on these topics litter the Internet like dung in a cow pasture. It was ever thus! In America, any reasonable estimate of such true-believers is above 50 percent—about the same number and the same people who accept creationism. The writers of the New Testament also believed they were living in the End Times of the apocalyptic age. In several passages from the Gospels, Jesus clearly says to his followers they are living in the last days. Consider Matthew 16:27-28 (KJV):

For the Son of man shall come in the glory of his Father with his angels; and then he shall reward every man according to his works. Verily I say unto you, There be some standing here, which shall not taste of death, till they see the Son of man coming in his kingdom.

Well folks, in case you haven't noticed, it didn't happen. And this has been a major embarrassment for Christians. Among other things, it proves Jesus wasn't omniscient—and this would seem to be a required attribute for any co-equal member of the Trinity. Rather than accept the obvious, Christians have done some enjoyable contortions to explain away this passage and others like it (Mark 8:38, 9:1 and Luke 9:26-27).

Undoubtedly, the most entertaining of these contortions is the whole-cloth invention of the legendary Wandering Jew. This myth has many forms and readily morphs into new ones. The standard story is of a Jewish shopkeeper who, seeing how slowly Jesus walked dragging the cross, stuck him on the back commanding him to move faster. "I go," Jesus replied, "but you will tarry until I return."

So for two thousand years this Jewish shopkeeper has wandered the earth unable to die so that Matthew 16:27-28 won't be proven false. The English poet *Shelley* penned verses about him; the French author Eugene Sue wrote a ten-volume biography of him; the American writer Walter Miller wrote a novel (*A Canticle for Leibowitz*) in which the Wandering Jew is the last person alive on Earth. But all around this legend are dark and menacing forms of horrific cruelty: Auschwitz, Treblinka, Buchenwald, Russian pogroms, Babi Yar, and a thousand unnamed places. The anti-Semite growls deeply at this shopkeeper who struck Jesus! Like the pre-World War II productions of the Oberammergau passion play, this myth was a powerful catalyst for European anti-Semitism. (*See* the Chapter Notes for a detailed literary history on this legend.)

Apparently unable or unwilling to learn from history, every age is convinced theirs is the last. Former televangelist Jerry Falwell was so certain he would be raptured—caught up in the clouds to meet Jesus on his return—that he once said he wasn't going to purchase a burial plot. I suspect he has changed his mind now, or what's left of it!

When I was younger—and that's most of my life—a door-to-door Jehovah Witness gave me a small book containing the *actual date* of the world's end. And this was very odd because that date had already passed. Furthermore, the book's publication date was also after the predicted dreadful day. I was confused. This must be a special and refined variety of reasoning with which I was unfamiliar. I still haven't mastered it.

In his entertaining book, *Did Adam and Eve Have Navels?* Martin Gardner summed up this special reasoning:

> For the past two thousand years, individuals and sects have been setting dates for the Second Coming. When the Lord fails to show, there is often no recognition of total failure. Instead, errors are found in the calculations and new dates are set. In New Harmony, Indiana, an Adventist sect called the Rappites was established by George Rapp. When he became ill he said that were he not absolutely certain the Lord intended him and his flock to witness the return of Jesus, he would think this was his last hour. So saying, he died. [4]

Modern manipulators of the Shakespeare Syndrome have mastered this art and taken it to new heights, or rather depths.

Hal Lindsey and Tim LaHaye are co-regents of this lucrative kingdom. Both authors conjure up Hollywood style apocalyptic visions of the End Times. In some manner, theirs is a terrifying death cult as Sam Harris points out:

> Or consider how you would feel if you learned that a nuclear war had erupted between Israel and its neighbors over the ownership of the Temple Mount. If you were a millennium-minded Christian, you would undoubtedly view this as a sign of Christ's imminent return to earth. This would be nothing if not good news, no matter what the death toll. There's no denying that a person's conception of the afterlife has direct consequences for his view of the world. [5]

Like Islamic suicide bombers, they foresee paradise after death rather than the reality of mold and mice. Hal Lindsey's first book *The Late Great Planet Earth* has sold an incredible 30 million copies! Tim LaHaye has sold upward of 90 million copies of the *Left Behind* series of books. Seven titles have reached #1 on the bestseller lists for *The New York Times, USA Today,* and *Publishers Weekly.* Mainstream authors can only hallucinate about such sales figures. All across America there is a great hunger to devour this junk food of the mind.

It doesn't add to our collective sense of security to know Ronald Reagan invited Jerry Falwell to National Security Council briefings. And it's positively frightening to learn that the President asked Hal Lindsey, the Armageddon activist, to instruct top Pentagon military strategists on nuclear war with Russia from a Bronze Age book written by near barbaric nomads. Furthermore, at least one other recent president had apocalyptic mindsets decorated with End–Time wreaths and Armageddon logos: George W. Bush. Any ideology that looks to a golden age after death inevitably devalues the only life we know surely— this one. The worst case situation is a fundamentalist Islamic state with long-range nuclear weapons. To doubt this is to portray Mahmoud Ahmadinejad, Iran's president, as a rational human being rather than a Holocaust denier who wishes to drive the Israelis into the sea. We can thank whatever gods may be that during the Cold War the Russians were atheists.

Hal Lindsey, Tim LaHaye, Jerry Falwell, Pat Robertson, Billy Graham, and their ilk find fatuous parallels between the Bible and modern world events. For this service, America's political elite prepared a place for them in the halls of power and at the elbows of presidents. All this from a book that either states or implies:

- The earth is flat.
- The universe was created in six days—creationism.
- The sun circles the earth—geocentrism.

We are drowning in a world awash in bad ideas while blowing bubbles in the foam.

Still unconvinced? Still believe the Bard polished the KJV Bible? Let's use the Shakespeare Syndrome on Shakespeare. As previously noted, Shakespeare died on April 23, 1616. Remarkably, on that same day, month, and year—perchance at the same hour—the greatest master of the Spanish language, Miguel de Cervantes, died and joined his English counterpart on the Happy Isles. Moreover, Shakespeare and the KJV share a curious synchronicity: the Bard wrote his last play, *The Tempest*, at the same time the King James Bible was released. Beyond even this, our best research informs us Shakespeare was also born on 23 April. So he came into the world on the 23rd, left it on the 23rd, for a sum of 46—our psalm number. Who would have thought?

WHAT IS TRUTH?

George Washington declared he could not tell a lie. Unlike the first President, I can tell a lie but I choose not to—a position requiring a choice and for this reason morally superior. As Mark Twain said, however, we sometimes tell a small lie just for the sheer refreshment of it. Nevertheless, we value truth; we seek truth. Lies are like counterfeit money. If we have too much, the currency is devalued as is the discourse. Ideally, for every dollar printed, the government has a matching amount in gold. If the government prints money wildly, then they devalue their own currency becoming a counterfeiter itself. This one-to-oneness between printed money and gold is analogous to the correspondence theory of truth.

Surprisingly, there are five other competing theories of truth. Let's list them with an example for each:

- Correspondence theory: *the Earth has a large moon*
- Coherence theory: *you cannot divide by zero*
- Relativistic theory: *dogs taste wonderful when barbecued*
- Pragmatic theory: *9/11 suicide bombers blow up the Twin Towers to get 72 virgins each*
- Universal cultural truths: *all men are created equal*
- Revealed truth: *God created man*

CORRESPONDENCE THEORY: This theory claims that *true* statements correspond to the actual state of affairs—attempting to put forward a relationship between statements on the one hand, and reality or facts on the other. This is the model of classical Greek philosophers such as Socrates, Plato, and Aristotle. When the average person speaks of "truth," this is what he/she means.

The many authors of the Bible's sixty-six books (KJV) saw truth differently. They had an agenda, a story to write for religious and tribal purposes. Anything was permissible if it advanced this agenda. Consider the first five books of the Bible: Genesis, Exodus, Leviticus, Numbers, and Deuteronomy often referred to as the Pentateuch or Torah. In Sunday school, we were all taught that Moses wrote these books. Old Testament authors insist on Mosaic authorship, as do numerous New Testament writers; the veracity of the Bible as a whole dissolves if Moses is not the author of the Pentateuch. This is a critical point.

How do you judge the veracity of a god? How many errors do you allow the creator of the universe before you relegate his "inspired" book to doorstop status? The answer is clearly none, nada, zilch!

The Torah offers such a supermarket of fraud it's difficult to choose from among its egregious howlers. Moreover, Israeli archeologists haven't uncovered a single piece of evidence for either the existence of Moses or the Exodus from Egypt. The broken tablets would be nice. Even Mount Sinai can't be located.

But for your consideration, I offer the following blooper: Moses records his own death, funeral, burial and thirty-day mourning period in Deuteronomy 34:5-8—a book he authored. Try hard and see if you can make yourself believe this. If you can accept that a man can write an account of his own death, burial, and mourning period, you probably have much larger problems than this book can solve.

COHERENCE THEORY: This hypothesis makes statements not about the real world but about other statements. Its practitioners endeavor not to contradict themselves like the comedian who says, "I never repeat myself . . . let me say that again." Coherence is the standard of truth in mathematics and chess where the rules and laws cannot be contradictory or the entire activity collapses. For example, if you allow division by zero, you contradict other rules.

Is the Bible non-contradictory? Consider the following famous line from Psalm 14:1 (KJV) with which the faithful relish confronting skeptics:

The fool hath said in his heart, There is no God.

The standards for the coherence theory of truth are incredibly high—identical to those we set for the veracity of the deity. If the theory has a single error, then the entire enterprise is abandoned. And we start over. There is no higher standard.

Now considering the following from Matthew 5:22 (KJV):

But whosoever shall say, Thou fool, shall be in danger of hell fire.

So which is it: Psalm 14:1 or Matthew 5:22? You can't have it both ways and claim to be coherent. Perhaps it's neither. Do we need a second example? I think not if God's "holy and inspired" book is to have the same high standard of truth as chess and mathematics. Hence, at some level, the Bible is incoherent.

RELATIVISTIC THEORY: This title covers many topics and areas. For our purposes we'll hold to relativistic arguments of truth as often heard in the saying, "That's true for you but not for me."

Its central claim is that truth of a statement depends solely on the views of the people, cultures, or religions, not on any correspondence to reality—this allows for geocentrism, flat-earth, and phrenology. Let's be clear from the beginning, relativism is something neither religion nor science can accept. This idea is a direct challenge to the correspondence theory of truth on which science bases its power. And the church sees relativism as an assault on faith and morals.

Through the scientific method, scientists work to discover *universal* truths. In this endeavor, they have succeeded beyond anything Archimedes or Newton could have dreamed of. As a species, the discoveries of *Homo sapiens* are so astounding that we might well be called the lords of creation. There is no Islamic chemistry or Protestant physics—there is only chemistry and physics, universal and enduring. We have *strong reasons*—and that makes all the difference—to believe that our chemistry and physics apply everywhere in the cosmos. This is the very antithesis of relativism.

Religion, on the other hand, is deeply parochial. Consider the maps we have all seen at the front of atlases, showing the major geographic areas of the world's religions: Islam, Buddhism, Christianity, Folk Religions, Baha'ism, Animism, Hinduism,

Religions of the World

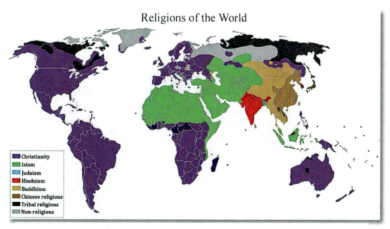

The Distribution of the Major Religions of the World Today

Judaism, Confucianism, Wicca, Sikhism, Jainism, and Shintoism. Religion cannot even transcend this planet, least of all lay claim to a cosmos neither their minds nor their "sacred" books comprehend or appreciate. This is religiocentrism; this is relativism.

Presently any such map of the earth's religions is something of an anachronism. Several of the religions I enumerated in the previous paragraph are not even shown: Baha'ism, Wicca, Jainism. Without doubt, a century ago this chart would have been more accurate. Today with world travel, the Internet, and communications of all kinds, these colors should be mottled sponges of different pigments; this trend will only continue at an accelerating rate. I am not saying this multicultural vector will succeed and mold us into a dreary monoculture like the North Korean nightmare. Satellite TV and the Internet are venues that may also keep people in touch with those sharing mutual values and beliefs.

The universe is large and full of wonders, and in its unimaginable complexity very likely contains numerous advanced civilizations. Do you really expect aliens, if they visit earth, to fall on their knees to Islam or any earthly religion? Would they genuflect to Mecca and Rome? The very thought causes fools to blush.

It may seem that relativism promotes tolerance, but it does so at the high cost of logic. It's not really a theory of truth for it denies the existence of objective reality. Believe whatever whimsy you wish, but expect no one to follow you. This is the realm of ghosts, sky-saviors, fairies, elves, and their kin. The ultimate destination of this fantasy is a padded cell with locks on the door. Complete relativism is a hollow drum—full of sound and fury; signifying nothing. Remember Jonestown!

Let's look deeper—a great dilemma exists with relativism just below the surface. This theory proclaims, "Truth is always personal and/or cultural; there is no objective reality." But *this statement* itself is a truth claim about objective reality—the very thing it cannot be. As Euclid would conclude, we have reasoned ourselves into ridiculousness—reductio ad absurdum.

PRAGMATIC THEORY: This proposal maintains a statement is true if it works for a particular person. So within the context of Islam, the prospect of seventy-two virgins may seem true to Mohammed Atta and help him blow up the Twin Towers. But for non-Muslims it is madness motivated by foolishness. (Some wag has noted that these virgins come with seventy-two mothers-in-law. Incidentally, what reward does Allah confer on female suicide bombers?) Pragmatism confuses utility with veracity.

Consider another example. You are in the forest and hear a rustling noise nearby. Is it the wind or a predator looking for lunch? Every time this happens, you hastily leave the area. Even if this is a false belief, 99 times out of a hundred, it's still useful. This is the modus operandi of most forest animals, even bears and wolves. So the use-value of a belief is clearly different from its truth-value.

A rationalist in a discussion with a theist will soon be faced with the following statements: "My religion makes me feel good, and I can't possibly go on living without it." Although these declarations are something of a conversation stopper, they're as sincerely held as stated. These are pragmatic utterances: they have a use-value even if they are false. You may point out that believers of the world's other religions say identical things, but this will be to no avail. Again, this is religiocentrism—their universe is small and full of trivialities. To more effect you could state that narcotic addicts say identical things: "Opium makes me feel so wonderful, and I couldn't live in a world without it." Recall that Karl Marx wrote, "Religion is the opiate of the people." He was right.

In his book, *The Selfish Gene*, Richard Dawkins introduced the concept of the *meme* (rhymes with cream) as a cultural unit of heredity—the counterpart of the *gene* in biology. Wearing your baseball cap backward to indicate heighted masculinity (or such) is an example. Valuing faith over evidence and reason is another. Religion is a very robust meme, and The Religions of the World map indicates where variations of this meme dominate. In the Indian Ocean tsunami of December 26, 2004, 230,000 men, women, and children perished in one of the deadliest natural disasters in recorded history. Larry King on his TV show asked George Bush senior if this cataclysm shook his faith. Immediately Bush replied, "No, no, Larry it increased my faith."

A common meme that confronts every rationalist is that Adolf Hitler was an atheist, and that this disbelief explains his demonic, evil behavior. This is false, horribly false. Hitler saw himself as doing God's work; the anti-Semitism of Martin Luther, the father of the protestant reformation, inspired him. In *Mein Kampf* he wrote, "I am convinced that I am acting as the agent of our Creator. By fighting off the Jews, I am doing the Lord's work." In 1938, Hitler affirmed, "I am now as before a Catholic and will always remain so."

Catholic anti-Semitism helped lay the groundwork for the emergence of 20th century racial anti-Semitism, and most German Christians saw no conflict between Christianity and their association with the Nazi Party. Below, two Catholic priests give the Nazi salute alongside Wilhelm Frick (hanged at Nuremburg) and Joseph Goebbels (committed suicide):

The death camps contained many atheists and other European intellectuals—independent thought was a crime in the Third Reich. The majority of interned Christians were Jehovah's Witnesses—pacifism was a crime in the Third Reich. Other Christians in the camps were Polish—resistance was a crime in the

Two Catholic Bishops, Unknown Soldier, Wilhelm
Frick, and Joseph Goebbels Giving the Nazi Salute.
Image courtesy of Bayerische Staatsbibliothek
München/Fotoarchiv Hoffmann

Third Reich. But the vast majority of Christians in the concentration and extermination camps were the administrators and guards. Every German soldier had a belt buckle that said *Gott*

Mit Uns or God With Us. My uncle brought one of these buckles home from the Italian front. As a child, I found the inscription confusing because I thought God was on our side. May I suggest that those who imagine Adolf Hitler was an atheist labor under my childhood delusion?

German Belt Buckle

Nazi Germany was anything but secular. Der Führer championed religious indoctrination in all public schools and sent the secularists to join the atheists and intellectuals in the death camps. But let the beast speak for himself on this point (Hitler, April 26, 1933, during negotiations, which led to the Nazi-Vatican Concordat of 1933):

> Secular schools can never be tolerated because such schools have no religious instruction, and a general moral instruction without a religious foundation is built on air; consequently, all character training and religion must be derived from faith. . . *we need believing people.*

Hitler wanted *believing people*, and with the help of his propaganda minister, Joseph Goebbels, he got them. The rest of the world got the most savage war in human history. Belief for the sake of belief leads to the darkest places in the human mind. We don't reason with the blood or stomach but with our brains. Belief alone may have efficacy, but it's often built on dogma, ignorance, and falsehoods like the anti-Darwinian nonsense of Aryan superiority.

The Polish Jew Jacob Bronowski made this point powerfully in his extraordinary book *The Ascent of Man*:

> It is an irony of history that at the very time when this [the uncertainty principle of Heisenberg] was being worked out there should rise, under Hitler in Germany and other tyrants elsewhere, a counter-conception: a principle of monstrous certainty.

When the future looks back on the 1930s it will think of them as a crucial confrontation of culture as I have been expounding it, the ascent of man, against the throwback to the despots' belief that they have absolute certainty.

. . . .

It is said that science will dehumanize people and turn them into numbers. That is false: tragically false. Look for yourself. This is the concentration camp and crematorium at Auschwitz. This is where people were turned into numbers. Into this pond were flushed the ashes of four million people. And that was not done by gas. It was done by arrogance. It was done by dogma. It was done by ignorance. When people believe that they have absolute knowledge, with no test in reality this is how they behave. This is what men do when they aspire to the knowledge of gods. [6]

UNIVERSAL CULTURAL TRUTHS: This proposition holds that we establish general truths over time—occasionally centuries; they transcend all religions and cultures. These are truths derived from experience, the distillation of the best of human thought. Their finished form arrives through discussion with our fellows: *all men are created equal.* Yet, they are not sacrosanct or above criticism: *all persons are created equal.* Universal cultural truths evolve, and evolution is never over.

In popular culture, the opening remarks of *Star Trek* the TV series have undergone a similar revision. In the original, Captain James T. Kirk says, "To boldly go where *no man* has gone before" whereas, the next series had Jean-Luc Picard say, "To boldly go where *no one* has gone before." Among rational people, changing your mind on the presentation of *good evidence* is considered a virtue; this is not, however, a universally accepted truth.

In our discourse with each other, amelioration of opinions is required for progress. It's fruitless to debate with fools and fanatics. Ask your fellow disputants if they could ever change their minds. If they answer no, just walk away.

The defining virtue of science is skepticism: to consider whatever conclusion you have arrived at as tentative and possibly erroneous. Similarly for the conclusions of others be they Newton, Galileo, or Einstein. Of all human communities, only the scientific holds this principle paramount. It's the fountain of progress. Practically everything biologists believed in in 1850 has been proven false, yet the company of biologists flourishes.

Science takes very human forms of knowledge—venturing forward, taking chances, often in error. A myriad of maxims show how to correct errors, but to repeat, Oliver Cromwell's underlies any hope of improvement: "I beseech you in the bowels of Christ, think it possible you may be mistaken." If you want fixed, eternal "truths," don't choose the sciences, but rather wade into the dogma of the church, synagogue, mosque, temple, or Capitol. In these "holy" places, changing your opinion, for whatever reason, is considered the very essence of weakness. Yet, it's the ultimate sign of our humanity that we can change our minds on the presentation of new evidence. To do less is dehumanizing. Never mistake reasonableness as a failing. As Jacob Bronowski wrote in *The Ascent of Man*, "Science is a tribute to what we can know although we are fallible."

If in our most exact sciences this skeptical attitude lies at the core, where can the rest of human discourse go but follow? You might be surprised at the tortuous paths religious believers can scurry along. Let's consider an example.

In their geography of the afterlife, Catholics recognize four regions: heaven, hell, purgatory, and Limbo. For 1500 years, Limbo has been the abode of unbaptized babies and virtuous pagans—this should also include all aborted fetuses, both medical and natural. In the *Inferno*, Dante called Limbo the first circle of hell. Catholic theologians, never ones to hastily admit a moral error, waited until 1994 to investigate whether sending blameless babies to Limbo was a good idea or not. Any layperson might have thought the answer was self-evident.

This conclave of clerics was even more absurd than the group that gathered for thirteen years to reexamine the trial of Galileo. Sam Harris brilliantly sums up the Limbo deliberations in the following scathing critique found in his *Letter to a Christian Nation*:

> Can we even conceive of a project more intellectually forlorn than this? Just imagine what these deliberations must be like. Is there the slightest possibility that someone will present evidence

indicating the eternal fate of unbaptized children after death? How can any educated person think this is anything but hilarious, terrifying, and unconscionable waste of time? When one considers the fact that this is the very institution that has produced and sheltered an elite army of child molesters, the whole enterprise begins to exude a truly diabolical aura of misspent human energy. [7]

After several years of investigation, the 30-man Vatican commission proclaimed in a 41-page document that there were *good reasons to hope* babies who die without baptism go to heaven. Here is the *first* sentence; try not to laugh . . . or cry.

The International Theological Commission has studied the question of the fate of un-baptised [sic] infants, bearing in mind the principle of the "hierarchy of truths" and the other theological principles of the universal salvific will of God, the unicity and insuperability of the mediation of Christ, the sacramentality of the Church in the order of salvation, and the reality of Original Sin.

For those masochists among us, see the Chapter Notes for a link to the complete Vatican document. When you sort through its stupefying concatenation of words, you ultimately discover the church *has not changed its mind* unlike what several major newspapers* reported. Catholics may still hold the concept of Lincoln. All this, every bit of it, applies to Roman Catholics only—the yellow bits on the Religions of the World map. According to them, all the other colors go to hell anyhow. Nor do you find the slightest awareness in this document of the deep anguish felt by Catholic mothers and fathers when their child dies unbaptized. If you're shackled to your theory and not to its consequences, this is how you behave. Jesus condemned this behavior in John 2:27, "The Sabbath was made for man, not man for the Sabbath." Dialogue with the church in gathering universal cultural truths seems unworkable when such a self-evident truth is slave to such a dreadful dogma.

_____

* *The New York Times* (April 20, 2007) "Vatican City: Pope Closes Limbo"

As noted previously, the defining feature of science is its willingness to change its position on the presentation of strong evidence. Science is a journey not a destination. Now the salient feature of religion is its absolute certainly and hence unwillingness to alter its dogma no matter what the evidence. The Magisterium—the divinely appointed authority in the Catholic Church—claims "converse" with the deity. (This could be a tad arrogant.) Religion is a destination not a journey. Those muddled minds who believe science and religion are compatible haven't been reading the news for the last two millennia. Religion and science hold different world views—a clash more profound than that between Islam and Christianity.

The following lines of doggerel are a comment on baptism, arrogance, and the nonsense of papal infallibility:

For the mothers of unbaptized babies
The situation is forever forlorn
There is no gentle mercy or kindness
From the temples of privilege and porn.

In the land of the steeple and spire
Where the priests give a wink and a nod
And the faithful help each other
But the Pope speaks only to God.

Just as I'm writing about universal cultural truths, this topic is flooding the world's news media. But for the Internet and the posting of two brave children begging for help, an horrific judgment would have gone unnoticed, and the apes that made it uncondemned. The Internet allows us to be jurors in the international court of public opinion—we have an ethical obligation to cry out against Stone-Age morality wherever it may be. Today it's in Iran. And the judgment is death by stoning! And these giant silverbacks* are the Iranian "legal" system. Can the reader speculate on the gender of the victim? Of course you can; you knew it was a woman—it almost always is. And the charge, you knew that too, is adultery. The man involved is likely in the local coffee shop being feted by his friends. The victim's name is

---

* I apologize to our jungle cousins for this comparison.

Sakineh Ashtiani; the mother of the two children fighting for her life—next month it will be someone else. Already she has survived 99 lashes plus incredible mental torture from her primate keepers.

Through the Internet, good people everywhere have joined with a single voice to have Ms. Ashtiani freed and stoning abolished. This is the power of people with a common humanity recognizing a universal cultural truth—stoning is evil. Here's a copy of the online petition.

We the undersigned are aware of the unjust treatment of Sakineh Ashtiani. WE CALL FOR SAKINEH ASHTIANI'S IMMEDIATE RELEASE.

We also call for the elimination of stoning as a practice in Iran, a practice which violates any and all definitions of human rights.

In as much as Iran is a signatory to the International Declaration of Human Rights and related Conventions, we call upon Ayatollah Ali Khamenei and the leaders of Iran to take responsibility for their commitments and intervene to free this woman who is being unjustly punished. WE also ask for the immediate end to stoning. No matter what the differences are in religious or political beliefs, Iran must participate, along with all other nations, in creating a world where basic human rights and fundamental humanity prevail.

Stoning is barbaric.... And it must be stopped.

Under world pressure, the apes responsible for her conviction and mistreatment are presently jabbering about suspending her stoning and just hanging her instead. By the time you read this, her fate will be known.

"Thou shall not follow a multitude to do evil" (Exodus 23:2 KJV) is a universal cultural truth. To stand against the wishes of the majority for good moral or intellectual reasons takes courage. Cowards cave and trot with the herd. Surely, gangs of thugs casting stones at a helpless human—wrapped securely in white robes and buried past their waist—is its antithesis. Bertrand Russell, the great rationalist, much admired this declaration, and he pursued it with great vigor. But what if the multitude is reduced to a single individual, and he's your superior? Shades of the Stanley Milgram experiment from Chapter 2. We know the great power of this situation to cause *most of us* to follow a superior to do great evil. And when the deed is done, the perpetrator usually claims the "Nuremburg Defense" or the "I was only following orders" justification. In the postwar trials, the Nazis frequently used this defense to little or no effect. The official version, called Nuremburg Principle IV, reads:

> The fact that a person acted pursuant to an order of his Government or of a superior does not relieve him from responsibility under international law, provided a moral choice was in fact possible to him.

The *unacceptability* of "I was only following orders" is a universal cultural truth developed over time. It's a variation on Exodus 23:2 implying we must take moral responsibility for our actions. How could it be otherwise!

REVEALED TRUTH OR REVELATION: On the wall before you is a huge map of the world, but you can't see it since you're blindfolded. In one hand you grasp a single dart that you must throw at the map. Where it lands will determine your birthplace, longevity, culture, language, and religion. This is a crucial moment! You hurl the dart. It drills through the air and lands on the Arabian Peninsula. So, you grow up speaking an Arabic dialect and practicing some form of Islam. . . . Suddenly your whole body shudders and you awake and know you were having a nightmare. Or were you?

The world calls you a Muslim child, rather than the child of Muslim parents. With this label your freedom of choice vanishes like the tip of the dart and at the same moment. You're a dutiful son, the best that parents could hope for. Studying the glorious Qur'an is your special passion; you have memorized entire Surahs (chapters). With your parents' blessing and their abundant wealth, you pursue your youthful passions into adulthood. You develop a scholarly reputation that spreads to other villages. Since the archangel Gabriel dictated the entire Qur'an directly to the illiterate Mohammed, these are the very words of Allah, the beneficent, the merciful. This is *revealed* truth in its literal mean-ing. You outgrow the meager intellectual resources of your vil-lage; you move to a larger town and then on to Medina, and fi-nally to Mecca itself. After a few years, even the heart of the sa-cred land and the sight of the Kaaba prove inadequate, and so you journey to the great centers of Qur'anic learning in Cairo, Istanbul, and Tehran. We'll call you Ishmael.

No matter where your personal dart landed, that will almost certainly determine your religion *forever*. This is the faith you will argue for, build temples, mosques, and churches for. (If you have the identical religion to your parents, ask yourself why.) Your theologians will pen weighty tomes on the profundities of its truth. Your poets will write magnificent verse in its praise, and musical geniuses will compose oratorios to your God's glory and transcendence. Reality has more possibilities, more choices, than any mere nightmare can conjure up. Most strongly held be-liefs are the result of your place of birth which is itself an acci-dent, a dart in the dark.

When I was a boy, it was unspoken but understood that we should never talk about sex, politics, or religion. As I grew older,

Sam Harris

I soon realized these were the most interesting topics and clearly in need of much discussion. Undoubtedly, sex and politics have abandoned the protected fold of forbidden subjects and entered common discourse. But religion, more exactly an individual's faith, is still considered a sacrosanct topic—immune from debate and crit-icism. Sam Harris in his brilliant book *The End of Faith* drives home this point and its grave consequences. With this prohibition in place, the church, mosque, and temple exercise a strong form of control over the faithful.

Faith is a conversation stopper. When individuals proclaim their faith, a curtain falls, their chins harden, their eyes fix, and all discourse ceases. It can be the precursor to something other than conversation. And it's the *sine qua non* of the religious elite and their grip over what they deem the great unwashed.

Hebrews 11:1 (NIV) defines faith as follows: "Now faith is being sure of what we hope for and certain of what we do not see." Google says it is "a strong belief in a supernatural power or powers that control human destiny." A rationalist might describe it as what true believers employ when their reasons run out. The reader can see there is some agreement among these definitions.

Revealed truth and faith are just two sides of the same coin—without one you can't have the other. Consider an example of this. The Bhagavad Gita is the most *sacred* and popular religious scripture in Hinduism. Their faith affirms it is a direct message from God in the incarnation of Lord Krishna revealed to Prince Arjuna in the middle of a battlefield. Despite the fact that almost one billion Hindus accept this, Mr. True Christian Believer (TCB) has *absolutely no faith* that the Bhagavad Gita is a divine revelation or any such oriental nonsense. He dismisses their revealed truth with the same gravitas he would a fly from his nose. TCB knows the real truth—his.

Consider another example. Enter Mr. True Muslim Believer (TMB), like Ishmael, whom we met a few paragraphs earlier. Since TMB claims descent from the biblical Abraham, he also recognizes Moses, Noah, and Jesus (Isa in Arabic عيسى) as important prophets. Muslims scorn the divine attributes of Jesus and reject Christian claims of his crucifixion and resurrection. Moreover—and here's the kicker—like all prophets in Islam, Jesus is considered to have been a Muslim. And they dismiss the Bible, the sacred text of Christians, as a corrupted document due to changes, omissions, additions, and so on.

Despite the fact that almost two billion Christians accept this, Mr. True Muslim Believer (TMB) has *absolutely no faith* that the Bible is a divine revelation or any such Western nonsense. Followers of Islam point out that Christians, even among themselves, cannot agree on which books are canonical. (*See* the following table for a summary of these discrepancies.) He dismisses their revealed truth with the same gravitas he would a fly from his nose.

RELIGIOUS DIVISIONS	ACCEPTED CANON
Judaism	24 books
Protestantism	66 books
Roman Catholicism	73 books
Greek and Russian Orthodox Churches	79 books

Mr. True Believer dismisses all other religions and their sacred texts—they barely enter his/her consciousness. Of course, if a religion has died out like Norse or ancient Greek, he treats it as mere mythology. Paradoxically Mr. TB is puzzled and hurt when other religions return the favor and ignore his scared truths. Mark Twain understood all this elevated foolishness and described it with great relish and insight in his essay "The Lowest Animal":

> Man is a Religious Animal. He is the only Religious Animal. He is the only animal that has the True Religion—several of them. He is the only animal that loves his neighbor as himself and cuts his throat if his theology isn't straight. He has made a graveyard of the globe in trying his honest best to smooth his brother's path to happiness and heaven. . . . The higher animals [nonhumans] have no religion. And we are told that they are going to be left out in the Hereafter. I wonder why? It seems questionable taste.

From an earthly perspective, all the fighting and bloodletting among religions is parochial. From a cosmic perspective, it's ludicrous. I guarantee the reader cannot comprehend the size of the universe—mere words beg a description. Yet I do guarantee the reader can picture the smallness, the pettiness, the sheer parochialism of all earthly religions. Each claims divine authority for its writings and real estate. And conversely, if my texts are holy and sacred then yours must be unholy and profane.

Contrast this behavior with that of scientists in any of their disciplines, say physics. There is no Japanese physics, Russian physics, or American physics. There is only *physics*! A discipline practiced worldwide and verified globally; we also have powerful evidence it is true throughout the entire universe and over all time periods. It is unquestionably true within our solar system, because physics* has enabled us to explore our "neighboring" planets and even to land spacecraft on some. This is one difference between parochial revealed "truths" and universal scientific truths.

This limited vision of the religious was noted by Carl Sagan in *Pale Blue Dot: A Vision of the Human Future in Space.*

> How is it that hardly any major religion has looked at science and concluded, "This is better than we thought! The Universe is much bigger than our prophets said, grander, more subtle, more elegant. God must be even greater than we dreamed?" Instead they say, "No, no, no! My God is a little god, and I want him to stay that way." A religion, old or new, that stressed the magnificence of the Universe as revealed by modern science might be able to draw forth reserves of reverence and awe hardly tapped by the conventional faiths.

Strangely, Dante, known for his restrictive vision of hell as an inverted cone, had the opposite vision of the starry universe. He wrote "Heaven wheels above you, displaying to you her eternal glories, and still your eyes are on the ground." The church should have listened to him; instead, they enjoyed too much the fiery punishments of hell visited on "sinners." Pope Saint Gregory, better known in English as Gregory the Great, wrote the following:

> The bliss of the elect in heaven would not be perfect unless they were able to look across the abyss and enjoy the agonies of their brethren in eternal fire.

Rather than the adjectives *Saint* or *Great*, surely this person should be described as a *sadist* or *sociopath*.

---

* In Nazi Germany in the 1930s, two physicists Philipp Lenard and Johannes Stark attempted to label Einstein's Relativity as *Jewish Physics* and have only *Aryan Physics* taught. Nonetheless, professors taught Einstein's theories without mentioning his name.

THE SUM OF ALL TRUTHS

Twenty times in the course of my late reading, have I been
upon the point of breaking out: This would be the best of all
possible worlds, if there were no religion in it!
John Adams (1735-1826), second U.S. President

We have explored the six theories of truth previously listed, and religion has been found wanting under all its headings. Let's list these theories again for convenience.

- Correspondence theory
- Coherence theory
- Relativistic theory
- Pragmatic theory
- Universal cultural truths
- Revealed truth

IN THE CORRESPONDENCE THEORY of truth, we saw that Deuteronomy 34:5-8 recorded Moses' death, funeral, and thirty-day mourning period. Now it's possible to write your own obituary but not of your own death and funeral. Of course, that's not the only howler in either Testament. Consider Joshua commanding the sun to stand still for a whole day so that the Israelites could continue slaughtering the Amorites (10:12-13 NIV).

On the day the LORD gave the Amorites over to Israel,
Joshua said to the LORD in the presence of Israel:
  "O sun, stand still over Gibeon,
  O moon, over the Valley of Aijalon."

  So the sun stood still,
  and the moon stopped,
    till the nation avenged itself on its enemies,
as it is written in the Book of Jashar.
The sun stopped in the middle of the sky and delayed
going down about a full day.

This statement is such a bundle of astronomical errors that I will leave it for the reader to unravel the web of nonsense.

Yet, there is always the possibility that poor Joshua was really commanding one of his male progeny to stop moving around, but this may be equally problematic. Cherry picking the Bible to find errors isn't necessary—its low-hanging fruit is found everywhere on the biblical tree of knowledge. Look for yourself!

And in case you think no one has ever taken this passage seriously consider the following. The miraculous account of Joshua stopping the movement of the sun was the basis for the Catholic Church's refusal to acknowledge Galileo's proofs that the earth went around the sun. The Inquisition members argued that the sun could not have been stopped if, indeed, it didn't travel around the earth. But as my logic professor at university was fond of saying, "From a false premise anything follows." And the condemnation of Galileo using the passage about Joshua is a prime example. This was one of the church's most shameful acts. This was "proof" by revealed truth.

INCOHERENCE OR SELF-CONTRADICTION is abundant in both the Old and New Testaments. In science and mathematics, one contradiction and the theory at hand is in serious trouble if not dead. I pointed out the biblical self-contradiction with the word "fool," but the faith heads ignore it and continue to clamber over the cliff of absurdity.

Consider a second, albeit unnecessary, example of the same problem. Jesus said he came to fulfill the prophecies of the Old Testament of the coming Messiah, and he acted in accordance with just that, or so we are told. So you would think that when he pointed out the Old Testament prophecy, he would get his reference correct. But oh no, we can't expect that level of consistency. In Mark 12:5 Jesus says that the law of the Old Testament states that the priests profane the Sabbath but are blameless. Nevertheless, no such statement is found in the Old Testament. The Bible contains thousands of flaws, absurdities, atrocities, less than questionable ethics, and even vulgarities. *See* the Chapter Notes for an online reference to these.

RELATIVISTIC THEORY, as I pointed out previously, is self-contradictory. This theory proclaims, "Truth is always personal and/or cultural; there is no objective reality." But *this statement* itself is a claim of truth about objective reality—the very thing it cannot be.

We know our truths are culturally colored. Nevertheless, science can recognize this tinting while religion sees the entire universe through the prism of faith, a faith peculiar to its time and geography, and hence with no prospect of universality.

PRAGMATIC THEORY: This is where a truth may have a use-value but lacks a truth-value. For example, I may believe the Hollywood sex symbol Megan Fox is secretly in love with me. This belief makes me feel fantastic—at least initially. I wouldn't want to live in any world where Megan Fox was not madly infatuated with me. And unless the reader is equally delusional, he/she must realize this fantasy has zero truth-value. This is what Daniel Dennett means by *belief in belief.* Implying that many think it is desirable to believe even if the belief itself is false. So perhaps I should continue with my Megan Fox fantasy or maybe I should just grow up and return to my true relationships. Short-lived daydreams or fantasies are probably harmless and perhaps even healthy. Unquestionably, long-term delusions are not, as I pointed out previously in the case of Nazi Germany.

UNIVERSAL CULTURAL TRUTHS: When humans come together, three options arise: talk, fight, or sulk. I would suggest the latter two are unproductive and the last often leads to the second. There is a saying—apocryphally attributed to Voltaire but actually written by English writer Evelyn Beatrice Hall (1868–1919)—that should be adopted as a universal cultural truth: "I disapprove of what you say, but I will defend to the death your right to say it." I endorse the sentiment more than the wording—but, of course, the statement itself is open to debate.

Those in a weak intellectual position have difficulty accepting a difference in opinions. And it has been my observation that Christians and Muslims really need their own faith confirmed by making converts. They secretly say to themselves, if the convert believes it, it must be true! Carolyn Baker, American professor of history and self-described "recovering fundamentalist Christian," wrote the following on this point:

I recall my own dependency on what "the Bible says." . . . I remember the need for the "fix" of the church service, the revival meeting, the prayer meeting. . . . But no "fix" was more deliciously validating than "winning souls for Christ"—that dramatic moment when I had manipulated someone else into a born-again experience. For this, the fundamentalist Christian addict lives and breathes. [8]

Pity the poor missionary. Leaving behind family, friends, and home, they ventured into countries whose customs and religion they neither knew, nor understood, nor wished to. Thousands died of malaria and yellow fever in Africa and still the heartless home churches sent more to replace them in what came to be called the white-man's graveyard. They went to their deaths as if soldiers charging out of the trenches with shouts of "convert the heathen*."

There are two ways to view history: one sees it as a brightly colored leaf on the forest floor and admires its beauty and patterns. The other turns the leaf over to see the decaying brown and moldy stench while the centipedes and earwigs scuttle away. It takes a great talent to look at the colored leaf and still comprehend the chaos and darkness beneath it. Mark Twain was such a man. What follows is one of his hilarious but double-sided paragraphs, this one on missionaries. Read it slowly, pausing over the punctuation.

Mark Twain

Sally—that's Sally Hogadorn—Sally married a missionary, and they went off carrying the good news to the cannibals out in one of them way-off islands round the world in the middle of the ocean somers, and they et her; et him too, which was irregular; it warn't the custom to eat the missionary, but only the family, and when they see what they had done they were dreadful sorry about it, and when the relations sent down there to fetch away the things they said so—said so right out—said they was sorry, and 'pologized, and said it wouldn't happen again, said 'twas an accident. [9]

---

* This is the supreme arrogance of believing they possess absolute universal truths derived from a Bronze Age cult of the Levant.

REVEALED TRUTH OR REVELATION: I believe Aristotle first opined that man was a rational animal. All my life I have searched for this mythical being, but as a rationalist I have come to doubt his/her existence. B. F. Skinner put human rationality under his thumb when he wrote, "Society attacks early when the individual is helpless." Clearly, Skinner's statement is a variant of Rousseau's "Man was born free, and he is everywhere in chains." If we are not free, surely we cannot discover the truth! Show me a society without freedom, and I'll show you a society dominated by lies. Falsity is an element in the evil of servitude.

Every human being values truth even those promulgating lies. Liars often believe their own lies. It is a large part of the human condition to be unaware of the sea of lies we live in. When General Eisenhower liberated one of the feeder camps for Buchenwald, he had every citizen of the town of Gotha personally visit the camp to view its atrocities. Having done so, the mayor and his wife went home and hanged themselves. Certainly, the majority of Germans did not comprehend the enormity of Hitler's egregious lies. Nor did the Russians glimpse the evil of Stalin's communism. Both dogmas had their holy texts, their revealed truth: *Mein Kampf* and *Das Capital*.

Do present-day Muslims understand the wickedness of their imams encouraging suicide bombers with hatred of the West? Do the Protestant and Catholic churches have any idea of the grandiose delusion of divine revelation they labor under? Both dogmas have their holy texts, their revealed truth: the *Qur'an* and *The Holy Bible*.

Imagine a large table in front of you covered with the world's holy books of *revealed truth*. A portion of the table is stacked with audiotapes for those whose divine revelations are still at the oral tradition stage[*]. You are amazed at so many different visions of god(s)—who would have thought? Moreover, all these versions of ultimate reality vehemently oppose each other; are even willing to kill over trivial disagreements. (Historically, consider the past centuries of Protestant and Catholic bloodletting; presently, reflect on the Sunni versus Shia bombings.) It is more accurate to think of these *revealed truths* as competing dogmas. Unlike science, there is no universal harmony here. Historians of the world's religions tell us these competing belief systems have only two dogmas in common:

- Higher being(s) exist.
- We should have dealings with them.

All else is conflict. The rational person is left with two choices: one of these texts is divinely revealed, or they are all man-made. This effectively eliminates more than 99 percent of them—so the rationalist and the religionist are in near perfect agreement. The former just takes the final micro step and says all sacred texts are man-made.

Although humans are not generally rational, they can be. See the cover of this book for nine famous examples. For the opposite conclusion, consider a recent survey by *Time* magazine that found 24 percent of Americans believe President Obama is a Muslim. Sic transit sanitas americanus.

Reflect on the following simple logical error we should all avoid. A man reports seeing a Sasquatch in the wilds of Washington State; the newspapers and TV networks pick up the story

---

[*] These "divine revelations" *never* contain any advanced technological information. For example, the number π to ten decimals would be nice and profoundly convincing. But oh no, I Kings 7:23 implies pi is three. Clearly, the Christian god failed math! Also, he failed the make-up test on the same topic in II Chronicles 4:3.

and run with it. CNN does a documentary on the many "sightings" of these creatures in the state and in neighboring Canada. In towns close to where the Sasquatch was sighted, believers flock into the streets demanding the government do something. Several others confirm the man's story with their own sightings of crepuscular creatures. But wait a minute! As Carl Sagan said, "Extraordinary claims require extraordinary evidence." The Sasquatch, a.k.a. Bigfoot, claims are so outlandish (note I did not say false) that the burden of proof is on the proponent of the proposition. And anecdotal evidence is nearly worthless. If someone claims anything extraordinary, weird, or peculiar, he/she is the one who must prove his or her case, not the listener.

The tellers of tall tales have to deliver tall evidence to support bizarre claims. Otherwise their stories are just more poltergeists, ghosts, goblins, fairies, trolls, yetis, space aliens, or other such fluff from the childhood of our species. Believe them at your peril because they are sensational, but in so doing you dehumanize yourself by abandoning the rational part of your brain that can be the glory of our species. Of course, the true masters of tall tales are the world's religions that feed on every human weakness. As we have learned, all these religions *claim the existence of unseen higher being(s)*. Let the claimants now provide evidence to support this Everest of tall tales fit for the crackling fireside on a cold, blustery, winter night in the forest.

Religion can come into your home as a day worker for special occasions like weddings and funerals; it may stay on as a permanent roomer. Eventually it will become a part owner of your home and ultimately the lord of the manor. The place in which you were once the master of your domain now has a new lord and you are his servant. This new master decides what you eat and when, whom you talk to or avoid, when you have sex or not, what you read and think, where you go to school or not, the curriculum of your school, how often you worship him with prayers and prostrations, and most importantly what you do with your money.

Too extreme you say! I respond that you haven't seen the lords of most religions. These faiths are an ever-present danger to your life, liberty, and happiness. The 2008 United Nations' *Human Development Report* ranks nations on a measure of "human development"—longevity, education, standard of living, and so on. It lists Denmark 14th and Sweden 6th. In contrast, the 50 *least*-developed nations are *all* highly religious. For those who mistake theocracy as the road to utopia, the data couldn't be clearer. Denmark and Sweden rank among the most well-developed, wealthiest, most democratic, most free, least corrupt, least violent, most peaceful, healthiest, happiest, best educated, most charitable, most environmentally aware, and *least religious* societies on earth.

The Creation of Adam by the Flying Spaghetti Monster titled
Touched by His Noodly Appendage ©, artist Niklas Jansson, 2005

The above anti-religious rant is true of every sect save one you may not have encountered: Pastafarianism. The prophet and founder of this new religion is Bobby Henderson who in 2005 revealed the Flying Spaghetti Monster (FSM) in a letter to the Kansas State Board of Education. Henderson, then a physics student at Oregon State University, later wrote out his divine revelation in the *Gospel of the Flying Spaghetti Monster* published by Villiard Press in 2006—available at fine bookstores everywhere.

Pastafarians' core belief is that an invisible and undetectable FSM created the universe (*see* the painting above) after a night of heavy drinking—hence the flawed nature of our existence. Followers are mainly young, bright university students from all over

Europe and America. Here is a representative quote from their gospel. Please forgive the vulgarisms—this is after all sacred text.

With millions, if not thousands, of devout worshippers, the Church of the FSM is widely considered a legitimate religion, even by its opponents—mostly fundamentalist Christians, who have accepted that our God has larger balls than theirs.

Even before the *Gospel of the Flying Spaghetti Monster* was written, other texts on Pastafarianism began to propagate over the Internet. Most were written in Olive Garden restaurants on linen napkins. A true believer called Solipsy compiled these into the *Loose Canon, a Holy Book of the Church of the Flying Spaghetti Monster*. And in an act of synchronicity that would have impressed even Carl Gustav Jung, the *Loose Canon*—just like the Bible—is divided into two parts: the Old Pastament and the New Pastament. With such a proliferation of these texts, a council similar to the Christian one at Nicaea in 325 CE will have to be convened to determine which are truly canonical. In the meantime, the reader may freely download all these as one PDF file (*see* Chapter Notes for the link). Even Gideon International, who put free Bibles in every hotel room as gifts for the guests, can't equal Pastafarian distribution. To give the reader a taste of the flavor of this sacred revelation here are two excerpts:

I am the Flying Spaghetti Monster. Thou shalt have no other monsters before Me. (Afterwards is OK; just use protection.) The only Monster who deserves capitalization is Me! Other monsters are false monsters, undeserving of capitalization.
Suggestions 1:1

"Since you have done a half-ass job, you will receive half an ass!" The Great Pirate Solomon grabbed his ceremonial scimitar and struck his remaining donkey, cleaving it in two. "Now get your ass out of here!"

Praised Be to His Noodly Appendages—and may the Sauce be with you!

Pastafarians, for no just reasons I can discern, have their critics, generally referred to as ante-Pastafarians many of whom belong to the human race. This group includes Christians, Jews, Muslims, Hindus, Buddhists, Republicans, and Baptists. The feeling is we are far too happy and need to tone it down—religion isn't meant to be this much fun*. We do enjoy our holy days of *Pastover* and *Dontgiveadamn*, but it's entirely spurious and a deliberate attempt to discredit Pastafarianism to link us with *Festavus for the Rest of Us*. With its feats of strength and airing of grievances, it's just a parody of a true religious holiday. We proclaim on the sacred balls of the FSM that in no manner whatsoever have we, or ever will we, celebrate *Festavus for the Rest of Us*.

Yet the most unfair and unwarranted criticism of all by these ante-Pastafarians is to demand we prove the existence of our God, the Flying Spaghetti Monster. Now we fully understand that an invisible and undetectable FSM—like the gods of all the Abrahamic religions—cannot be proven. So why should we have to do what the mainline religions have never done, or been asked to, or even can do—verify the existence of a deity. These demands are monstrously unfair, hypocritical, and a complete double standard. We can, of course, always fall back and say, as all religions do, that this is *our faith*. Bobby wrote it, I believe it, that's the end of it!

THE LAST WORD

Pontius Pilate asked, "What is truth?—Quid est veritas?" but didn't stay to hear Jesus' reply. We have developed some answers to this historic question. For scientists and citizens "truth" is the correspondence of statements with reality. A famous example is "the Earth revolves around the sun." Truth implies freedom and power; falsity entails servitude and helplessness. When you witness slavery and servitude, the truth is nowhere present—consider North Korea. All dictatorships are the product of propaganda, another word for lies. Truth must be earned by imagination, insight, and research, and above all by a willingness to change your mind on the presentation of new, strong evidence.

---

* As Alfred North Whitehead commented, "The total absence of humour in the Bible is one of the most singular things in all literature."

As we know, religions rarely if ever do this, and then only on a glacial timescale. There is no royal road to truth by divine revelation or dancing prophets. History is witness to this truth. In John 8:32 (NIV) Jesus declares, "Then you will know the truth, and the truth will set you free." He was right; it will set you free—free of the gods from the childhood of our race with its long nightmare of religious belief.

CHAPTER—6

GOD'S MESSENGERS

*Those who can make you believe absurdities
can make you commit atrocities.*
Voltaire (1694-1778)

Where is Allah? Where is Yahweh? Where is God? The Islamic madrassas, Jewish theological seminaries, and the Christian Sunday schools tell us they are *everywhere*. Religious scholars like to say He/She/It is omnipresent, and for good measure, omniscient and omnipotent. Let's consider the first of this triumvirate of supreme attributes. The Qur'an (Authorized English Translation or AET) Surah 2:115 declares:

> *To GOD belongs the east and the west; wherever you go there will be the presence of GOD. GOD is Omnipresent, Omniscient.*

The Bible proclaims in Psalm 139:7-8 NIV:

> *Where can I go from your Spirit?*
> *Where can I flee from your presence?*
> *If I go up to the heavens, you are there;*
> *If I make my bed in the depths, you are there.*

It's clear that all the Abrahamic religions pronounced the deity's omnipresence. But what does this magnificent attribute entail? A reasonable person would inquire if there were any evidence for omnipresence. Of course there isn't; nor could there be. We can't even imagine how such empirical data could be found, but proving it false requires just a single point without God. Theologians like to endow their deities with every supreme attribute even though evidence for any of these is missing. Religious "scholars" are often like ancient court sycophants sucking up to the BIG Guy.

Let's imagine He/She/It is omnipresent and see where this assumption leads. Not only highly religious people have maintained this position. The famous scientist Max Planck, in his 1937 lecture "Religion and Naturwissenschaft," expressed the view that God is omnipresent. Thomas Aquinas pontificated that He/She/It stepped out of eternity into time—whatever that means. It's unclear how St. Thomas arrived at this insight. If He (for convenience I'll normally drop the She and It), was at Wal-Mart last Friday for the special sale and again this Friday, then He is *in time* not out of it. Therefore, perhaps St. Thomas had a minor difficulty with omnipresence, so let's look deeper.

The Qur'an and the Bible[*] forcefully inform us that Allah, Yahweh, and God hate homosexuals. Since most of us in the West know the biblical injunctions against gays, let's consider the Qur'anic. As well as the Authorized English Translation or AET of the Qur'an, we will use the older Marmaduke Pickthall translation or PT.

And Lot! (Remember) when he said unto his folk: Will ye commit abomination such as no creature ever did before you?
Lo! ye come with lust unto men instead of women. Nay, but ye are wanton folk. Surah 7:80-81 (PT)

What! Of all creatures do ye come unto the males, and leave the wives your Lord created for you? Nay, but ye are forward folk. Surah 26:165-6 (PT)

Since the archangel Gabriel, according to tradition, dictated the entire Qur'an directly to the allegedly illiterate Muhammad, these are the very words of Allah, the beneficent, the merciful, or so we are told.

Now the residents of Sodom and Gomorrah, known as the people of Lot or Lut, gave rise to the Arabic words for homosexual behavior *liwat* and those who practice it *luti*. Amazing, isn't it! Allah dictated the identical story to Muhammad as Yahweh told Moses. Either they need new material or the Prophet Muhammad was plagiarizing.

[*] *See* Leviticus 18:22, 20:13, and Romans 1:26–27

Nevertheless, preachers and Sunday school teachers seldom mention the *complete* story of the "virtuous" Lot and the "depraved" residents of Sodom and Gomorrah. For example, Lot's drunkenness and incest with his daughters are entirely absent from the Qur'an—Muhammad plagiarized selectively. To this day, Muslims venerate both Lot and his uncle Abraham. Even the Apostle Peter proclaimed the former a righteous man. But as the song says, "It Ain't Necessarily So."

The unexpurgated story follows. Two angels arrive at Sodom, and Lot prevails upon them to stay at his house. The locals (the Sodomites) come to Lot's door and demand that he send these foreigners out "that we may know them." In Genesis 19: 6-8 (NIV), the ever-virtuous Lot offers his daughters instead to be gang raped:

> *Lot went outside to meet them and shut the door behind him and said, "No, my friends. Don't do this wicked thing. Look, I have two daughters who have never slept with a man. Let me bring them out to you, and you can do what you like with them. But don't do anything to these men [angels], for they have come under the protection of my roof."*

I would have thought that the protection of his virginal daughters would have been more important than that of two strangers who had angelic powers, but apparently not. Furthermore, Genesis 19:30-36 also tells us Lot had sexual intercourse with these daughters on two successive evenings, but he blamed it on his drunkenness. In biblical and Qur'anic terms, from Eve onward women were always at fault for any sexual wrongdoing between genders. Muhammad wanted no part of these drunken, incestuous stories in his schoolboy copying so he simply omitted them.

Let's return to our main theme of problems and paradoxes with omnipresence. Since we have established that all the Abrahamic deities abhor homosexuality, and they are everywhere at all times, then are they not in bed with every gay and lesbian couple? This would then be a most curious ménage à trois, or a gross case of peeping tomism. This conclusion, of course, is ridiculous only because the idea of omnipresence is ridiculous. *From a false foundation, any foolishness follows.*

With a twinkle in his eye, H. L. Mencken once said, "Conscience is the inner voice that warns us somebody may be looking." And with a big-brother deity who is omnipresent, you know you are being watched—literally. Like the ubiquitous Santa, He's making a list and checking it twice; Gonna find out who's naughty and nice. This is the universal police state; the mindset of all those who want absolute control, where at any time you may be called to account for a life-long rap sheet. The Qur'an emphasizes this last judgment or rap-sheet day by numerous references and names: the Day of Reckoning, the Hour, the Last Day, Day of Judgment, the Day of Resurrection, or *Yawm al-Qiyāmah* in Arabic. This is the day all Muslims labor for; this is the day all Muslims fear; this is the day suicide bombers pray for; this is the day that *ruins this life* in preparation for the afterlife. Because of this day, all Muslims sacrifice the only life they truly know for the fabled next. This is one consequence of Allah's omnipresence! Islam is the path of obedience; even the word itself means to give up, to surrender to God—the way of all slaves. The word *abd* in Arabic means slave and hence *Abdullah* means slave of God. The prefix *abd* occurs 81 times with different names for Allah in the Qur'an but the implication is always the same—slavery.

Omar Khayyám succinctly summed up the debate on the two worlds—this life and the afterlife—in quatrains 27 and 49 of his *Rubáiyát*:

Why, all the Saints and Sages who discuss'd
Of the Two Worlds so wisely—they are thrust
Like foolish Prophets forth; their Words to Scorn
Are scatter'd, and their Mouths are stopt with Dust.

Strange, is it not? that of the myriads who
Before us pass'd the door of Darkness through,
Not one returns to tell us of the Road,
Which to discover we must travel too.

Theologians often tell us that hell—among other things—is the absence of God. Remember God, Allah, or whomever, made hell for evildoers, unbaptized babies, and virtuous pagans.

Since none of these deities, most unfortunately, ever goes to hell, they are not truly omnipresent. But let's not worry about such contradictions because God, in particular Allah, seems to love hell. An incredible 87 of the Qur'an's 114 Surahs speak of hell. Allah virtually salivates on the prospect of torturing people for eternity. Consider just two horrific examples of this incredible psychopathology:

> *Surely, those who disbelieve in our revelations, we will condemn them to the hellfire. Whenever their skins are burnt, we will give them new skins. Thus, they will suffer continuously. GOD is Almighty, Most Wise.* Surah 4:56 (AET)

> *As for those who disbelieve, they will have clothes of fire tailored for them. Hellish liquid will be poured on top of their heads. It will cause their insides to melt, as well as their skins. They will be confined in iron pots. Whenever they try to exit such misery, they will be forced back in: "Taste the agony of burning."* Surah 22:19–22 (AET)

Educated people in the West no longer believe in hell. They dismissed this wretched concept through morality, reason, and laughter. In the auditorium of the Earth, however, this laughter hasn't yet reached the Muslim world. The following reworked chestnut, in a weak effort to initiate such:

> A little Muslim girl was talking to her teacher, the Imam, about whales. The precocious little girl said it was physically impossible for a whale to swallow a human because even though it was a very large mammal its throat was very small.

> The Imam stated that the Qur'an said a whale swallowed Jonah (Surah 37:139-144). Irritated, the little girl reiterated that a whale *couldn't* swallow a human; it was physically impossible.

> She said, "When I get to heaven I will ask Jonah." The Imam asked, "What if Jonah went to hell?" The little girl replied, "Then you ask him."

Thus far, I've concentrated on reason and laughter to point out the problems with the attribute of omnipresence. Amongst the majority of people, however, reason has no power in the realm of religion. So we'll consider deep moral issues. Being everywhere at all times implies that Allah, Yahweh, and gods in general have witnessed every atrocity, every abuse, every murder, every genocide that history's dark story records. We will consider one.

As you plunge down through the cesspool of human depravity, you eventually discover a floor constructed with the concrete blocks from the Killing Room at Auschwitz. When the Jews and others arrived from one of the feeder camps, the SS guards lined them up. Younger people were sent to the right; older people and children deemed too weak to be good workers were sent to the left, meaning the gas chambers. To prevent panic, the Nazis guards told them they would be taking a shower and made them strip naked. Instead, Zyklon B gas, made from hydrogen cyanide crystals and formed into pellets, discharged from the showerheads, killing the helpless. Look below; see for yourself. This is where dogma, ignorance, and arrogance lead. This is the concrete death chamber at Auschwitz.

Auschwitz Crematorium Killing Room

Imagine you are there! You enter through the small door—the only door—seen on the left side of the end wall in the above photograph. This windowless cavity held hundreds, perhaps as many as a thousand naked bodies. The children wonder why all the adults had taken their clothes off. When the room was full and the door closed and sealed, the "showers" turned on. Within seconds, those closest to the cyanide spewing showerheads realized what was happening. From these epicenters a crescendo of panic quickly spread to engulf the entire cavity. And then a headlong rush to the door began with screams that could easily be heard in the surrounding corridors. Those few at the door itself ripped the nails from their fingers in a futile attempt to open it. Those further away surged toward it as a mass of naked flesh. Civilization fell away; the primal drive to survive surfaced in a climax of shrieking fuelled by cyanide, chaos, and defecation—but still the door was sealed.

The God of the Jews, Yahweh, saw all this. Allah saw all this. Jesus saw all this. All omnipresent Gods were witnesses to this unspeakable horror. Yet, none opened the door. No mercy! No kindness! No compassion! You need not be omnipotent to open this door, just moral, simply decent.

With overwhelming confidence, I can tell you I would have opened that door and so would you! Nothing within my power would have prevented me. Absolutely nothing! Where does that leave Yahweh, Jesus, and Allah? Quite simply with all those without sympathy or even a touch of human kindness. They were worse than the SS guards who carried out their orders with Teutonic efficiency! "God moves in a mysterious way His wonders to perform" as the old hymn by William Cowper says—as do all psychopaths. This is where the attribute of omnipresence ultimately leads. It is wiser to conclude, as all the evidence shows, that such Gods do not exist, and if they do, they are devils. Yahweh, Jesus, and Allah are either everywhere at all times or nowhere at any time! Make your choice! All sky-gods deserve the attribute of nihil-presence. Incredibly, the synagogues, churches, and mosques still hold up these deities as paragons of virtue to teach us morality.

RELIGION AND ASTRONOMY

He also made the stars.
Genesis 1:16 NIV

All peoples have creation myths. We read them in primary school. Even as children, we saw some parallels among them.

Yet, the significant similarities are those of time, place, and people rather than those of character and content.

From the earliest times, all people also have believed they were at the center of creation, perchance fashioned even in the image of God. As noted in Chapter 3, the Eskimos still call themselves *Inuit* and the Cheyenne Indians of the Great Plains called themselves *Tsistsistas*, both meaning "The People." The Hebrews have long referred to themselves as "The Chosen People." Science has paved a broad path of withdrawal from this anthropocentrism, and the retreat has disturbed the equilibrium of the faithful. Copernicus and Darwin were only two—possibly the most important two—who laid the scientific bedrock for an objective view of humankind's true place in the universe.

Islam, Judaism, and Christianity have no appreciation for the magnificent discoveries of astronomy, ancient or modern. No theologian, rabbi, priest, bishop, cardinal, pope, monk, imam, mullah, or grand ayatollah, past or present, dared to whisper otherwise. The very few who advanced conflicting astronomical ideas were horribly punished: Galileo who discovered evidence for heliocentrism with his telescope and Giordano Bruno who imagined the stars were other suns scattered through an infinite universe. The first suffered permanent house arrest while the second was burned alive at the stake. At that time, scientists and thinkers got the message and withdrew from Catholic Europe to the friendlier Protestant north.

The images of the Hubble Telescope present a universe so much grander than anything in the creation fables of Genesis or its copies sprinkled throughout the Qur'an. Genesis 1:16 NIV sums up this biblical inadequacy when it says, almost as an afterthought, "He also made the stars."

> God made two great lights—the greater light to govern the day
> and the lesser light to govern the night. He also made the stars.

Of course, the moon shines only by reflected light. And the sun is just an ordinary star, one of 300 billion, in a small arm of an out-of-the-way spiral galaxy, a minor part of the Local Group of Galaxies, a minute fraction of the Virgo Super-Cluster, one of innumerable such clusters—a mote in the eye of the universe.

The Qur'anic "astronomy" is worse. When Muhammad isn't cribbing from the Old Testament, he spews the following scientific nonsense:

And verily We have beautified the world's heaven with lamps, and We have made them missiles for the devils, and for them We have prepared the doom of flame. Surah 67:5 (PT)

Instead of throwing snowballs, Allah creates the stars to hurtle at the little devils, or they are lamps set in the sky to light man's way at night. Allah needs to get out more and see what the universe He created is really like. All this sounds very like sixth-century Arabia rather than the wisdom and knowledge of an omnipotent creator.

Lo! We have adorned the lowest heaven with an ornament, the planets; With security from every forward devil. They cannot listen to the Highest Chiefs for they are pelted from every side, Outcast, and theirs is a perpetual torment. Surah 37:5-9 (PT)

Now the planets, like the stars, are ornaments for us to enjoy from our anthropocentric armchair. And again, Allah bombards the devils with stars so that they cannot eavesdrop on his conferences (with whom?). Of course, the Qur'an mentions hellfire once more—Muhammad's favourite vacation spot for infidels and apostates.

None of these comments are meant to disparage the astronomical achievements of the Islamic Golden Age, traditionally dated from the mid-8th century to the mid-13th century. More on this later.

Carl Sagan

Carl Sagan, shown at the left, was an extraordinary human being with innumerable achievements. A whole generation was introduced to him through *Cosmos: A Personal Voyage,* a thirteen-part television series with Sagan as presenter and co-writer. It's still the most watched PBS series in the world and has been broadcast in more than sixty countries and seen by over 500 million people. Who better to give us an appreciation of our universe? He comments on the extraordinary blindness of all Western religions to the wonders of our fantastic cosmos:

> What we are seeing here are more galaxies beyond the Milky Way [see next page]. In fact, there are more galaxies in the universe than stars within the Milky Way Galaxy. Most of the objects you see here are not stars but galaxies; spiral ones seen edge on, elliptical galaxies, and other forms. The number of external galaxies beyond the Milky Way is at least in the thousands of millions and perhaps in the hundreds of thousands of millions, each of which contains a number of stars more or less comparable to that in our own Galaxy. So if you multiply out how many stars that means, it is some number—let's see, ten to the . . . it's something like one followed by twenty-three zeros, of which our sun is but one. It is a useful calibration of our place in the universe. And this vast number of worlds, the enormous scale of the universe, in my view has been taken into account, even superficially, in virtually no religion, and especially no Western religions. [1]

We have found our true place in the cosmos by a journey of ever-widening perception from the micro to the macro universe. We began in the womb and progressed to the nursery and on to our home, neighborhood, and city. Most of us advanced to seeing ourselves as citizens of our birth country and a very few go even further and view themselves as citizens of the world. But this is only the barest beginning. Let's take the final step in a highly enjoyable manner by watching the YouTube video* produced by author, comedian, and singer Eric Idle listed in the footnote.

Earlier I wrote about our inconceivable smallness on the vast scale of things; coupled with this is the fact that we are not at the center of anything. The universe doesn't have a center even though it is expanding (see Chapter 3 for an explanation of this seeming paradox). Nonetheless, as we grew up we realized quality was not proportional to quantity—we valued the dime

---

* *Google* "Eric Idle"+NASA.

more than the larger nickel. And do we really need to be at the center of anything? Are we still children? It appears the deity thought otherwise concerning our size and position for He created us miniscule in an outer arm of a forgotten galaxy.

Yet, we are privileged to have a vision of creation built on evidence, and not on the daydreams of "sacred" texts. We are splendid creatures! Sagan wrote that you and I are rolled out of stardust, baked in the furnace of broken symmetry. As the Bard[*] said, "What a piece of work is a man! how noble in reason! . . . in action how like an angel! in apprehension how like a god!"

Hubble Ultra Deep Field Infrared View of Galaxies

---

[*] Hamlet, Act II, Scene 2

THE MUSLIM MESSENGER

The love of the world is the root of all evil.
Prophet Muhammad—peace be upon him

The prophets of Islam are those men chosen by Allah to teach His word. The followers of Islam believe *every* prophet was a Muslim as well as those they preached to—that certainly means many of my readers.

The world is large and full of wonders, but none so much as the creator of the universe being interested in us. Except perhaps the even stranger and over-powering desire—demand if you will—He has for our praise and worship. Some make a career out of praising Him, others, the lucky ones, need only genuflect five times daily. Consider the following. Allah is walking on an endless beach somewhere in His infinite universe of innumerable planets when He reaches down and picks up a single grain of sand. This He says of all possible grains is a special grain, and I will call it Earth.

The year is 610 CE and the endless beach is Arabia. Supposedly on this grain of sand are millions, if not billions, of mites. Allah picks a single mite on the grain and thinks to Himself "I will reveal everything to this mite so that it can tell all the other mites how gloriously magnificent I am and worship me forever and ever in complete and abject subjugation." (For some reason using the JumboTron at the World Cup or a Super Bowl game was never an option.) As Christopher Hitchens is fond of saying, "See if you can make yourself believe this. Try harder. Try again."

Well, apparently many people can manage to believe these incredible stories: 1.57 billion at present. We call them Muslims. The mighty mite who managed all this was the Prophet Muhammad, God's messenger. Before Allah chose Muhammad, He had chosen others to tell the world how wonderful He was. You know them: Adem (Adam), Nuh (Noah), Ibrahim (Abraham), Lut (Lot), Musa (Moses), Yunus (Jonah), Isa (Jesus). They were all Muslims according to Islam (perhaps that's what Adolf Hitler meant when he said Jesus wasn't Jewish).

The deity, like any big shot, deals with this mite through an intermediary. Accordingly, He sends a strangely androgynous Gabriel (*see* picture below) to reveal what is in His heavenly book, the Glorious Qur'an to the *apparently* illiterate Muhammad. This annunciation was not done in public where others might confirm or deny its reality but in a dark cave called Hira about three kilometers from Mecca.

Gabriella and Muhammad

Muhammad described this event in the following manner: Gabriel, using extremely unorthodox teaching methods, hugged Muhammad three times shouting, "Recite." Finally, the Angel said these momentous (?) first verses:

In the name of thy Lord Who createth,
Createth man from a clot.
And thy Lord is the Most Bounteous,
Who teacheth by the pen,
Teacheth man that which he knew not.
Surah 96:1-5 (PT)

So Muhammad then repeated these verses.

If these are the first verses given to Muhammad, the reader may wonder why they don't come first in the Qur'an. This "holy book" is not chronological but organized roughly according to chapter size, largest to smallest.

However, these initial verses are a revelation of sorts in that they teach us absolutely nothing new! Allah's first scientific utterance on the creation of man is false, utterly false. We learn nothing about history, health, astronomy, human relations, literature, or anything else. The words express merely braggart praise upon the speaker. All this sounds suspiciously like a human currying favor from a sky-god modeled on earthly despots similar to Muammar Gadhafi and Saddam Hussein.

What could the creator of the universe have said to truly impress us? How about something that for 610 CE would have settled *for all time* the divine nature of His revelation in the Qur'an. Here are three simple suggestions:

- pi to 50 decimal places
- the theory of germs
- Mars* has two small moons; Jupiter has four large ones

Unlike the Bible, where pi is implied as 3 in I Kings 7:23, the Qur'an says nothing about this number. Nada! Nil! Zilch! Historians of science often rank how advanced a society is by the number of decimal places it has calculated for pi. The Egyptian Rhind Papyrus of 1650 BCE had pi as 3.1; the Bible implied 3 in 600 BCE, while the Greek genius Archimedes pegged pi at approximately 3.141 in 250 BCE. Yet the Qur'an 800 plus years after Archimedes says or implies nothing. In light of the absence of anything new, up to date, or even mildly interesting in Allah's first words, this Surah sounds just like a seventh-century native of Mecca on an ego trip.

Despite the fact that the world's most famous number doesn't make even a cameo appearance, either explicitly or implicitly in the Qur'an, many Arabic language scholars believe this book has a profound number pattern. The leader among these devotees was Dr. Rashad Khalifa, who made the Authorized English Translation. He claims the many coincidences involving the number "19" in the

---

* Johannes Kepler, Jonathon Swift, and Voltaire all predicted Mars would have two moons.

Qur'an are beyond chance, and prove its divine origin. *Google* "19 in the Qur'an" for more on this foolishness.

What are we to make of Muhammad? A man who at forty years of age goes into a dark cave for days finally emerging to say he talked to Gabriel. Yes, talked to an angel! And this angel dictated God's holy book from heaven to him, an illiterate supposedly. From this "revelation" sprung a major religion now with 1.57 billion followers. Amazing? Incredible? We must answer the question, "Who was Muhammad, really?"

GOD'S MORMON MESSENGER

But before we do that consider that America has had its own Muhammad, Joseph Smith, who once said, "I will be to this generation a second Mohammed." Smith founded the modestly titled The Church of Jesus Christ of Latter-day Saints hereafter called the LDS or Mormons. He adopted the fierce motto either "the Alcoran [Koran] or the Sword." It has been pointed out that Smith was too ignorant to know that *al* is the definite article and hence *the* is redundant. Comparing Smith and Muhammad is instructive and at times entertaining.

Both men claimed an angel talked to them. In the case of Joseph Smith, this creature had the unfortunate name of Moroni. Both men were allegedly illiterate although we know Smith could read a little. Both men were prolific polygamists: Muhammad had thirteen wives while Smith had a veritable herd of thirty-eight. Nonetheless, both men still had time to dictate a "holy" book and energy to found a religion. Both these books are wonderful soporifics for insomniacs. Mark Twain who owned a copy of the Book of Mormon wrote, "It is such a pretentious affair and yet so slow, so sleepy, such an insipid mess of inspiration. It is chloroform in print." Even one of its fifteen books is appropriately titled the Book of Ether. Doubtless neither book has the power or majesty of the King James Bible.

Twain went into some detail about the deficiencies of Smith's book; he could just as accurately have been writing about Muhammad's. The following quote is from his marvelous volume *Roughing It: A Personal Narrative.* It's one of the best on the

American West, full of intriguing characters such as miners, treasure seekers, cowboys, rowdies, and Mormons:

> The book [Smith's] seems to be merely a prosey detail of imaginary history with the Old Testament for a model followed by a tedious plagiarism of the New Testament. The author labored to give his words and phrases the quaint old fashioned sound and structure of our King James translation of the scriptures. The result is a mongrel, half modern glibness and half ancient simplicity and gravity. The latter is awkward and constrained, the former natural, but grotesque by the contrast. Whenever he found his speech growing too modern, which was about every sentence or two, he ladeled in a few such scriptural phrases as, "exceeding sore," "and it came to pass," etc. and made things satisfactory again. "And it came to pass," was his pet. If he had left that out, his bible would have been only a pamphlet.
>
> If Joseph Smith composed this book, the act was a miracle. Keeping awake while he did it, was at any rate. If he, according to tradtion, merely translated it from certain ancient and mysteriously engraved plates of copper, which he declares he found under a stone, in an out of the way locality, the work of translating it was equally a miracle for the same reason.

To repeat, what are we to think of men like Muhammad ibn Abdullah and Joseph Smith, Jr. who talk to angels, dictate holy books, and found religions? In 1844, Smith ran for the presidency of the United States until assassinated. And by the time of Muhammad's death in 632 CE, all of the Arabian Peninsula was under the yoke of Islam due to his military and political leadership. Both men dreamed on a grand scale, leaving entire mythologies behind them. Then as now, there were always Borg-like followers forever busy in the hive of their small minds in their small world. Reason tells us there are three possible answers to the initial question: *these men were either frauds, delusional, or a strange combination of both.*

Let's deal with the easier case first. There can be little doubt that Joseph Smith was a disorderly person and an impostor because he was convicted of such in March 1826 in Bainbridge, New York. The evidence? Smith *admitted his guilt.* He also confessed to being a necromancer and treasure hunter using his secret "seer stone"—all this was just four years before the angel Moroni revealed the location of the golden plates. (Mark Twain

Smith dictating the Book of Mormon by "reading" reflections in a seer stone at the bottom of his hat

wrote that the plates were copper, but Smith did everything on a grand scale, and a base metal just wouldn't do.) Smith dictated the Mormon Bible and other works while wearing his "sacred spectacles" and gazing at his seer stone in the bottom of his hat. The gold plates were never present but kept away from prying eyes in a secret hiding place—perhaps on another planet. Sometimes he dictated from behind a curtain, and you can be assured the golden plates were never present there either. Perhaps "speaking through your hat" is a variation of "talking off the top of your head." The Prophet, as Mormons call him, gleaned many gems. Not the least of these was the location of the Garden of Eden in Jackson County, Missouri, and the place of construction of Noah's Ark in South Carolina—remember it's warmer there.

Now if you can possibly make yourself believe any of this foolishness, there is no point in you reading this book—or any other book for that matter. Oh, and by the way, Smith never let anyone see these golden plates, despite testimonials to their reality; they later mysteriously disappeared. They always do!

The Prophet had his troubles with the law. At least ten charges against him are known—two for treason. The extent of his culpability, due to the anger of his accusers, is uncertain, but as hard as the LDS faithful may research his rap sheet there is no pony in here. Ultimately, an enraged mob assassinated him while he was running for president and in jail for destroying a newspaper office, which had printed unflattering facts about him.

And then there were his wives—thirty-eight plus or minus a couple depending on your reference. He was evidently charismatic, personally charming, and affectionate to his Mormon friends and followers, especially their wives, for he married nine of them while they were still wed and continued to be so to their "saintly" husbands. So he was into polyandry as part of his polygamy. Today we would label him a "swinger," but back then he was just a spectacular womanizer. Smith called these "celestial marriages" to gain the bride a high seat in heaven later at the cost of some terrestrial hanky-panky now. The Prophet's private prayer might well be "Lord, lead us not into temptation, but don't keep it too far away."

Many of the beliefs and practices of Mormonism—as well as Islam—are so hilarious that they deserve mentioning if just for comedic value. Consider Mormon sacred magic undergarments. Only after having undergone the Temple Endowment Ceremony was a member permitted to wear these special undies. The juxtaposition of "undergarment" and "endowment" was entirely fortuitous, or so we are told, and they don't like to talk about it—at least Mitt Romney doesn't. Smith himself designed these for both men and women and they come in one or two-pieces outfits of unbleached cotton. Each breast and the navel bear Masonic symbols and there is a special slit in the lower right leg area so "every knee shall bow." LDS members tell miraculous tales of those so adorned: soldiers who survived while all those around them perished; survivors who lived when all others died in fires, airplane crashes, and car accidents. Who needs Kevlar when a thin layer of unbleached cotton will do the job? The origin of this tale is part of Mormon folklore.

When authorities in Carthage, Illinois, arrested Joseph Smith and his brother Hyrum plus John Taylor and Willard Richards for demolishing a newspaper office in 1844, the miracle began to unfold. About 200 armed men, their faces painted black with wet gunpowder, assaulted the jail. Smith wrongly thought they were his followers come to rescue him. Immediately one gunman blasted Hyrum in the face, but Joseph, who had a smuggled gun, shot three of his attackers before the mob killed him. Taylor received numerous bullet wounds but lived. Willard Richards, who was the only one wearing his magic underpants, escaped unscathed and a legend was born of impeccable logic. (God's miracles always seem somehow incomplete. Couldn't they all have been wearing their magic undies?)

The story continues in the best traditions of Hollywood Westerns. Legend says Taylor's pocket watch saved him by interrupting a gunshot, directed at his chest. The LDS Church History Museum in Salt Lake City proudly displays this timepiece (the hands stopped at 5:16). Unfortunately, modern analysis reveals Taylor merely fell against a windowsill and damaged it. This tale at least, unlike the magic undies, has some plausibility.

In the real world, Smith discharged all six rounds from his pepperbox pistol although three misfired. He reportedly wounded three men, two of whom died. The Prophet wasn't into turning the other cheek unless it was those of his backside as he jumped from the jail's second-story window. Smith was likely dead when he hit the ground; nonetheless, his attackers hurriedly assembled a firing squad and shot him several more times.

Joseph Smith's name may be common, but his life was extraordinary, and in one area he has been the very best in the world. Let's find out what that was. To do this we'll examine the LDS claims that the Book of Mormon is the word of God.

In 1841, the Prophet declared the Book of Mormon (hereafter BoM) to be "the most correct of any book on earth, and the keystone of our religion." When Mark Twain wrote, "Man is the only animal that blushes—or needs to," he must have been thinking of Joseph Smith. What follows is a minimal list of errors, boo-boos, and fubars from this most "perfect" book.

- *Redundant phrases*: for example, "and it came to pass" happens over 1200 times; "behold" and "therefore" occur to serious hypnotic effect.
- *Misspelled words in the original BoM*: consider, "yars" for years, "phrensied" for frenzied, and "adhear" for adhere
- *Grammatical errors*: in the original BoM, for example, "I have wrote to them."
- *Anachronisms*: referring to cows, horses, and asses in First Nephi 18:25 (590 BCE). But Europeans introduced these animals 2000 years later.
- *Neologisms*: for example, "numerority" for a large number and "consigned" for convince

- *Plagiarisms*: only the Qur'an can surpass the BoM in this area. In First Nephi, there are eighty-seven examples of direct copying from the Bible.
- *Inconsistencies*: people die in an early chapter only to be alive in a later one. For instance, in the original BoM, King Benjamin dies in Mosiah 6:5 but lives later in Mosiah 21:28. To spare themselves needed embarrassment, the LDS faithful corrected this for all later editions.
- With each new printing of the BoM, the LDS faithful make significant corrections and updates (some enumerators say over 4000). Why didn't the angel Moroni just hand Smith a Xeroxed copy of the BoM in perfect English—a little short on technology in heaven perhaps?

As egregious as all these errors are, any competent copy editor would have found and corrected them. That said, copy editors don't generally analyze *ideas* in a manuscript, however, this is what we'll do next for the BoM.

I suggest the reader be seated, take a deep breath, and prepare themselves for the following incredible tale. The BoM speaks of two groups of people who traveled from biblical lands to America by boat—Smith calls them barges, the first in 2500 and the second in 600 BCE. The initial group, the Jaredites, was destroyed. The latter group landed in South America and migrated to Central and then North America. Time and circumstances divided them into two warring nations, the Nephites and the Lamanites but both descended from the lost tribe of Manasseh, or so we are told. In old Hollywood Westerns, the good guys wear white hats and the bad guys wear black hats. It's the same in the BoM, where the Nephites are white and "delightsome" and the poor Lamanites are dark and "loathsome"—their words, not mine. Jesus came to America in 30 CE and preached the Gospel so there was peace in the valley for two hundred years. After becoming enemies again in 385 CE, the Lamanites defeated and killed the Nephites, and since God cursed them with dark skin, they became the ancestors of the North American Indians[*]. Moroni was the last of the surviving good guys and he wrote their

---

[*] And strangely enough, the Polynesians as well.

story on the golden plates which Joseph Smith later found and transcribed. (I assure the reader, I did not make this up.)

Modern archaeologists have uncovered nothing of their cities and towns, nothing of their bones, tools, or middens. Nothing! It's not as though there is a missing link here, but rather the entire chain has vanished. It's as if they never existed. Who could have guessed? One man who did was Michael Coe, the preeminent archaeologist of the New World who, in 1973, wrote the following in an article for *Dialogue: A Journal of Mormon Thought*:

> The bare facts of the matter are that nothing, absolutely nothing, has even shown up in any New World excavation, which would suggest to a dispassionate observer that the Book of Mormon, as claimed by Joseph Smith, is a historical document relating to the history of early migrants to our hemisphere.

But geneticists do know the *deep ancestry* of the Amerindians, the pre-Columbian inhabitants of North, Central, and South America—and it's not Jerusalem. It is the Chukchi, an indigenous people inhabiting that part of Siberia closest to Alaska. The Amerindians and the Chukchi have identical genetic markers. (A genetic marker is a DNA sequence arising from a mutation with a known location on a chromosome.) When two geographically distant species have the same genetic markers, we know that these species are related. Unbelievably, our DNA would stretch to the moon and back more than 3000 times, so the probability that these two peoples have identical markers by accident is effectively zero. Bye bye Lamanites.

Presently the National Geographic Society is collecting DNA samples (mouth swabs) from every continent, except Antarctica, to create the earth's first "genographic" map. This map shows the migration routes of all peoples out of Africa approximately 50,000 years ago. That's only about 2000 generations, not long enough for any major genetic variation to occur. If the reader wishes to know their deep ancestry, *Google* "genographic" and participate in this landmark study. Add your DNA to this unique map of the continental wanderings of humankind.

MORMON COSMOLOGY

I began this chapter by asking, "Where is God?" The Abrahamic religions all proclaim He is omnipresent, and we have seen the moral and intellectual problems that concept entails. The Mormons are different, of course the Mormons are different, and different can be good—but not in this case. They give a definite (?) location for the deity in a retirement home of sorts. Joseph Smith revealed this magnificent secret in his "Book of Abraham" from the modestly titled *Pearl of Great Price*, another canonical LDS text "translated" from some controversial papyri. Here are chapters 2 and 3:

> And I saw the stars, that they were very great, and that one of them was nearest unto the throne of God; and there were many great ones which were near unto it;

> And the Lord said unto me: These are the governing ones; and the name of the great one is Kolob, because it is near unto me, for I am the Lord thy God: I have set this one to govern all those which belong to the same order as that upon which thou standest.

So, Mormon cosmology teaches us God lives on a planet near a great star called Kolob. (Mormon "sacred" texts often confuse planets and stars; possibly both Joseph Smith and God didn't know the difference.) Further reading tells of God's many celestial wives, with whom he continually has sex to keep them perpetually pregnant, producing "spirit children," not to be confused with "spirited children." Kolob sounds much like the fictional pleasure planet Risa from the TV series *Star Trek: The Next Generation* but has less reality. Amusingly, the star Kolob and Mormonism have an even closer connection to space fantasy. In another science-fiction television series *Battlestar Galactica*, some of the plot comes directly from the Mormon beliefs of its creator Glen A. Larson. The story revolves around the *planet* Kobol as the ancient and distant home world of the human race. And the word *Kobol* is a simple anagram for *Kolob*. Of course, modern astronomy knows nothing of Kobol or Kolob, but science fiction is the rightful home of both. Perhaps Larson was doing more satire than drama.

These factual fubars of Mormon theology are entertaining to expose but of little actual importance. On a deeper note, LDS lifestyles are not all Donny and Marie or bunnies and butterflies. Many of their practices—especially those based on Smith's "sacred" texts—have a cruel and morally corrupt influence. Consider the demeaning impact of polygamy on the *first* wife. For those husbands who can't appreciate the painful force of this

practice, reflect on how you would feel if your wife cuckolded you with twenty-six different men. Well, that's precisely what the bearded Patriarch Brigham Young did to his first wife, Emmeline. Polygamy is simply a method to have sex with as many women as possible and to avoid being labeled an adulterer. Male, and sadly female, LDS members will point to scriptural approval for this practice;

Brigham Young

Patriarch Young did, and on January 21, 1846, he married four women, two before lunch and two after!

The Mormons have had a turbulent history with the US federal government over polygamy. The first collision occurred in the mid-19th century when this Mormon practice was the reason the government denied statehood for Utah seven times. In 1890, when the government was about to seize the assets of the LDS, Wilford Woodruff, fourth president of the Church, received a timely revelation from God. This "Great Accommodation" postponed the practice of polygamy until heaven; with this, the government backed off and Utah became the 45th state of the Union. This timely revelation was a *deus ex machina* whereby God abruptly solves an impenetrable problem—the Mormons were masters of this device. How convenient, how transparently self-serving. Money talks!

The reader can be certain, polygamy *is still* widely practiced in Utah and the surrounding states, plus lower British Columbia, and northern Mexico. Warren Jeffs, the breakaway leader of the Fundamentalist Church of Jesus Christ of Latter-day Saints (hereafter FLDS) is currently in a federal prison for having sex with prepubescent girls, committing incest, and rape. When the

saints come marching in, the wise hide their daughters, especially the younger ones. After all, these saints would say, Joseph
Smith approved of it and God practices it.

There are more rotten eggs in the Mormon nest of together-
ness; one of the most putrid is racism. This also has divine sanction—remember the loathsome Lamanites. Little did we know
that they weren't all Indians, they also include blacks. You do
not need reasons in religion; recall that from a false premise (for
example, divine texts) anything can follow and usually does.
LDS faithful see the biblical Cain as black and they subscribe to
the nonsense that Noah's cursed son Ham and all his descendants
were also black (*see* pages 128-29 of Chapter 4). Heaven truly
does hate H/ham.

Brigham Young, in one of his more compassionate moments,
opined the following gems[*] on interracial marriage and slavery:

> Shall I tell you the law of God in regard to the African race? If
> the white man who belongs to the chosen seed mixes his blood
> with the seed of Cain, the penalty, under the law of God, is
> death on the spot. This will always be so.

> You must not think, from what I say, that I am opposed to slav-
> ery. No! The negro is damned, and is to serve his master till God
> chooses to remove the curse of Ham.

George Romney was a popular Governor of Michigan from
1963-69 and the father of Mitt Romney. Unlike his son, he was
an ardent supporter of the Civil Rights Movement and Act. As
we might expect, Romney's advocacy of civil rights brought him
into conflict from the LDS church. In January 1964, the Quorum
of Twelve Apostles member Delbert L. Stapley wrote Romney a
letter stating the proposed civil rights bill was "vicious legislation." And unbelievably telling him "the Lord had placed the
curse upon the Negro," and it was not for humans to abolish it.
Romney refused to change his position and increased his efforts
towards civil rights. This letter is so unctuous to Romney, so
patronizing to blacks, so worshipful to "holy" texts, and so

incredibly ignorant that every white person should read it*. Then you will know in every part of your being why black Americans needed the Civil Rights Act. Stapley's antepenultimate sentence says, "This letter is for your personal use only (also Lenore [Romney's wife]), and is not to be used in any other way."

Because of the Civil Rights Act of 1964, the LDS felt pressure during the 70s arising from their institutionalized racism—such as the prohibition on black males entering the priesthood. All "worthy" white male members can receive the priesthood, but females of any color, just as the blacks, need not apply, after all, the LDS are a patriarchy. The Internal Revenue Service was threatening to cancel the church's non-profit tax-exempt status. This pressure was relieved on June 6, 1978, when President Spencer W. Kimball, chief prophet (or is it profit?), of the church received a miraculous and timely revelation from the Lord to end the practice of discrimination against blacks or Negroes as they say. For reasons no Mormon can explain, Lincoln got his message about freeing blacks more than a hundred years before Kimball. Again, how loudly money talks to Mormon prophets while conscience and kindness are mute.

Apparently, not all the telephone lines were open to the Lord on June 6, 1978. The convicted child molester and FLDS leader Warren Jeffs is still uttering pearls like the following:

> So Ham's wife that was preserved on the Ark was a Negro of the seed of Cain and there was a priestly purpose in it, that the Devil would have a representation [on earth] as well as God.

> So the Negro race has continued, and today is the day of the Negro as far as the world is concerned. They have influenced the generations of time; they have mixed their blood with many peoples, until there are many peoples not able to hold the priesthood.

All religions want money from those who do *real* work. Some pass the basket, others have donation drives, televangelists do endless appeals selling "holy" water and "sacred" relics, but the Mormons turned giving into a science. They call it tithing:

---

* *Google* "Delbert to Romney letter".

you give 10 percent of *everything* you earn to the church. Shakespeare called it "carrying coals to Newcastle," or the poor giving to the rich. The church holds yearly accounting sessions to make certain that all payments are up to date. If not, you and your family will be restricted from entering the temple voiding any hope of getting to the Celestial Kingdom. This practice and others similar have caused many Mormons to question their faith. Ex-Mormons, those recovering from this hive mind, refer to the church as the Morg (*Mormon Org*anization): comparable to the Borg, those mindless cybernetic drones from the TV series *Star Trek: The Next Generation*.

In one activity Joseph Smith, as noted previously, might have been the very best in the entire world. Perhaps the reader has figured out what that is. Well, he wasn't just an ordinary con artist, he was a world-class con artist and swindler of unbelievable proportions. And the LDS leadership have greatly profited from this Prophet's teachings.

In the world cup competition for the most fraudulent and ridiculous religion, the Mormons are prominent contenders. They certainly beat out Islam in this crowded field, but the winner is a group to be mentioned later. But never count the LDS out; they may yet win the prize as the least *rational religion*— after all that is an oxy-mor(m)on.

MUHAMMAD'S MALADY

Let's return and examine the visions and character of God's greater messenger, Muhammad. He, of course, knew nothing about Smith and the Book of Mormon; Smith knew almost nothing about Muhammad and the Qur'an. Had they been contemporaries, they would have assigned each other to the hottest places in their respective hell—to be forever tortured by demons and devils, as Smith would sermonize, or djinns and genies, as Muhammad would harangue. Even in hell, however, there are degrees of punishment, just as in Dante's *Inferno*. For Mormons in the deepest pit, the ultimate mental agony is to read and reread the Book of Mormon for all eternity. Alongside them are the Muslims, on their knees, in equal torment, endlessly rereading

the Qur'an. Satan reserves these punishments for the truly wicked. Both messengers, Smith and Muhammad knew they were
absolutely right or fabricated as much. But that cannot be. Either
one is God's messenger and the other isn't, or they both aren't!

The evidence for Joseph Smith's hucksterism and fraud are abundant and clear to all but the blind, the dead, and the indoctrinated. For
Muhammad it's not so simple. I think he was sincere in that he *did
see visions* although they were all in his head because of epilepsy.
Christian "scholars" have made this accusation so frequently that
some commentators consider it simply malicious propaganda. The
present writer, however, can't be faulted on that ground, so let's take
a closer look. To condemn the patient for his/her actions when he/she
has a *severe* mental disorder is positively medieval and Christian. We
are not driving out demons as fundamentalists presently do, or devils
as the full-time Vatican exorcists do.

Chief exorcist* Father Gabriele Amorth says the Devil is in the
Vatican—of that, I have no doubt. In Matthew 8:28-37, Jesus casts
the demons out of two men and into a large herd of swine, which
then dashed violently into the sea and drowned. (Incidentally, the
Gadarene townsfolk then pleaded with Jesus to leave their area
before he destroyed any more of their livestock.) Clearly, Jesus
thought pigs were unclean; apparently, Muhammad thought dogs
were unclean—today the SPCA (Society for the Prevention of
Cruelty to Animals) and PETA (People for the Ethical Treatment
of Animals) wouldn't be happy with either of them.

We cannot see the brain; we only see the results of the brain's
activity, i.e., the mind. We will attempt to show, the common-
place observation, that if the results of the mind's activity appear
unwell then the brain itself is unwell, perhaps even diseased, or
injured. If you have a parent with Alzheimer's disease, you know
there is progressive *brain* damage. If you have a child with au-
tism, you know it has a genetic basis in the brain. The *mind* is
simply the chemical and electrical activity of the brain, and this
activity is wondrous indeed. René Descartes was mistaken:
there is no mind-body or mind-brain duality. There is only the

---

* The Catholic Church does between 1,000 and 1,500 exorcisms each
year; Pope John-Paul II did one personally in 2,000.

incredible brain. To demonstrate how specific areas of the brain map to specific visions in the mind watch a short reenactment* of neurosurgeon Wilder Penfield's famous experiment, "I can smell burnt toast." Conclusively, damage the brain in a very specific area and you get a very specific result in the mind. To be gross, see how well your mind works if your brain is removed. Q.E.D.

A modern civilized society treats, or should treat, all those with mental disorders kindly; various types of therapy are available from surgery to drugs, from discussion to exercise. None of these involves driving out demons by exorcism, which is as close to modern psychiatry as astrology is to astronomy, numerology to mathematics, or alchemy to chemistry. Remarkable, isn't it that whether Muhammad or Jesus, they never vary from the common practices of their times: it's always drive out the demons and all will be well. It's probably foolish of us, but we would have thought that anyone in direct contact with the creator of the universe, whether through visions or prayers, would have something insightful to say about mental illness—but no, never. It's always *drive out the demons!*

Modern medicine informs us there are more than forty varieties of epilepsy. Each brings its own set of symptoms: loneliness or a feeling of connection with the universe, fear or a sense of being invincible, sorrow or overwhelming ecstasy. Some have likened this altered state of consciousness to stepping into a Salvador Dali painting—skewed objects, everywhere images, slowed time; you are a stranger in a strange land. These hallucinations have often been life changing, and they have fueled decades of creativity. We will marshal strong circumstantial evidence that Muhammad had the most interesting and visionary form of this disease, *temporal lobe epilepsy* (TLE) with a twist.

Furthermore, TLE is sometimes associated with a constellation of symptoms known as the *Geschwind syndrome*—the twist. This personality is characterized by the following traits: hyperreligiosity, hypergraphia (strong need to write or talk), altered sexuality (usually lowered), aggression, pedantry, and humorlessness. The syndrome can vary from mild to severe and may be more common than we realize.

---

* *Google* "I can smell burnt toast."

What do we know of Muhammad's epilepsy, if indeed he actually had such a condition? A Christian monk named Theophanes (752-817 CE), noted in his Chronography that the Prophet was afflicted with epilepsy. Muslims, of course, see this as vile Christian propaganda against their revered Prophet, may peace be upon him. But they need not be so smug, because much of the evidence for his diagnosis comes from their second holy book, the Hadith: a collection of accounts said or done by Muhammad and his companions. Here are two reports from the Hadith of Bukhari, the most respected of the redactors:

> Sometimes the Angel [Gabriel] comes in the form of a man
> and talks to me [Muhammad] and I grasp whatever he says.
> Bukhari 1.2

> He [Muhammad] fell unconscious on the ground with both his
> eyes towards the sky. When he came to his senses, he said, "My
> waist sheet! My waist sheet!" Bukhari 5.170

The first seven symptoms itemized below were present in Muhammad during the moments he was supposedly receiving revelations. The final three, occurring in the intervals between seizures, are major indicators for temporal lobe epilepsy with the Geschwind syndrome. All these points come from the canonical Hadith of Bukhari:

- He had visions of seeing an angel or a light and of hearing voices—sometimes even Satan's.
- He sweated even during the coldest days.
- He had trembling and twitching in his neck muscles.
- He had uncontrollably strange lip movements.
- He endured bodily spasms and agonizing abdominal pain.
- His face, flushed; his countenance was troubled.
- He was overcome by sudden emotions of fear and anxiety occasionally resulting in seizures.
- He had the tendency to see significance in everything.
- He had an *irrepressible* urge to talk about his visions.
- He also exhibited hyperreligiosity.

All the indicators for TLE epilepsy are in the Hadith—all but the name itself. Muhammad's diagnosis is clear.

THE DIVINE SICKNESS

Epilepsy is the stuff of legend and literature. Dostoyevsky, who had an ecstatic form of this affliction, gave it to four of his characters for dramatic effect. He once declared he would gladly trade ten years of his life for just one more visionary seizure. The list of creative people with epilepsy seems inordinately long. Here are a few: George Gershwin, Vachel Lindsay, Vladimir Lenin, Socrates (?), Edgar Allan Poe, Sylvia Plath, Leo Tolstoy, Lewis Carroll, Gustave Flaubert, Richard Burton (actor), and Vincent van Gogh. Some of these epilepsies were substance induced.

Writers, composers, and painters will often resort to almost anything for a visionary, creative experience, be that drugs, alcohol, mushrooms, or whatever—the kind of moment that arrives unexpectedly for those with TLE (temporal lobe epilepsy). Consider William Blake's celebrated poem *Auguries of Innocence* where he sees importance in minute things—a telling sign of epilepsy. Nevertheless, it's not known if Blake was on anything or had TLE.

To see a world in a grain of sand,
And a heaven in a wild flower,
Hold infinity in the palm of your hand,
And eternity in an hour.

In a similar vein, Samuel Taylor Coleridge wrote his immortal poem *Kubla Khan* in a dream-like trance while under the influence of opium, which promotes visual imagery and mild ecstasy:

In Xanadu did Kubla Khan
A stately pleasure-dome decree:
Where Alph, the sacred river, ran
Through caverns measureless to man
Down to a sunless sea.

Aldous Huxley ushered in the modern era of psychedelic drugs with his 1954 book *The Doors of Perception*. It details his heightened state of awareness from experimenting with mescaline, a hallucinogenic drug derived from the flowering heads of a Mexican cactus and long used in Indian religious rites. Coincidently, the book's title comes from another of Blake's poems *The Marriage of Heaven and Hell*.

But the true users of hallucinogens—the real inveterates—arising from ancient times, have always been those who claim to communicate with the gods. The Delphic priestess sat on a tripod to inhale sulfurous fumes until rendered unconscious at which times she is said to have conversed with Apollo. For all the mystery cults of Europe and the Middle East, the drug of choice was the magic mushroom, *Amanita muscaria,* cheap and readily available. This was the hallucinogen in John Allegro's provocative book on Christianity, *The Sacred Mushroom and the Cross*. Shamans, witchdoctors, and voodoo practitioners all pursue altered states of consciousness through chemicals. Monks, gurus, and swamis starve themselves until they faint from low blood sugars and then they are said to talk to God. Some with seizures are born to it, others suffer it by way of a head injury; we call it temporal lobe epilepsy. The unimaginative call it the "falling sickness," but the ancient Greeks knew better, so they named it the "divine sickness," recognizing its many religious features.

Modern medicine would correctly say drug users aren't reaching too far—not outside their skulls. This pharmacopeia of chemicals induces everything from mild euphoria to full-scale electrical storms in the brain's neurons. You aren't speaking to God, merely chatting to yourself!

MUHAMMAD'S PERSONALITY

Muhammad had exceptional abilities as a political and military leader. During his lifetime, he united the squabbling tribes of the Arabian Peninsula into a single political unit under the aegis of Islam. This was an unusual accomplishment for a recluse who often spent his days in a small cave in the Meccan hillside. What propelled him out of this cave onto the world stage to become one of the most important and enduring men in history? We know the answer! It's a small thing—the ultimate example of the Butterfly Effect noted in the second chapter—the misfiring of neurons in Muhammad's brain because of his temporal lobe epilepsy. He knew he was conversing with God's angel Gabriel, and that changed his world and ours forever.

Because of his temporal lobe epilepsy (TLE), Muhammad had a transformative experience with Gabriel in the cave, and that gave birth to Islam. For all those who reject this deduction based on the argument from incredulity—meaning it's just too preposterous to be true—consider the following, consider yourself. You, dear reader, are wholly improbable. The possible genetic combinations—disregarding your environment—that made you and not a gazillion others is beyond unbelievable. (Incidentally, scientists now know that even "identical" twins are genetically distinct.) Also, consider the arrow of time, where it has been, and where it's going. Most people who have ever lived are now dead. And only a miniscule number of those who could exist in the future will have that opportunity. Here at this moment in time, with our particular combination of genes, you and I are alive. In the universal lottery of life, we have won the biggest prize possible: existence! As noted earlier, every birth is unique; every life is original. In his book *Unweaving the Rainbow*, Richard Dawkins elegantly phrases this idea:

Richard Dawkins

We are going to die, and that makes us the lucky ones. Most people are never going to die because they are never going to be born. The potential people who could have been here in my place but who will in fact never see the light of day outnumber the sand grains of Arabia. Certainly those unborn ghosts include greater poets than Keats, scientists greater than Newton. We know this because the set of possible people allowed by our DNA so massively exceeds the set of actual people. In the teeth of these stupefying odds it is you and I, in our ordinariness, that are here. [2]

The argument from incredulity may be true or false—it all depends on the evidence. The evidence for Muhammad's temporal lobe epilepsy is abundant and clear. In the scholarly

Encyclopedia of Islam, Alford Welch comments on the Prophet's seizures:

> Muhammad is reported to have had mysterious seizures at the moments of inspiration. . . . the graphic descriptions of Muhammad's condition at these moments may be regarded as genuine, since they are unlikely to have been invented by later Muslims.

This diagnosis explains his physical ailments and gives a motivation and a framework for his success. Muhammad profoundly believed in what he did, and regrettably, absolute certainty energizes absolutely.

Ibn Ishaq (8th century) was a Muslim historian who wrote the first hagiography of Muhammad from collected oral traditions titled the *Life of the Messenger of God.* The following quote from this work is revealing because Muslims cannot disregard it as the ravings of a Christian or Jewish infidel:

> In order to gain his ends he [Muhammad] recoils from no expedient, and he approves of similar unscrupulousness on the part of his adherents, when exercised in his interest. He profits utmost from the chivalry of the Meccans, but rarely requites it with the like. . . For whatever he does he is prepared to plead the express authorization of the deity. It is, however, impossible to find any doctrine which he is not prepared to abandon in order to secure a political end. [3]

By combining his particular TLE with a willingness to do whatever it took to achieve his ends, the Prophet had a distinctive—and never imitated—method of dealing with his harem. That is, he simply *faked seizures* to get what he wanted.

To stop his wives from quarreling, all he needed was a quick word with the deity via Gabriel (*see* Surah 33:30). Ditto to have the wives accept another new bride in their midst (*see* Surah 33:28). Truly, most of the harem thought his act was hilarious and said so. As the old English proverb declares, "No man is a prophet in his own country." And certainly not among his dozen or so wives who knew him all too well.

Muhammad must have had a low sperm count because despite all these wives, he produced few children and *none* of the boys lived to adulthood. Realizing he mightn't have a male heir, the Prophet adopted a youth. Yet, less than two weeks after this young man was married, Muhammad lusted after the new bride, his daughter-in-law. In an act of celestial pimping, the Prophet suddenly had a seizure and received a revelation from Allah declaring it proper to take another man's wife (*see* Surah 33:37). Joseph Smith, as we have seen, had a similar itch, but a different solution. Nevertheless, Muhammad did him one better for he lusted after his followers' daughters as well. Abu Bakr was Muhammad's senior companion and his first Muslim convert outside his family; he later succeeded him. Now Bakr had a daughter Aisha whom the Prophet married when she was only six years old. In an act of surpassing magnanimity and sexual restraint, Muhammad didn't have intercourse with this child until she was nine and he was in his fifties. Let the record show that after his penile penetration, Aisha went back to playing with her little toys.

PAUL OF TARSUS

Most of us recall only a few ideas from our high school, college, or university courses. I remember one memorable evening class when our professor pointed out the egocentrism in each of us with respect to our accomplishments. He said, "Whatever you have done that you acquit as unique almost certainly is not." He then drew a bell curve on the blackboard and continued. "You are somewhere on this curve with thousands, if not millions, of others; *between* you and the mean [average] is an unbroken parade of fellows who have identical, or nearly identical, accomplishments." You could be an extreme *outlier*, that is several standard deviations from the mean, but nonetheless, between you and the mean are others of similar abilities.

This idea has broad applications. For thousands of years we have all thought our planet was unique in the universe. Religions expound that it's the very apple of God's eye. Copernicus and Galileo began the long retreat from this position, which continues to this day. In present times, modern astronomers have found dozens of earth-like planets existing in what scientists call the Goldilocks or liquid water zone. Solar systems are the norm; planets like Earth are common; perhaps life is the norm!

Let's apply this idea to religious prophets other than Muhammad. Did any of them have TLE? The historical record clearly confirms that many of them did.

Some religious groups and cults have developed very peculiar doctrines concerning the 144,000 from the Book of Revelation. The Jehovah Witnesses are a prime example. Evidently they believe only 144,000 saints will go to heaven, while the remaining faithful will live on Earth and never die. But as Christopher Hitchens points out, "That which can be asserted without evidence, can be dismissed without evidence."

A more fascinating group is the Seventh-Day Adventists. Their charismatic prophetess, Ellen Gould White, with her husband James, founded the Adventist movement around 1850. As a child of nine, Ellen suffered severe head trauma and spent three weeks drifting in and out of consciousness. She meets the criteria for TLE: extreme religiosity, excessive tendency to write or dictate (100,000 pages in over 4,000 articles), sameness of her message, a lowered sex drive, and a sharp sense of moralism.

Professing divine authority for her many writings, Mrs. White would often fall into a trance with upward rolling eye movements from which she would later awake with "great" religious revelations. In one of her early visions, she claims to have seen the 144,000 saints standing on a sea of glass arrayed in "a perfect square." Regrettably, for Mrs. White, it's impossible for 144,000 people to arrange themselves into a perfect square. Why? Because only numbers with exact square roots (like 9 and 25) may be so arrayed, and the square root of 144,000 is far from exact. In fact,

$$\sqrt{144,000} = 379.473 \dots$$

This must cast grave doubts on either the source of her visions or on her honesty. Certainly, someone had a problem with his or her arithmetic. I can hear readers objecting that I'm being picky, picky, picky. That would be the case if religious conversations with the deity didn't need to reach the level of truthfulness scientists and mathematicians demand in their disciples.

In all of Western civilization, the most celebrated instance of TLE happened on the road to Damascus: the conversion of Saul of Tarsus to St. Paul of Everywhere. Below is Michelangelo's conception of this event, which was followed by temporary blindness—a not uncommon side effect of TLE.

Detail from the *Conversion of Saul*
by Michelangelo

Did Paul have any of the other symptoms seen in Muhammad and White? In particular, did Paul have any additional seizures? Some say he simply suffered a case of heat stroke; others maintain this was a unique intervention by God to transform the prosecutor into the great defender of Christianity. Paul undoubtedly saw this experience on the Damascus road as transformative. In this respect, it had all the features of *ecstatic* TLE; the type of experience Dostoyevsky was willing to trade a decade of his life for. But this was not a one-time event; it was a chronic illness as Paul himself asserts several times in the New Testament. Consider this example from 2 Corinthians 12:1-7 (NIV). Paul writes:

I will go on to visions and revelations from the Lord. I know a man in Christ who fourteen years ago was caught up to the third heaven. . . . was caught up to paradise and heard inexpressible things, things that no one is permitted to tell. I will boast about a man like that, but I will not boast about myself, except about my weaknesses. . . . because of these surpassingly great revelations. Therefore, in order to keep me from becoming conceited, I was given a thorn in my flesh, a messenger of Satan, to torment me.

In the second sentence above, the Apostle is clearly speaking of himself in the third person.

This often mentioned "thorn in my side" was most likely some ongoing side effect of his seizures. Although Bishop Spong in his book *Rescuing the Bible from Fundamentalism* suggests Paul may be referring to homosexual desires, this seems unlikely since TLE usually results in lowered sexuality; however, there are exceptions like Muhammad. Paul's legendary misogyny*, that needn't be repeated here (*read* 1 Corinthians 11: 2-16), lends some credence to Spong's view. Those countries that harshly repress female rights, like Saudi Arabia, Iran, and Afghanistan, are also the most sternly homophobic—surely, this isn't a coincidence. Perhaps Paul was a gay man with TLE.

What about the overwhelming need to write or dictate, the symptom so unmistakable in Ellen Gould White and Muhammad? Paul wrote one-third of the entire New Testament, more than any other contributor, and this doesn't include the problematic Epistle to the Hebrews. As for hyper-religiosity and excessive moral pickiness and pedantry, Paul was the very model of the modern moral prig. He loved laws and rules more than people; no nuanced morality for the man from Tarsus. In Chapter 4, *Of Human Bondage*, we saw where he returned the runaway slave Onesimus in accordance with Roman law—even immoral laws transcend human decency, it would seem. In his eyes, every man, woman, and child was a sinner whom only the acceptance of Jesus and His sacrifice on the cross could redeem. "Bow, worship, bend, fall on your knees, and stay there" could have been on his family crest. Paul had it all, the complete syndrome of temporal lobe epilepsy with the twist, and we have no cure.

This man did something to European civilization from which even after two millennia it has yet to recover. He saw himself as

---

* The church he founded built his misogyny into its hierarchical structure. The early church "father" Tertullian (c. 200 CE) laid a few big bricks of his own. According to him women were "the gateway to hell" and "a temple built over a sewer."

God's messenger to the gentiles, and he pursued this obsession with incredible vigor from that day on the road to Damascus until his death in Rome. What did he do? He introduced another form of Middle Eastern mysticism into the Roman Empire: *his version* of Christianity. It's very doubtful Jesus would have endorsed Paul's version of his message. And since Jesus considered Gentiles to be dogs and pigs (*see* Matthew 7:6), it's even more doubtful he would have approved taking his message to them. Consider the following quotations from the NIV. Jesus speaks:

> *Do not go among the Gentiles.* Matthew 10:5
> *I was sent only to the lost sheep of Israel.* Matthew 15:24
> *Salvation is of the Jews.* John 4:22

The man from Tarsus changed Jesus' message so much that the man from Galilee is barely discernible in his writings. The heirs to Paul's legacy are the hell-fire, Bible thumpers, and ideological preachers and priests found across Europe and the megachurches of America. They put more emphasis on Daniel and Revelation than the Sermon on the Mount or loving your neighbor as yourself. Albert Schweitzer wrote the following on Paul:

> Where possible Paul avoids quoting the teaching of Jesus, in fact even mentioning it. If we had to rely on Paul, we should not know that Jesus taught in parables, had delivered the sermon on the mount, and had taught His disciples the "Our Father." Even where they are specially relevant, Paul passes over the words of the Lord.

The historian and philosopher Will Durant was harsher:

> Paul created a theology of which none but the vaguest warrants can be found in the words of Christ. Fundamentalism is the triumph of Paul over Christ.

THE BELLS ARE INSIDE THEM

The circumstantial evidence is strong; the verdict is in. Islam and Christianity are both the direct result of TLE in its founders. The visions they saw and the gods and angels they spoke with were all in their heads. To them it was real, immediate, and intense. But as Dylan Thomas wrote in "A Child's Christmas in Wales," "I mean that the bells the children could hear were inside them."

We have made large claims for the effects of TLE with the Geschwind syndrome—at least in certain individuals. We have also provided solid evidence for their condition. Nonetheless, unless you actually have TLE, you cannot truly know it—know it from the inside. This situation is analogous to attempting to describe the colors of the rainbow to someone completely colorblind, or to communicating the delicious flavor of chocolate to somebody who has never tasted it. Fortunately, there is a way to pass from the objective study to the subjective experience of TLE: by wearing *the God helmet*. This device, when placed on the head of the subject, stimulates the brain with changing magnetic fields.

Dr. Michael Persinger of Laurentian University, Ontario, Canada has almost *single-handedly* invented a new field of research called neurotheology associated with the "God helmet." His work in the last few decades builds on the results of Wilder Penfield mentioned earlier.

The theoretical basis for his work is simple, at least on the surface. Every human activity—meditation, paranormal experiences, listening to music, and so on—generates particular brain waves as measured by an electroencephalography (EEG). By generating weak electromagnetic fields inside the "God helmet" directly on the subject's temporal lobes, Persinger is able to produce the feelings of the human activities listed above. In particular, if you duplicate the brain waves for mystical experiences, you get people who have feelings of an unseen presence and other paranormal phenomena. Here's what Persinger said in a December 2009 interview:

> Our research starts on the basic premise that all experience is generated by brain activity. Now, the critical thing is that all experience means your experience of love, or memories, or having a mystical experience, must be associated with specific patterns of brain activity. That brain activity in large part is determined by the brain structure. Many of these things, because structure dictates function, may be relatively unique to the human being itself.

Now, although that's our assumption, the most powerful tool of science is the experiment. So if we want to understand these experiences and how they are generated by brain activity, we have to reproduce them in the laboratory. So the basic approach then was, okay, if people have mystical experiences and they're associated with brain activity then if we imitate them in the laboratory and we understand the physical conditions that produce them, we should be able to 1) understand the areas of the brain and the patterns of activity responsible for these experiences, and 2) we should be able to control them.

And if they're natural phenomena, and we think that mystical experiences, including the God experience, the God belief, are natural phenomena, we should be able to reproduce them easily if we have the correct parameters in the laboratory, control them and understand how they may be manipulated by others with less honorable goals. [4]

And Persinger has reproduced all manner or religious experiences in his laboratory with electromagnetic stimulation of the temporal lobes. *See* for yourself; *Google* "God helmet" and watch at least two of the YouTube videos*. I highly recommend you do this—Persinger's work is a major breakthrough in our time. Approximately, 80 percent of all his participants experience a benign presence, angels, demons, or other supernatural phenomena. The particular experience is contextually and culturally dependent: Catholics, Protestants, and Muslims all see *different* things. Richard Dawkins, who belongs to none of these three groups, experienced nothing out of the ordinary. He's a 20 percenter.

Speaking to the Society of Neuroscience in 1997, Dr. Ramachandran, Director of the Center for Brain and Cognition at the University of California, San Diego, commented, "there is a neural basis for religious experience." Ramachandran's declaration projected neurotheology into the public spotlight. His report and the work of Dr. Persinger aroused the somnolent fundamentalists

---

* Michael Shermer of *Skeptic Magazine* went to Laurentian University to try the God helmet. *See* the remarkable results online at *Google* "God Helmet"+YouTube.

from their state of ease, to protest on the Laurentian University campus calling Dr. Persinger and his helmet "demonic."

Religion claims scientists are opening Pandora's Box with this neurotheology; others say we are marching triumphantly into the lost city of El Dorado. As these neurotheologians explore the streets and houses of El Dorado, new discoveries will abound. The graveyard with its tombstones is of special interest. Over the city's only cemetery is a sign, which reads, *This is Necropolis, Home of the Immortal Gods.* Here is a vast area, out of all proportion to the city's size. Thousands of large and small headstones lie in neat rows across an immense plain. The names of these dead gods are almost all unknown. Near the end of one row, we see the name *Zeus* with a lightning bolt, and in an out-of-the-way spot, someone finds a gravestone in the form of a hammer with *Thor* chiseled on it. An overwhelming number of other immortal gods lie buried here, not so much forgotten as unknown to us. Someone commented that we were fortunate the Hindu deities are buried elsewhere because there are over 330 million of them. After days of scouring every part of this place, the neurotheologians find three modest markers, side by side; they say, "Here lie the immortal gods, *Allah*, *Jesus*, and *Yahweh*." And in the middle of this joyous necropolis is the largest monument of all. It reads "To All Unknown Gods."

Stephen Hawking

Religious authorities have forever attempted to quash human curiosity and scientific research—demanding we don't look behind the curtain lest we find the wizard is a charlatan. Catholic priests refused to look through Galileo's telescope lest they saw something questioning their faith. The attitudes of the Magisterium haven't changed since then. During a conference on cosmology in Rome in 1981, all the participants, including Stephen Hawking, were granted a group audience with John Paul II. He instructed them it was all right to study the evolution of the universe after the Big Bang, but they should *never examine* the moment of creation itself because that was the work of God. Not wanting to share Galileo's fate,

Hawking apparently was pleased the Pontiff didn't know the subject of his talk at the conference. Here was a man in a tall pointless hat wearing a dress, yet dictating research limits to the world's greatest living scientist. Authority as evidence is religion; evidence as authority is science.

JUDAISM AND TLE

Let's reach back into deep time, past Ellen Gould White, beyond Muhammad, even before Paul of Tarsus, all the way back to Genesis and its author(s). As noted in Chapter 5, Moses was a fictional creation in order to give the Israelites a heroic past. If he existed at all, it was not as recorded in the Pentateuch a.k.a. the Torah (Genesis, Exodus, Leviticus, Numbers, and Deuteronomy) that legend says he wrote. Moses was as real as Achilles.

There isn't a single secular sentence corroborating the existence of Moses. Modern Israeli archaeologists, after decades of research and diligent digging, haven't found a toothpick to indicate his reality, the Egyptian enslavement, Exodus, his desert wanderings, Mt. Sinai, the holy tablets, or any artifacts whatsoever. The Egyptians, who were extensive record keepers, never mentioned Moses or the Jewish captivity. It's as if he and it never existed! At least Achilles had Troy—several of them.

Any literate person, who scans Genesis 1 and 2, can tell these are distinctly different creation stories. Genesis 1 is all about counting the six days of creation and resting on the seventh. Even the first verse has 7 words composed from 28 or 7+7+7+7 letters. God created man and woman *after* all the animals and on the last day. In the original Hebrew, the word used for God is *Elohim*, the plural form of *Eloah*, the royal *we*. It is notable that the author used a plural subject *Elohim* with the singular verb *created*. This God is distant and impersonal like all royalty.

In Genesis 2, however, God breathes life into a clump of earth to create Adam in his own image *before* all the plants and the animals; Eve is fashioned from Adam's rib as an afterthought to be his troublesome helpmate. Remarkably, both have real names, as does God. Here the author calls the creator *Yahweh*, his personal name in the Pentateuch, and conspicuously, there is no seven numerology.

Each creation story has a different literary style, uses unique structures, different vocabulary, and distinct phrases. Some critics judge the stories of Genesis 2 to be superior to those of Genesis 1. So, which is it, 1 or 2—*Elohim* or *Yahweh*?

This analysis of Genesis poses a huge problem for religious conservatives who insist Moses wrote the Torah. Let's assume for a moment he did. Then only one conclusion is possible: he became senile in the latter part of his 120-year lifespan and forgot he had already written a creation story. Repeating himself, evidently with increasing irritability, was standard practice for the old geezer. I noted his tendency for repetition earlier—*see* Chapter 4, starting at page 91—where he proclaimed the Ten Commandments in four different places, in three different versions, and usually more than ten. To posit *single authorship* for the Torah must be embarrassing for both the prophet and the deity! So which is it, two distinct authors, or a distinctly senile Moses?

All but those impossible to embarrass would choose multiple authors for the Torah. Detailed scholarly work during the 19th century revealed four different sources plus a compiler, which researchers denote by five capital letters: J, E, D, P, and R; These are summarized below from oldest to youngest:

SOURCES OF THE TORAH

- J: Yahwist   c. 950 BCE   Source of Genesis 2 and about half the rest.
- E: Elohist   c. 850 BCE   Source of Genesis 1 and more.
- D: Deuteronomy   c. 600 BCE   Source of Deuteronomy.
- P: Priestly   c. 500 BCE   Source of Leviticus with its laborious stress on censuses, genealogies, dates, numbers, laws, and more laws from the Book of Numbers.
- R: Redactor   c. 400 BCE   Redactor or editor who assembled it all.

Documents J and E contain all the best writing and most memorable stories, the ones we know and love. D is a recapitulation of what went before, a replay of earlier material. R provides the bridges or segues between documents. And P, the Priestly source, is more than twice as long as J, E, D, or R. It consists of 20 percent of Genesis, almost all of Leviticus, and large parts of Exodus and Numbers. Which parts? All the nasty bits and those of least literary value even in translation: pointless genealogies, endless lists, sexually repressive laws, boring repetitions, pedantic minutiae, aggressive style, extreme religiosity, and verbosity. Formulaic writing was a standby in the P document: the author used the word *seven* or words containing *seven* about sixty times just in Leviticus. Too harsh you say—well maybe you haven't read this stuff lately. Somebody once remarked that the strongest defense against Judaism and Christianity, or indeed any "holy" text, are their very texts. Fundamentalists of all faiths are incredibly ignorant *of* and selective *from* their Bibles and Qur'ans. Consider the following quotations from one of the world's most "sacred" books: Leviticus (NIV):

> *If a man has sexual relations with a man as one does with a woman, both of them have done what is detestable. They are to be put to death.* Leviticus 20:13

> *Anyone who curses their father or mother is to be put to death.* Leviticus 20:9

> *If a man commits adultery with another man's wife—with the wife of his neighbor—both the adulterer and the adulteress are to be put to death.* Leviticus 20:10

> *If a man has sexual relations with his father's wife, he has dishonored his father. Both the man and the woman are to be put to death.* Leviticus 20:11

> *If a man has sexual relations with his daughter-in-law, both of them are to be put to death.* Leviticus 20:12

> *If a man has sexual relations with an animal, he is to be put to death, and you must kill the animal.* Leviticus 20:15

> *If a priest's daughter defiles herself by becoming a prostitute, she disgraces her father; she must be burned in the fire.* Leviticus 21:9

> *No man who has any defect may come near [altar]: no man who is blind or lame, disfigured or deformed.* Leviticus 21:18

[A]nyone who blasphemes the name of the LORD is to be put to death. The entire assembly must stone them. Leviticus 24:16

If in spite of this you still do not listen to me but continue to be hostile toward me, then in my anger I [God] will be hostile toward you, and I myself will punish you for your sins seven times over. You will eat the flesh of your sons and the flesh of your daughters. Leviticus 26:27-29

The preceding were not the deranged ravings of an al-Qaida suicide bomber about to depress the *on button* to get the seventy-two virgins. And no, this was not Osama bin Laden, Adolf Hitler, or Pol Pot spewing their "put to death" venom. I wish I could say this short list of monstrously immoral ravings was a complete fabrication. But no, these sayings come from the core scriptures of Jews and Christians, the people of the book as the Arabs call them. No living Jew or Christian, of course, subscribes to this insanity—at least I hope not, but one can never be certain. Civilized people don't follow these ancient prohibitions because morality isn't fixed and carved in stone, chiseled into tablets, or written on parchment. It evolves! And the forces that cause it to evolve are always secular. So how do Christians and Jews accommodate their present beliefs with the founders' lunacies? They just completely ignore them as most of my readers have already done.

The authors of the Torah decree 613 commandments or rules for every aspect of human behavior—in large part, these come from Leviticus. (Even the avaricious Ferengi of *Star Trek* fame have only 286 Rules of Acquisition.) Freedom cannot flourish here but slavery and servitude find a welcome home. Religion, particularly monotheism, relishes regulating life in bizarre ways. In Islam, there are twenty-five rules on how to use the toilet. Since the Jinns and other evil spirits live in these filthy places (no plumbing remember), the user, however urgent, must always enter with the left, or sinister, foot first while reciting prescribed verses aloud; fortunately singing wasn't required.

Leviticus—the Torah's most fanatically religious book—was the product of an unknown author; however, the shadowy person behind the text is revealed in the writing. And prophets rarely invent a God bigger or better than themselves. Although we have no *personal* knowledge of him or any seizures, we can with assurance say he had every feature of that special form of TLE referred to as the Geschwind syndrome. You know its features: hypergraphia (uncontrollable urge to write), extreme religiosity, hyposexuality (a distaste for sex and a drive to control it), aggressiveness, pedantry, and tiresome repetition. The author of the Priestly Source is the earliest known individual to have this unattractive form of TLE—he had it all.

EZEKIEL'S WHEEL

In 2001, at a meeting of the Society for Neuroscience in San Diego, Dr. Eric Altschuler* started a firestorm by presenting evidence that Ezekiel had temporal lobe epilepsy. The Internet reaction to this seemingly scholarly research was so intense you might think the good doctor had labeled the gloomy prophet an atheist. Let's look at his evidence.

We know Ezekiel had visions—he wrote about them in amazing detail. Consider his famous apparition of the wheel within the wheel. Some modern believers interpret this as the world's first recorded UFO (*read* flying saucer) sighting. It comes early in Chapter 1:

> *This was the appearance and structure of the wheels: They sparkled like topaz, and all four looked alike. Each appeared to be made like a wheel intersecting a wheel. As they moved, they would go in any one of the four directions the creatures faced; the wheels did not change direction as the creatures went. Their rims were high and awesome, and all four rims were full of eyes all around.* Ezekiel 1:16-18 (NIV)

Now, the rational reader has a choice. Either this was a spaceship (from Yahweh if you wish) or Ezekiel was on a space trip of his own by the rivers of Babylon. Certainly, something or someone was on a trip and flying high.

This prophet also had long periods of speechlessness, on one occasion for seven days. Interestingly, St. Paul went blind after

---

* *See New Scientist* for November 17, 2001, for the article "Seized by God" by Alison Motluk on Altschuler's ideas.

his seizure as did Ellen Gould White; Ezekiel became speechless after his visions—are we seeing a pattern here?

> *Then the Spirit came into me and raised me to my feet. He spoke to me and said: "Go, shut yourself inside your house. And you, son of man, they will tie with ropes; you will be bound so that you cannot go out among the people. I will make your tongue stick to the roof of your mouth so that you will be silent and unable to rebuke them, for they are a rebellious people.*
> Ezekiel 3:24-26 (NIV)

The binding with ropes could easily imply Ezekiel became violent, and for their own protection and that of others, the people restrained him. Today we would put him in a straightjacket.

The Book of Ezekiel is the third largest in the Bible, however, later scribes trying to make sense of nonsense may have written some parts, but this only resulted in redundancy. Assuredly, Ezekiel was a compulsive writer. Much of this book passes the boundary into incoherence unless you are such a committed Christian you believe the Book of Revelation is as clear as a column of addition. Visions overflow while Yahweh's bizarre and punishing commandments proliferate, such as lie on your left side for 390 days and cook your food with your own feces (Ezekiel 4:4-12 NIV*). That the Creator of the Universe, the Lord of countless worlds, has such a profound and peculiar interest in scatology surpasses all understanding.

And by the way, Ezekiel had a 40-day period on his right side afterward. Only a severe mental disorder can begin to account for such gibberish. He preached aggressively, wrote compulsively, talked pedantically, and fainted frequently. He had the whole package of the Geschwind syndrome within an uncompromising case of TLE.

But wait a minute, many readers are quietly saying, "Where's the sex?" Recall that a major indicator of the Geschwind syndrome is an altered state of interest in sex—usually lowered. So where is it? Well, as Christians claim, the Bible truly has it all so here it is in Ezekiel 23, holy pornography. The graphic imagery

---

* In Ezekiel 4:12 the KJV says, *"And thou shalt eat it as barley cakes, and thou shalt bake it with dung that cometh out of man, in their sight."*

here can rival any pornographic writing in America today. It's so explicit that Sunday schools and Sunday preachers dance around it as if it were the Black Death, and they have no posies.

> *There she lusted after her lovers, whose genitals were like those of donkeys and whose emission was like that of horses.*
> Ezekiel 23:20 (NIV)

For Ezekiel the most abominable of all human activities is sex, and he weaves his loathing into a metaphor to condemn the sin—it's always some perceived sin or other—of Israel. He writes of Israel as two whoring sisters fornicating with Assyria and Egypt to bring idol worship into Jerusalem. The following verse displays his fondness for breast imagery and ejaculation:

> *She did not give up the prostitution she began in Egypt, when during her youth men slept with her, caressed her virgin bosom and poured out their lust on her.* Ezekiel 23:8 (NIV)

Elsewhere and often, he turns from this in pathological disgust. So, yes, Ezekiel had the whole nine yards of the Geschwind syndrome and some take-home cloth as well.

A GLANCE BACK — A LOOK FORWARD

Neurotheology may prove to be as important to our century as natural selection was to Darwin's. And as surely as civilization is waging a rear-guard action against no-nothing creationists today, we will be battling no-nothing anti-neurotheologists in the future. The main founders of Judaism, Christianity, and Islam had TLE and that unique cluster of symptoms experts identify as the Geschwind syndrome. Unquestionably, the author of the Priestly Source as well as Ezekiel, Paul of Tarsus, and Muhammad displayed every feature of it.

Just so that the reader is clear on what I'm saying, I don't *believe* any of this! That's right. I don't *believe* it. We reserve the word *belief* for those situations lacking evidence and hence requiring acceptance by faith alone. This is not one of those cases. Here we have presented solid evidence, often in the patient's own words. As Bertrand Russell wrote in the famous passage quoted in Chapter 3, page 61, I wish to reiterate the radical proposition that *belief* be directly proportional to the *evidence* for its veracity.

These "sacred-text" authors were certainly *sincere,* and they were certainly *mistaken.* As I understand it, those who have TLE-induced visions are profoundly moved by their experience just as those who tested Dr. Persinger's God helmet were. This can be a life-altering experience, so intense you hardly question its reality. Joseph Smith's sincerity, however, is in question; he will not be in their number when the saints go marching in. It is patently clear he was just a charlatan in magic underpants.

The unquestioning and obedient followers of God's messengers deserve the greater censure. The messengers received the message from their visions; the followers received the message from the messengers—the ones with the affliction.

In recent years, the news media had an example of this blind obedience. A very elderly preacher from California, one Harold Camping, predicted May 21, 2011, as the day of the rapture when the world would end. According to Camping, who has/had all the attributes of an Old Testament prophet without TLE, this was certainly based on his biblical calculations. "Certain I tell you!" The reader, of course, knows Camping was a little short because that date has long passed. Forgive him for he knows not what he does, perhaps because of a sprinkling of Alzheimer's disease. But his supporters were the true fools, the ones who gave up their jobs, homes, and money to follow and spread Camping's lunacy. They were like the sheep that still trail behind St. Paul and Muhammad and trust in the Torah. They were the real losers.

On the day after, nothing was heard from Camping—he was hiding in an obscure motel room because of embarrassment while most of us had been hoping the Lord had raptured him. By May 23, however, he had fully recovered from his discomfiture and proclaimed:

We had all of our dates correct, we had all of the proofs correct. . . . Every proof, every sign is all correct. The only thing is, God had not opened our eyes yet to the fact that May 21 was a spiritual coming where as we thought it was a physical coming. But he has come.

To assuage his deep disappointment, Mr. Camping set the new absolutely certain date for the destruction of the Earth to be October 21, 2011—153 days after May 21. Why this number you ask? That's the quantity of fish St. Peter caught in the net recorded in John 21:10, and with that revelation, everything became crystal clear! Unfortunately, that date has also passed without incident, but Camping is probably still babbling. In case you're wondering about the millions of dollars donated to his church, he kept it, and it's tax-free too—all Americans paid for that.

Rather than just admit his biblical calculations were wrong, Camping, by making another prediction, set himself up for a second embarrassment. After nearly a century of bogus predictions of the world's end, even the Jehovah's Witnesses have given up on this foolish enterprise. Now, I ask the reader, is there anything other than re-re-calculating the date of the rapture or apocalypse that would have been more humiliating for Camping? What could that possibly have been? What if he had said God told him to lie on his left side for 153 days while cooking his food with (or eating) his own feces? That should do it! Harold would have been quickly shut away somewhere warm and comfortable and heavily drugged for his remaining years. No one, not even his most rabid followers, would have seen him as anything other than delusional. He would not have been an Old Testament prophet in modern times, but just an old man with mental problems.

The outstanding question now is "Why don't we see Ezekiel in exactly the same manner?" Since Copernicus and Galileo, we no longer accept Ptolemy's astronomy. We criticize Aristotle's classification of plants and animals. We laugh at ancient physics with their four elements of earth, air, fire, and water. We are stunned by the sheer childishness of Pythagorean number beliefs. Why should we give God's ancient prophets privilege and protection from criticism and analysis? The American revolutionary thinker Thomas Paine noted, "The Bible is a book that has been read more and examined less than any book that ever existed." But no sacred texts, principalities, or persons should be above criticism. Does time produce veracity? Of course not, it just silences criticism. Ezekiel was just another Bronze Age prophet with the Geschwind syndrome—less rational and less humane than his modern counterpart Harold Camping.

MONOTHEISM

Abraham on his way
to sacrifice Isaac

Abraham had two sons, Isaac and Ismael. The latter he sent into the desert with his mother, Hagar, probably to perish. The former he decided to sacrifice because God had commanded it (Genesis 22:2). This hallowed patriarch also took firewood with him to roast the carcass of his sacrificed son because Yahweh enjoyed the aroma of burning flesh. Legend says that at the moment of execution, Abraham happened to see a ram caught in some bushes nearby, and he interpreted this as a sign from God to sacrifice the animal instead. We are to believe that this last minute change of mind meant God was just testing Abraham's faith and that made the whole episode all right. It's doubtful, however, that Abraham will ever be nominated as father of the year.

Christians spend a good deal of time dancing around this incredibly barbarous commandment and its "true meaning." No such dancing was required for the tens of thousands of lambs and other animals who had their throats ceremoniously cut[*] for the same purposed: to diminish the fury of an implacable God. Why Yahweh glories in blood and gore is another of those divine mysteries surpassing all understanding.

Abraham is also the eponym of the Abrahamic religions, among which are Judaism, Christianity, Islam, and others (e.g., the Baha'i Faith). The pride and glory of all these religions is their claim to be monotheistic or so they believe. This is problematic for Yahweh who clearly knows there are other gods as is evident in his First Commandment from Exodus 20:3 (NIV):

You shall have no other gods before me.

---

[*] In front of the Temple (I Kings 7:23) were huge cauldrons of water so that the priests could wash the blood and gore from their bodies and vestments. Special drainage canals in the stone flooring carried away the spurting blood from the animals' sliced throats.

He did not say there were no other Gods just that he was the first. This implies Yahweh is a henotheist, that is, one who believes in many gods but worships only one.

Henotheism is a halfway house for those unable to abandon polytheism; similarly, agnosticism is a home for timid atheists. Some wags have suggested monotheism is heading in the right direction and it only needs to take one or two more steps. The next line summarizes this progression of beliefs in sky-gods:

Polytheism → Henotheism → Monotheism → Agnosticism → Atheism

It seems apparent that the concept of the Trinity—Father, Son, and Holy Ghost—is a polytheistic fossil the Christian Church is still attempting to bury and resurrect simultaneously. Isaac Newton was an avid anti-Trinitarian—he wrote numerous pamphlets on this topic. Only the Unitarian Church has committed to the final step of downgrading Jesus from God to man. And no one knows where the Holy Ghost is, but then we never did.

The Muslims, on the other hand, have been uncompromising in their monotheism from the beginning. Muhammad's tribe was traditionally such, so the Prophet was simply spreading his tribal ethos throughout the Arabian Peninsula.

Why is monotheism superior to polytheism or indeed all other isms? Is this the result of cultural evolution or traditional delusion? What are the social and political consequences of believing in a single, all-powerful deity? The American writer and historian Gore Vidal has an answer to this question:

> The great unmentionable evil at the center of our culture is monotheism. From a barbaric Bronze Age text known as the Old Testament, three anti-human religions have evolved—Judaism, Christianity, and Islam. These are sky-god religions. They are, literally, patriarchal—God is the Omnipotent Father—hence the loathing of women for 2,000 years in those countries afflicted by the sky-god and his earthly male delegates. The sky-god is a jealous god, of course. He requires total obedience from everyone on earth, as he is not just in place for one tribe, but for all creation. Those who would reject him must be converted or killed for their own good. Ultimately, totalitarianism is the only sort of politics that can truly serve the sky-god's purpose. Any movement of a liberal nature endangers his authority and those

of his delegates on earth. One God, one King, one Pope, one master in the factory, one father-leader in the family at home.

Vidal has compellingly summed up the failure of monotheism to benefit humankind. Totalitarianism is the top-down command structure for monotheism—on Earth as it is in Heaven. Regrettably, these are the governments the Middle East still has. We in the West and the Far East have had our share of such wretched systems: Nazism, Fascism, Communism, Maoism, and so on. In the shadowy background of every religious and ideological commandment is the silent but unspoken 11th supreme mandate: *Thou shall not question!* To question shows disobedience and this makes God's delegates on earth panic and their sky-gods rage. It also infuriates earthly dictators and has their minions scrambling for cover. If you question, you will be silenced—to the extent your society allows. Because of secularization in the West since the Inquisition, the punishment is usually little or nothing; in the Middle East, however, the price of apostasy is death[*]. It's about freedom. It was in the past, it is in the present, and will be in the future—it always has been. Freedom to think! Freedom to question and write! Freedom to discuss! This is the great divide between good and evil.

To contrast the freedom in the West with the subjugation of the Middle East, no clearer example exists than the Salman Rushdie fatwa. It was falsely rumored that Ayatollah Khomeini, the Supreme Leader of Iran, had no sense of humor. But on *Valentine's Day*, 1989, he issued the following fatwa (Islamic religious verdict) against author Salman Rushdie and all those connected with the publication of *The Satanic Verses*:

> [T]he author of *The Satanic Verses* book which is against Islam, the Prophet and the Qur'an, and all involved in its publication who were aware of its content, are sentenced to death. I call on all zealous Muslims to execute them wherever they find them, so that no one will dare to insult the Islamic sanctions. Whoever is killed on this path will be regarded as a martyr, God willing.

---

[*] An Afghan Christian convert was jailed for months awaiting the death sentence under Afghanistan's apostasy law before being released.

Incredibly, Khomeini offered his own money to anyone, Muslim or not, who would assassinate Rushdie, a private citizen of another country. Although the author publically apologized to Muslims for any perceived offence, the fatwa wasn't revoked. Khomeini expounded:

> Even if Salman Rushdie repents and becomes the most pious man of all time, it is incumbent on every Muslim to employ everything he has got, his life and wealth, to send him to Hell.

Some in the West suggested the Supreme Ayatollah show Rushdie the path to the underworld by going first, and perhaps we can assume he has.

Like drunken sailors streaming to a brothel, religious leaders of all faiths plunged headlong into the controversy to condemn Rushdie. That's right, the victim is guilty! Rather than criticize Khomeini for hiring others to do murder, they pounded on freedom of expression—a basic tenet of Western civilization. Christopher Hitchens names a few of these leaders in his book *god is not Great*: the Vatican, the archbishop of Canterbury, the Chief Sephardic Rabbi of Israel, Cardinal Archbishop of New York, and many Falwell and Robertson types across the American wasteland of fundamentalism.

And Muslim mobs reacted in a frenzy of seldom seen irrationalism thereby killing many—thirty-seven burned to death in a Turkish hotel fire. These religious thugs, in an egregious case of special pleading, claimed *they have a right not to be offended*. Let's be certain we comprehend their "logic." We must give up the bedrock values of Western free expression so as not to offend them; otherwise, they have a right to murder and mutilate. Who are these troglodytes that the brightness of the Enlightenment so dazzles them that they must shield their eyes? History has met them many times. They are the people of the night.

In the parallel disciplines of politics and religion, they see each other as comrades in arms. Of course, in almost all Muslim countries these are the same people. They're theocracies, not democracies. Is there an authoritarian regime anywhere, other than that competing religion of communism that the Catholic Church hasn't supported? Pope Pius XI (1857-1939) said, "Mussolini is a wonderful man. Do you hear me? A wonderful man."

Possibly, the present pope would opine that Pius XI* wasn't speaking ex cathedra—or perhaps his infallibility date had expired. The successor to the leader of Mussolini's fan club was Pope Pius XII, the World War Two-era pope, whose indifference during the Holocaust was indefensible. During these years, dozens of writers had their books put on the Prohibited Index and the Pope disciplined or defrocked numerous priests and theologians for being too liberal. Nevertheless—and this is nearly too incredible to believe—not a single Nazi, not even Adolf Hitler, a Catholic, was censured in any way by the church. After the war, the Magisterium was a vocal supporter of amnesty for Nazi war criminals. They helped smuggle many to South America including the notorious Angel of Death Joseph Mengele and the architect of the Holocaust Adolf Eichmann. In 2000, Pope John Paul II started Pius XII on the road to sainthood by elevating him to "Venerable." Now all they need are a couple of easy miracles and he'll be canonized. Recently Jewish leaders reacted with shock to Pope Ratzinger's comments in his modestly titled new book *Light of the World* that Pius XII "saved more Jews than anyone else." Surely, the lunatics have taken over the asylum.

Add a few gods to your lonely pantheon of one. Now it becomes difficult for any single deity to be supreme and lord it over the others. Consider the polytheism of Greece with its dozen Olympian Gods and numerous demi-gods and heroes. Zeus was often a figure of fun, notably when his wife, the goddess Hera, would catch him with yet another nubile nymph. Many philosophers have pointed out that one of the great misfortunes of Western civilization is that along with Greek art, science, and politics we didn't adopt their religion as well. At least they would have given us marvelous comedic relief instead of pain now and punishment later. If this had happened, our mythology would be Greek, not Judaic.

---

* This pope personally blessed the Italian airplanes going to bomb helpless Ethiopian villages in Mussolini's "glorious" 1935 war of imperial conquest.

Other than comedy, there are at least two main benefits to a crowded pantheon. History shows us polytheistic societies are less warlike and far less authoritarian. Recall, totalitarian Persia invaded Greece, not the reverse. Although Alexander the "Great" made up for that later, but by that time, he thought he was a god. Initially Adolf Hitler invaded Austria, the Sudetenland, and Poland, but the Allies soon returned the favor. Of course, to Americans the most outstanding example of this is the unprovoked attack on Pearl Harbor by the "God-Emperor," Hirohito. Ultimately, the U.S. responded in kind but with greater force. Conclusively, dictators, whether earthly or celestial, are warlike and authoritarian—it's their nature.

It cannot be an accident that democracy was born in a polytheistic society—Greece. The word itself is of Greek origin. This same society first questioned—no, condemned—slavery while all the world's "great religions" were silent. It's not because their "sacred religious texts" are ancient that they were mute on slavery and unable to envisage democracy. Joseph Smith published the Book of Mormon in 1830 and it's no better, worse in fact. You could not find democracy in the dark streets and alleys of Jerusalem with its religious devotees banging their heads on the Temple walls, nor in the mindless circumambulations of the Kaaba by Muslims. It required the open agoras and wide amphitheaters of Greece with its easy polytheism to let ideas flow.

Homo sapiens existed for at least 150,000 years without Muhammad, Jesus, Moses, or any of God's other messengers. During this vast time, hundreds of millions of human beings—men, women, children, and babies—died agonizing deaths from disease, famine, floods, earthquakes, plagues, and other calamities before God decided to help us with his "inspired" prophets. Recall that this omnipresent being was at the Auschwitz's killing rooms when the Nazis gassed millions, and would not open the door. Both times perhaps He was vacationing on Kolob or maybe the pleasure planet Risa. Nothing improved after the prophets arrived—much the opposite. These men and their holy books gave us religious wars, crusades, massacres, pogroms and so millions more were slaughtered. Religions and all dogmatic ideologies retard social progress wherever they go. Only the development of modern science cured diseases, increased food production, improved hygiene, and performed miracles by vaccinating the whole earth. Come, stand with us in the light.

CHAPTER—7

MORALS AND MAN

When I do, I feel good; when I do bad,
I feel bad, and that is my religion.
Abraham Lincoln

Never let your sense of morals prevent
you from doing what's right.
Isaac Asimov

In the mythology of the Abrahamic religions, God created Adam[*] in his image and Eve as an afterthought and a bit of ribbing. The young earth creationists assure us this took place in the not too distant past. And by eating the fruit of the tree of the knowledge of good and evil—sometimes called the tree of conscience—Adam and Eve gained an awareness of their nakedness. This knowledge or loss of innocence was a prerequisite for their moral or immoral behavior. The killjoy Catholics, however, label this "sin" and tie it closely to sex. Like all mythologies, there are several possible interpretations. This is one.

For reasons best known only to God, the eating of this fruit angered him greatly, and he thought it appropriate to curse *all humans* for generations or perhaps forever—a slight overreaction. For the Abrahamic religions, in some sense, we can say independence was born when Eve picked the fruit and Adam ate it. On the other hand, Yahweh's ferocious reaction reveals him as an immoral, vindictive tyrant. He needs to double up on his Prozac—and by the way, this is a repeat prescription.

I can hear the shouts of readers protesting that I've evaded the true cause of Yahweh's fury—DISOBEDIENCE. Adam was commanded not to eat the forbidden fruit and Eve was aware of this stern warning. Yet what could God truly expect. He puts two naked people in a beautiful garden and all they do is eat a little fruit—I would say they were well behaved.

---

[*] This is the second or Yahwist creation story from Genesis 2.

Incidentally, the word *Satan* does not refer to a specific person or entity like "Tom Collins" or "Ryan Coke." It's a general noun meaning "an adversary" who could be anyone or anything. Satan as such doesn't even appear in the Old Testament; it's a fiction of translation. So it's an anachronism to see the serpent as Satan in the sense that the New Testament does.

John Milton in his epic poem *Paradise Lost* dramatically sums up the traditional interpretation of this "rebelliousness" in the poem's initial sentence:

Of Mans First Disobedience, and the Fruit
Of that Forbidden Tree, whose mortal tast
Brought Death into the World, and all our woe,
With loss of Eden, till one greater Man
Restore us, and regain the blissful Seat,
Sing Heav'nly Muse

The alliteration of *First*, *Fruits*, *Forbidden* and the Latin sentence structure with the verb "sing" third last is a powerful construction.

God's terrifying reaction to this minor disobedience by his children is not an aberration but a biblical standard. It occurs at least twice in the Torah: Leviticus 20:9 and Deuteronomy 21:18-21 (NIV):

Anyone who curses their father or mother is to be put to death.

There's no nuanced response or detailed reasoning here; just a simple kneejerk totalitarianism—it's my way or death. In the eyes of tyrants, the child is never right, the rebel is always wrong. Anyone who challenges authority is to be put to death. This is *madness parading as morality.*

On the other hand, the mythical "rebellion" of Adam and Eve is deeply representative of our nature. We are neither sinful nor depraved, but a curious species with profound need to explore—it's our nature. We leave the concept of original sin to the sick and the dead. We will seek. We will find. We will explore. In fewer than 2,500 generations, we have expanded on foot over the whole earth, from the heart of Africa to the tip of South America.

We have explored the floor beneath the sea to the bottom of the Mariana Trench, a 6.8 mile deep abyss. We have walked on the moon, we have traveled the surface of Mars with robotic rovers; we have sent a spacecraft right out of our solar system—Voyager 1 it is the farthest man-made object from Earth in the universe. The fabled rebellion in the Garden of Eden set us on our heroic path to explore the universe; that's who we are as a species. That's the meaning I take from Adam and Eve's naked stroll in the Garden.

The lessons here are not those synagogue, church, or mosque would teach. So we must look elsewhere for the birthplace of morality, perhaps even to the creatures we are told God gave us "dominion over."

THE ORIGINS OF MORALITY

The higher animals have no religion. And we are told that they are going to be left out in the Hereafter. I wonder why? It seems questionable taste. Mark Twain (1835-1910)

I'm very fortunate to live much of each year in the wild hinterlands of Ontario. Not on a busy lake with noisy powerboats and water-skiers but in fields of wildflowers, bumblebees, deer, and all those animals we were given "dominion over."

A decade or so ago, I came upon a considerable mystery. It was a fall afternoon and while walking down the road toward my home, I couldn't help but notice enormous undulations on the dusty road. A snake perhaps? Now I knew no part of Ontario, or indeed any place on earth, held a snake that huge, at least I hoped not. The sinusoidal outline was approximately thirty inches wide, but its length was uncertain. I thought this thing must swallow deer for breakfast and dine on moose for lunch. My imagination was racing. To add to the mystery were occasional patches of dark blood—the remains of prey perhaps? As the days passed and grew shorter, I often thought about this mystery. What if I run into this creature on my daily rambles? Eventually the first snow fell overnight, and on that very morning, while checking for animal tracks, I came upon this fantastic winding trail for a second time—and it was close by my home! And once again there were dark blood stains, this time on pristine snow.

Should I be alarmed? I thought not, because anything that large without legs couldn't move quickly. On the other hand, if that were the case, how does this creature capture its prey? My mind was racing again. The mystery deepened when I observed fist-sized footprints in the snow on both sides of the undulations. If I had totally lost my mind, and I wasn't quite there yet, it's possible to imagine this as the serpent from the Garden of Eden. The creature God cursed and made legless to slither on its belly and eat the dust of the earth. In the real world, some snakes, particularly pythons, have external vestigial legs. What was happening? How could I solve this enigma?

I have a few additional delusions. In my imagination, I'm an excellent wildlife photographer, but more interested in the picture's subject than its quality. That is, I would prefer a poor picture of a moose, say, to an award-winning photograph of a landscape. I have a special camera that takes photographs automatically when it senses both heat and motion. While this is happening, I'm usually at home drinking a single-malt scotch.

This unique camera was attached to a tree overlooking the extraordinary snow track observed previously. I activated it and departed. Days passed, the snow melted, yet nothing happened: no photographs, no new tracks. I decided this camera trap needed some bait. Feed them and they will come, or so it hoped. I placed a large quantity of cracked corn on the off chance the creature was a herbivore, and four pounds of hamburger in case it was a carnivore—the more likely choice. The following morning I could hardly wait to check the site. As I approached I saw that all the food was gone, every bit of it, and that there were tracks everywhere, including those of this undulating monster. More significantly, the display window on the camera revealed it had taken 186 photographs. Jackpot!

I replaced the memory chip and ran home to boot up my computer and Photoshop Elements software to view these pictures. And what did I see? Bears, black bears, lots of them but no undulating monster. One large mother bear or sow came early in the evening with her two small cubs—probably females. (Each photo is imprinted with the date and time it was taken.) Four hours passed before a second mother bear arrived with her two larger cubs—probably males. But still nothing to explain the strange undulations I had seen. What was I missing? Here are the photographs of the two different sows. Where's the monster?

Large Sow and her two small female cubs

Mother Courage and her two large male cubs

Then I saw the problem. The solution to the mystery was obvious, but so incredibly improbable. The mother bear in the bottom photograph had no use of her hind legs. She was a paraplegic. Note the worn-away fur and exposed flesh on her back legs plus their unnatural position. Unbelievably, *she was dragging herself everywhere*, and this was the source of the undulations. There was no monster, just a mother bear of inconceivable endurance determined to feed her cubs and herself. I decided to call her Mother Courage. There never was a monster, just a delusion in my mind like the bells in the children's heads and the religious visions of God's messengers with temporal lobe epilepsy.

I contacted the Ontario Ministry of Natural Resources (MNR) about what we should do to help this injured bear. "We" quickly became "me." But they did suggest that if this sow made it to hibernation, about two weeks away, the cubs would have a better chance of surviving the winter—it can be 40° below zero where I live. Until then, I decided to feed Mother Courage and her cubs, and to do it outside my back window so that I might observe their behavior. After this, they came *every night*; however, I never saw the large sow and her two small cubs again. Two weeks passed, and then two more. Would she ever hibernate? I telephoned the MNR to ask if my feeding was inhibiting them from going into hibernation—they said not! Another two weeks came and went; it was now the middle of December, and this family often arrived during a blizzard. The cubs were always first by several minutes until this heroic animal dragged her bleeding backside out of the deep forest only to collapse in exhaustion. On many occasions she never ate—she just watched her cubs devour the cracked corn and dog food. Her mothering instincts could challenge those of many humans.

I became curious about the location of their wintering den. With the broad blood-spotted trail she had imprinted on the snow, I surmised finding her lair would be easy. It must be close; after all, how far can an animal drag itself? Yet, it took me more than an hour of arduous scrambling to negotiate my way through a nearly impenetrable tangle of fallen trees and branches. Finally, I reached an embankment sloping down to an ancient glacial lake, and located her den. This daily journey—both ways—would have intimidated Shackleton. Yet Mother Courage had done this daily trek for weeks, perhaps even months. I was stunned by the magnitude of her endurance and the power of her instincts. Neither torn flesh, nor exhaustion, nor death itself I thought would prevent her daily rounds. Some will say I am anthropomorphizing; I would say it is simple empathy with a fellow mammal in great anguish.

It's almost impossible to accurately assess an animal's weight by sight alone, but by comparing my first photographs to the later ones, Mother Courage appeared to be losing body fat. So, on December 17, I decided *not to feed* her and her cubs anymore hoping to force them into hibernation, lest she die crawling. It was a sad evening for everyone. They came. They searched. They left. And I never saw them again. Below is the final photograph of that snowy evening.

Mother Courage (on the left) and her family

Early in the New Year, I snowshoed to the den and was elated to find they were all safely asleep—or as asleep as hibernating bears ever truly get. The den entrance was encrusted with ice crystals caused by their emanating body heat. My flashlight revealed a bear's back almost completely blocking the entrance in an effort perhaps to retain this heat. In my imagination I took this to be Mother Courage in her ultimate act of protection for her cubs. She, of course, knew none of this. She was following those deep instincts that had preserved her genes through a million years of evolution.

Clearly, this mother bear was exhibiting behavior that can only be described as *moral*. And just as clearly, this behavior was preserving her genes by passing them on through her two male cubs. There was pressure for moral behavior, stemming from natural selection, because this behavior is adaptive for the preservation of genes, which are life itself. In his book *Darwin's Dangerous Idea* Daniel Dennett calls evolution by natural selection "the best idea anyone has ever had."

A vast literature exists on these topics, not just anecdotal stories like mine on Mother Courage. Scientists define this topic as follows:

> Sociobiologists accept as true that human behavior, as well as nonhuman animal behavior, can be partly explained as the outcome of natural selection. They maintain that to fully understand behavior; it must be analyzed in terms of evolutionary considerations.

At my latitude, the average date for bears to come out of hibernation is April 10, so, about two weeks after this date, I revisited the den site. The Ministry of Natural Resources had assured me that this sow (Mother Courage) would not exit the den alive—I had to see for myself. With some difficulty—everything appears different without snow—I found the den again. It was empty, completely empty; the entire family had left. In the distance was a kettle of turkey vultures, and I wondered if they were recycling Mother Courage. I suspected as much, but I declined to investigate. In my mind's eye, she will always be the most heroic creature I have ever known.

Male bear cubs will depart from their natal territory—an instinctive taboo against incest by *Ursus americanus*. By leaving their home area, they require a larger size since trespassing on the territories of other male bears (boars) can be hazardous. On occasion they will have to stand and deliver and it's good to be near or in the same weight division. Genetics tells us that inbreeding is generally detrimental to the gene pool. And again natural selection is the source of our discomfort and bears' avoidance of this practice. It's significant that sows will share territory with their female cubs since there is no danger of incest.

Morality arises in a social context, but even hermits have a need for it in their relationship with nature's wild creatures. All herd or pack animals have a large moral repertoire: whales, elephants, and, as we shall see, wolves.

In Western society, if you wish to conjure up a nightmare of slobbering immorality, of heartless cruelty, and mindless killing, the image is always that of the wolf. From nursery rhymes to adult fiction, the beast from the primeval forest is *Canis lupus lupus.* Never was a creature more maligned than this great grandparent of *Canis lupus familiaris,* the family pet. Yet there isn't a single authenticated case of a wolf killing a human in all of North American recorded history.

The Algonquin Wolf

On the other hand, we have poisoned, trapped, slaughtered, run down with snowmobiles, and shot from helicopters so many wolves they are virtually extirpated from the lower forty-eight states. Under great protest, a few have been reintroduced to Yellowstone Park. But often we know who the top predator is, the slobbering mindless killer—we need only look in the mirror.

Experts have long thought wolf-pack size was determined solely by the abundance of food. In my region the average pack of five or six wolves hunts over an area of approximately 100 square miles. Yet even in the presence of an overabundance of prey, pack size is relatively fixed. Why? All species of wolves live in tight-knit social groups. If the pack grows too large, the group disintegrates because they are not able to bond closely enough with each other. Curiously, the number of relationships grows more quickly than the actual pack size. In a pack of five there are ten relationships, however, in a pack of ten this number jumps to forty-five—far too many for close bonding. The chart below shows how quickly the number of relationships rises in proportion to the pack size:

Pack Size	1	2	3	4	5	6	7	8	9	10
Number of Relationships	0	1	3	6	10	15	21	28	36	45

The common paradigm for wolf behavior comes from Tennyson's *In Memoriam* when it says "red in tooth and claw." But if this were true, the pack would quickly disintegrate from death, injury, and animosity. You cannot risk your life every day or you will soon lose it. Approximately 90 percent of wolf-pack interactions are prosocial. That is not to say that wolves, like our military or our entire social order, don't have a strict hierarchy, which accounts for the remaining 10 percent.

In social groups with a hierarchical structure, a method is needed to release the tension caused by the restrictions on freedom. Ancient Rome developed the yearly feast of Saturnalia where masters served slaves. To be sure the slaves, nonetheless, prepared the food. Wolves have an analogous game where the dominant individuals "handicap" themselves in role reversals with lower ranking wolves by showing submission and permitting them to play bite. If a wolf bites too hard, it will "play bow" to ask forgiveness and the play resumes. This is a clear demonstration of fairness, and so pack tensions are released and bonding is reinforced. Unlike the Saturnalia, which was a yearly festival, wolves, play fight regularly. Their bonds are tight-knit and compassionate especially around any new-born pups where every wolf is a parent of sorts: older siblings from previous litters, aunts, and uncles. If the alpha female happens to die in pup-birth or otherwise, various aunts will care for the young, and these females will even lactate.

Marc Bekoff, Professor Emeritus of Ecology and Evolutionary Biology at the University of Colorado, claims that without a moral code governing their actions, these kinds of behaviors would not be possible. With co-author Jessica Pierce, bioethicist, they have cogently argued this point in their book *Wild Justice: The Moral Lives of Animals*.

Naturally moral differences exist between humans and other animals just as they do among all individuals of the same species including *Homo sapiens*. It's a matter of degree not of kind.

Many readers may have wondered how Mother Courage came to be a paraplegic. Only two reasonable speculations are possible: she was either hit by a car or shot by a hunter. It was bear hunting season when I first noticed the undulations on my dusty road. Hunting or "harvesting" as the euphemism goes is from the first of September until hibernation—almost three months. However, "harvesting" season on humans is always closed. All biology textbooks describe bears as "shy woodland creatures," and they are very rarely dangerous to humans. No records exist of anyone being killed by a mother bear defending her cubs, mauled yes; killed no. World black bear expert Lynn Rogers says the following on his website (www.bear.org):

> Black bears have killed 61 people across North America since 1900. This no longer worries me. My chances of being killed by a domestic dog, bees, or lightning are vastly greater. My chances of being murdered are 60,000 times greater. One of the safest places a person can be is in the woods.

Humans, however, have slaughtered hundreds of thousands of bears. We hunt bears, bears do not hunt us.

With our so-called God-given morality, we have driven hundreds if not thousands of species to extinction, and another universe must pass away before such creatures will ever come again. Remember the Bible tells us God gave us dominion over all life and we have taken it with a vengeance. I am not a vegetarian, but I would speak against the *senseless* slaughter of all those who cannot speak for themselves.

> *A dog starved at his master's gate,*
> *Predicts the ruin of the state*
> "Auguries of Innocence" by William Blake

Some moral behaviors exist outside of, and independent of, humans. Even among those who didn't hear Moses fresh back from Sinai where God gave him *another two tablets* and said call me in the morning[*]. If as a species, we had never existed or had gone extinct—and 99.9 percent of all species have—morality in terms we could recognize would still be flourishing on this planet.

For those who have heard Moses' message and swallowed the tablets whole, their environmental awareness is abominable, better yet, immoral. Because of his eschatology, Jesus made this same point in Matthew 6:25-28 (KJV):

---

[*] R_x swallow whole; do not smash   Repeats: 0

Therefore I say unto you, Take no thought for your life, what ye
shall eat, or what ye shall drink; nor yet for your body, what ye
shall put on. . . . Behold the fowls of the air: for they sow not,
neither do they reap. . . . Are ye not much better than they? . . .
And why take ye thought for raiment? Consider the lilies of the
field, how they grow; they toil not, neither do they spin:

Statements like this run through the New Testament implying
the end of the world—the Apocalypse—is at hand. These beliefs
give an immoral imprint to Jesus' sayings because they degrade
the lives of Christians and the environment. This world view is
anti-life or plainly pro-death. Christians and Jews have forever
believed we are living in the End Times. So nothing matters except Christ's message. From pulpits across America, preachers
shout, "Consider not the birds of the air, the animals of the forest,
nor the oceans of the earth—they matter not for the end is nigh."

This rapture nonsense and the Second Coming silliness both
feed this worldview. It's not just the Muslims who hate this life so
much that they frequently take the express route to the seventy-
two virgins; it's all the Abrahamic religions with their inherently
apocalyptic views. The last verse of Revelation 22:20 (NIV) before the final amen says:

> *He who testifies to these things says,*
> *"Yes, I am coming soon."*
> *Amen. Come, Lord Jesus.*

Well, evidently he's quite late—in fact by two millennia. Occasionally someone comes along who so starkly states this world
doesn't matter that even latent believers are shocked. James Watt,
Secretary of the Interior in the Reagan Administration Responsible
for National Policy regarding the Environment, was such a man.
Today he is remembered for the following gem, "We don't have
to protect the environment; the Second Coming is at hand."

When not at his job, which was most of the time, he'd go to
Charlotte, North Carolina. There he would regularly appear on
the *PTL Club* (PTL short for "Praise The Lord"), an opulently set
religious show hosted by televangelists Jim and Tammy Faye
Bakker. Jim was later convicted of stealing massive amounts of

church donations—185 million dollars—for his personal use and sentenced to eighteen years in jail. Some wags suggested *PTL* meant "Pass The Loot."

Watt continued to drop so many gems that some thought he must own the crown jewels of England. During a dinner in 1991 organized by Wyoming's Green River Cattlemen's Association Watt said, "If the troubles from environmentalists cannot be solved in the jury box or at the ballot box, perhaps the cartridge box should be used."

In 1995, Watt was charged by a federal grand jury on twenty-five counts of felony perjury and obstruction of justice. The indictments were due to lies he told to a grand jury investigating influence peddling. As part of a lawyer-engineered deal, Watt pleaded guilty to one count of withholding evidence. And he was sentenced to five years' probation and fined $5,000 plus ordered to perform 500 hours of community service. Undoubtedly James Watt was the worst Secretary of the Interior in American history.

What percentage of Americans believes in the rapture and the Second Coming? According to a June 2010 poll by the Pew Research Center, 41 percent are certain Jesus will return before 2050. This number rises to 52 percent in the South; that's more than 100 million people. *Newsweek* magazine in their cover story for May 24, 2004, "The New Prophets of Revelation" put the Rapturites at 55 percent. Even more astonishing are the 62 million copies of the "Left Behind" series of apocalyptic novels sold by Tim LaHaye and Jerry Jenkins—the most successful writing collaboration in publishing history. These beliefs have a devastating impact on all aspects of American society, but in particular the environment.

As governor of Alaska Sarah Palin never saw a wild animal she didn't want to kill. To that end, she reestablished the long-abandoned policy of a bounty for every wolf shot. In a gruesome act, the "hunter" received $150.00 for the left front wolf paw hacked off, and brought it in.

This "sportsman-like" activity was often done from the comfort of a helicopter with a hot toddy in hand, while the dark bodies of the exhausted wolves against the white canvas of snow made easy targets. Environmental scientists consider aerial shooting of wolves (and bears) a savage practice masquerading under the euphemism of predator control. Palin exudes concern for the hunters saying wolves are stealing food from their tables. But before humans were in Alaska straightening out these problems, predator and prey were unbelievably abundant.

Palin is an enemy of science and reason. She strongly advocates the teaching of creationism in public schools and believes global warming is a hoax. Her understanding of biology is childlike because of her Christian fundamentalism; she can't or won't comprehend the explanatory power of natural selection.

In some sense, predator and prey have created each other. Each depends on the other for its health and long-term survival. The wolves run on through the evergreen forests in their eternal pursuit of the deer. And for their part, the deer lead the wolves on a deadly chase. Each hones the other to perfection by natural selection. It's not only the weak and the old who falter and fall; it's the inefficient. To those who do the dance, whether deer or wolf, belongs the day. It's not a good day to die. It never is. And so the wolves run on through the evergreen forests.

Despite individuals like Bakker, Watt, and Palin the majority of people behave well towards animals and each other. Occasionally under the control of some fanatical religious or political ideology, we descend to levels unknown in the natural world: genocides, pogroms, ethnic cleansings, and religious persecutions. All these horrific crimes are committed in the name of some higher good, either political or religious.

The most fascinating behavior between animals—human or otherwise—is reciprocity*. You scratch my back and I'll scratch yours. Or, unexpectedly, I'll scratch yours even if I don't know you or will never see you again. Another name for reciprocity is the Golden Rule. I enumerated a list of these from the world's religions and cultures in Chapter 4, nonetheless, animals had it first, long before the Bible reiterated it, or Moses staggered down Mt. Sinai in a rage.

To the shock of those who are stony faced and stony minded, the evidence that humans, apes and monkeys, whales, elephants, wolves, and even rats and mice inherit ethical behaviors honed

---

* *Google* "Richard Dawkins on altruism and reciprocity".

by natural selection is profoundly disturbing. But should it be? We are a part *of*, not apart *from*, all life on earth. We are not descended from angels but ascended from apes. As I have said elsewhere, ours is a heroic past, at times so close to extinction that a wink might have made it so. Darwin would be pleased to witness this expansion of his great idea.

I am not saying *all* human morality is inherited. That's false, foolishly false. Much of ethics is cultural in its origin and development. Exodus 23:2, "Thou shalt not follow a multitude to do evil" is a powerful injunction against group thought and herd instinct. Its spirit is individuality and freedom, two of my main themes. Or for example, consider a modern variant and refinement of this, the Nuremberg excuse, "I was just following orders" mentioned previously—a repulsive cop-out and Western civilization has declared it such.

If *all* moral values were inherited, then we would hopefully see a world-wide standard of human rights, but plainly we do not. Inherited morality acquired through natural selection is one key to understanding human ethics, but it doesn't open every door. So let's find some new keys.

THE WORLD'S DIRTIEST WORD

Freedom, morality, and the human dignity of the individual consists precisely in this; that he does good not because he is forced to do so, but because he freely conceives it, wants it, and loves it.
Mikhail Bakunin, *God and the State*

In American society what is the single most derogatory term you can call someone? It's considered worse than being unemployed or on welfare. It's worse than being called a fag, queer, or homosexual. In one of his more lucid moments George Bush senior (*see* Chapter Notes) said, "I don't know that [they] should be considered citizens, nor should they be considered patriots." Even child molesters are not so reviled as these wretches. Muslims consider them lower than Christians; on the other hand, Christians deem them beneath Muslims. It's more dreadful than that first disobedience of Eve and Adam. We call them *atheists*. Yet different cultures have different arch-villains.

In the ninth and final circle of Dante's *Inferno* was Lucifer with three faces on one head. Unexpectedly, he is frozen in ice up to his waist; even more unexpectedly are the three arch-sinners he gnaws on—one in each mouth. Judas is head first in the middle mouth, but anyone unfamiliar with this poem will never guess the remaining two: Brutus and Cassius, Caesar's assassins. In Dante's mind all three are bound by their treachery; to the poet, this was the greatest of all sins. The conception of what is the supreme sin has the troubling habit of morphing over times and cultures. But the name "atheist" describes a different but related offence.

Even beneath the rebels and traitors and all the others is a final layer of "depravity"—so vile that some in America refuse to pronounce the word: Christians call them atheists, those who deny God's very existence. Muslims call them infidels. Sam Harris[*] has suggested that this word is beyond rehabilitation and atheists should abandon it:

> I didn't even use the term in *The End of Faith*, which remains my most substantial criticism of religion. And, as I argued briefly in *Letter to a Christian Nation*, I think that "atheist" is a term that we do not need, in the same way that we don't need a word for someone who rejects astrology. We simply do not call people "non-astrologers." All we need are words like "reason" and "evidence" and "common sense" and "bullshit" to put astrologers in their place, and so it could be with religion.

Daniel Dennett prefers the unfortunate word *bright* as a substitute; Christopher Hitchens refers to himself as an *anti-theist*. Undoubtedly an aura of negativity exists around the word *atheist*, so I prefer the positive and inoffensive designation *freethinker*. Remember anti-abortionists wisely renamed themselves as pro-lifers. Harris, however, wishes to avoid all labels for atheists and chooses no name whatsoever—he may be right.

Pronounce yourself an atheist and almost immediately you will be informed, by those more knowledgeable than yourself, that that belief leads directly to demons like Adolf Hitler. Since I have dealt with this burr previously, let's not dwell on it again.

---

[*] *Google* "Sam Harris on atheism."

Quick on the heels of this comes the inevitable old saw of Dostoevsky, "If God does not exist everything is permitted*." My first reaction is to point out that neither Dostoyevsky nor any of his characters said precisely that. The answer to this pseudo-Dostoyevsky question is emphatically, yes! Many more things will be permitted but *not everything*. What follows is a partial liberation list of what freethinkers would allow that either are now or have been thought to be forbidden by "holy" texts, churches, mosques, and synagogues:

- Full and free access to birth control materials and pro-choice options
- Stem-cell research
- Equal rights for women
- Same sex marriage
- Anesthetics for childbirth
- Taxes on all church donations to ease the debt crisis
- All decisions made on the basis of science and reason, not faith or religious dogma.

Now here is a partial list of things we would NOT allow that religions either presently support or have in the past whether with or scriptural backing or not:

- Genital mutilation—either male or female
- Religious crusades and jihads
- Child marriages
- Honor killings
- Religious indoctrination of children
- Slavery—physical and sexual
- Stoning to death
- Sexual abuse of boys and girls by the clergy.

Startling isn't it that those with faith would reverse these lists. These are just a small sampling from the historic record. But the thrust of the Dostoyevsky pseudo question is where do freethinkers

---

* Some translators of Russian to English use *lawful* not *permitted*— giving this question a human nuance.

get their morals? Well, I have already shown that much of it—those primal instincts and more—come from our evolutionary heritage of living in groups, herds, packs, and pods. But be certain that even after the detailed answer to follow in the next few pages, these burrs, or memes, of popular religion will cling to us. Cut them out if you wish, they will return.

The most frequent criticism leveled against the New Atheists—Dawkins, Harris, Dennett, and Hitchens—is they are recycling old arguments. This implies that whoever is casting this barb is familiar with hundreds, if not thousands, of these arguments—a most doubtful situation. But even if they were what matters it? It's not just arrogance that needs a second and a third lesson; it's all the world's religious fanatics. On the other hand how many times have you and I heard, "Jesus died for our sins" or "God so loved the world he gave his only begotten son." So I realize my bulleted lists on the previous pages have mostly been said before and by none more illustrious than the philosopher Bertrand Russell. Here are his words on the relationship between religion and morality from his *Why I Am Not a Christian*:

Bertrand Russell

That is the idea—that we should all be wicked if we did not hold to the Christian religion. It seems to me that the people who have held to it have been for the most part extremely wicked. You find this curious fact that the more intense has been the religion of any period and the more profound has been the dogmatic belief, the greater has been the cruelty and the worse has been the state of affairs. In the so-called ages of faith, when men really did believe the Christian religion in all its completeness, there was the Inquisition, with all its tortures; there were millions of unfortunate women burned as witches; and there was every kind of cruelty practiced upon all sorts of people in the name of religion.

You find as you look around the world that every single bit of progress in humane feeling, every improvement in the criminal law, every step toward the diminution of war, every step toward better treatment of the colored races, or every mitigation of slavery, every moral progress that there has been in the world, has been consistently opposed by the organized churches of the world. I say quite deliberately that the Christian religion, as organized in its churches, has been and still is the principal enemy of moral progress in the world. [1]

GOD VERSUS HUMANITY: A MORALITY PLAY

Mankind is not likely to salvage civilization unless he can evolve a system of good and evil which is independent of heaven and hell.
George Orwell

Burrs also cling to the cloak of God and all totalitarians: Do my subjects actually love me or are they just terrified into an obedient simulation of love? The job of the inquisitors, morality enforcers, and secret police is to ferret out the freethinkers and discipline or eliminate them.

Imagine two families, one Muslim, the other freethinkers; both have two children. It's inevitable that each desires to pass on their values and morals—one religious the other non-religious and cultural. How do they do this? The Muslim family does this in a quiet and loving manner, but the children soon discover that any deviation from the Qur'an will bring eternal and horrific punishments in hell.

Surely, those who disbelieve in our revelations, we will condemn them to the hellfire. Whenever their skins are burnt, we will give them new skins. Thus, they will suffer continuously. GOD is Almighty, Most Wise. Surah 5:56 (AET)

This is Islam's major theme scattered across 87 of the Qur'an's 114 chapters. Nearly 500 such verses speak of hell. Its message is clear and profoundly troubling and voices anger so deep that no punishment is enough for those who disbelieve. This is the mind-destroying lesson all Muslim children must learn.

These children will live their entire lives for the Day of Judgment; everything else is of lesser or no importance. They live the only life they know, for the wished for life hereafter hoping and fearing their good deeds will outweigh their bad when they stand before Allah. Their loving parents are aware of all this because they too live under this inhuman threat. For a Christian to emotionally comprehend this he or she would have to have been raised in the 14th century. Ayaan Hirsi Ali maintains that Muslim suicide bombers martyr themselves to get a direct ticket to bypass hell and not the seventy-two virgins I've satirized so often. Her earliest memories are terrifying tales of eternal hell-fire, and relatives still point to her grim future. Their eternal chant is repent, repent, repent! This childhood indoctrination of fear is the driving force behind so many Westernized Muslims returning to Allah's little tent of horrors in later life.

In the freethinker's home things are easier, simpler, and more natural. Morality comes deeply out of who we are as a species, both genetically and culturally. By love and example their child will grow up to be a moral human as children have in billions of homes over 100 thousand years since we first came out of Africa. Morality is that strangely good feeling we all have when we behave well. This feeling, like an orgasm, keeps us coming back for more, and binds the group and helps ensure its survival. Morality is its own reward. Winston Churchill once said, "We make a living by what we get, but we make a life by what we give."

FIRST ROUND: God 0, Humanity 1

MORALS AND THE OLD TESTAMENT

If the Old Testament were a reliable guide in the matter of capital punishment, half the people in the United States would have to be killed tomorrow. Steve Allen

It's a paradox that the most religious nation among the developed countries knows the least about its "sacred" text, the Bible. It would be an exaggeration to claim American biblical knowledge is just a veneer, it's virtually non-existent. Americans are profoundly religious but at the same time deeply ignorant on matters of faith, religion, and theology.

Consider the following sad examples. More than one in ten believes Joan of Arc was Noah's wife. (Perhaps the ARCangel Gabriel was their son.) The majority of high school seniors think Sodom and Gomorrah were husband and wife, and

270/ Allah, Jesus, and Yahweh

they're probably waiting for the sex tape to come out. On the *Tonight Show*, Jay Leno once asked his audience to name just one of Jesus' twelve apostles; they could not. And incredibly, fully two-thirds of Americans *believe* Billy Graham preached the Sermon on the Mount not Jesus. During the 2004 presidential primaries, a befuddled Howard Dean was asked to name his favorite New Testament book; after much deep cogitation, he blurted out the "Book of Job." But the most telling idea and one directly opposed to the Golden Rule is the following gem believed by 75 percent of Americans—that's approximately 170 million people. This most often quoted "biblical" passage[*] is "God helps those who help themselves." Unfortunately, this quote cannot be found in either testament, but is commonly attributed to Benjamin Franklin; however, it occurs in Aesop's Fables and the dramas of the Aeschylus, Sophocles, and Euripides. Of course, this quote goes directly against the generally accepted interpretation of the Bible. It's as if a prominent physicist denied Newton's laws, or a mathematician said the Pythagorean Theorem was false. If Americans are this uninformed of their own religion, one shutters to think what they know about Judaism, Islam, or Pastafarianism.

So religion in America has collapsed to counter-biblical concepts that would make Paul of Tarsus blush and Jesus angry. Megachurches concentrate almost exclusively on things non-biblical: how to invest your money, personal weight-loss programs, tension-releasing practices, and so on. Typically these palaces for profit have drive-through latte stands and Krispy Kreme doughnuts at every service. They forget or ignore the core message of the Gospels instead dwelling almost exclusively on end-time gibberish from Daniel and the Book of Revelation. Remarkably, the top two religious states, Mississippi and Alabama, are also the top two most overweight states—too many Krispy Kremes perhaps.

All the above is preamble to my central question. If Americans have shunned Jesus central message from the New Testament, what do they take, if anything, from the Old Testament? Three points immediately come to mind that born-again Christians would broadly confirm, and that I will examine in turn:

---

[*] From the Book of Zion of which only invisible fragments survive.

- The creation story
- Homophobia
- Morality

CREATIONISM: Only a single *verified* theory of evolution exists. Previous competitors have all been defeated in the marketplace of ideas and reason—Lamarckism from France and Lysenkoism from the Soviet Union are two such fallen contestants. Darwin's theory of evolution by natural selection stands alone, undefeated and now unchallenged. Since its historic publication in 1859, *The Origin of Species* has continued to gather strength and verification from related branches of science. It is now firmly established as one of the greatest ideas of all time and as certain as heliocentrism.

Thousands of creation myths exist, however, even the Torah has two: the first in Genesis 1, the second in Genesis 2 (*See* pages 234-35). None of these tall tales agree in the fine print. Creationism isn't a theory with proof; it's a theory with poof. In the beginning there was no universe, then God said *POOF* and there it was.

Darwinian evolution is like chemistry, physics, and mathemathics in that it works everywhere on Earth, Mars, and the far reaches of the universe, even as far as most of this year's Republican presidential candidates and perhaps, just perhaps, to Kansas. Instead creationism, creation science, or intelligent design, or whatever it's called now, is parochial.

Acceptance of evolution by examining the evidence, not by belief, is a bellwether of how well a civilization is thriving. Show me a nation that rejects evolution on the basis of some religion—it's always religion—and I'll show you a society in trouble. The chart on page 60 reveals that at least 40 percent of the adult US population believes evolution is false, and another 20 percent is confused about the issue. *See* for yourself! In a plunge for the bottom of the pile, the US beats out Turkey, the only Muslim country on the chart. Here the American creationists are among friends, their fellows from Iran, Iraq, Afghanistan, Jordan, Saudi Arabia, the Emirates, Yemen, Somalia, Syria, and so on. These are your intellectual bedfellows—now lie down with them. In Kazakhstan just 28 percent of the people believe evolution is false compared to 40-60 percent in

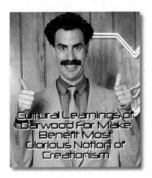

Borat

the USA. And this may be behind the confused reasoning of Borat when he said, "Cultural Learnings of [Charles] Darwood [Darwin] for Make Benefit Glorious Notion of Creationism."

HOMOPHOBIA: The Bible contains only 6 condemnations of homosexuals but an incredible 362 reprimands for heterosexuals. Obviously the straights were having too much fun and God had to stop that. Remember, it's pain now, pain later. Perhaps the paucity of chastisements for gays was the result of strict observance of Leviticus 20:13 to kill them. Although there is no direct injunction to kill homosexuals in the Qur'an, as in the Bible, it comes close enough in Surah 7:80-81 quoted previously.

A country that severely represses female rights, like Iran, is also the most severely homophobic and that surely is their policy. As of September 2007, Amnesty International calculated that 200 people had been executed in the previous nine months—many of them homosexuals. While speaking at Columbia University that year, their most glorious president, Mahmoud Ahmadinejad said to peals of uproarious laughter, "In Iran we don't have homosexuals like in your country." Perhaps he thinks he's killed them all.

Canada has recognized gay marriage for several years and despite the calamitous predictions of Mr. and Mrs. Sodom and Gomorrah and by the Born Agains, nothing—absolutely nothing—has happened. By recognizing gay marriage, the US, state by state, is progressing from Abrahamic Bronze Age bigotry to enlightenment. Having said that, if you *Google* "Kill Homosexuals," you get about thousands of sites. What's going on here? Almost all these websites quote the Bible or Qur'an to support their position—and they are correct in doing so. The aptly named televangelist Jimmy Swaggart, strutting about on his blood-red carpeted stage, clearly expresses the biblical position:

> I've never seen a man in my life that I wanted to marry . . . . I'm
> going to be blunt . . . If one of them ever looks at me like that
> I'll kill him and tell god he died.

Along with his other mental impairments, Swaggart is losing his
memory: the sixth commandment says, "Thou shall not kill" or
"You shall not murder." Nonetheless, he is correct about homosexuality. It's right there in Leviticus; it always has been.

We will leave these expressions of hate and homicide to the
sick and the dead—those brutes who remain true to the Bible and
Qur'an. Once again Americans are bedfellows—pun intended—
with their homophobic kin in the Middle East. Since then, the
majority of us have grown up and departed from such savagery.

MORALITY: In the late Roman Empire, when almost every aspect
of their government was in need of reform, Romans concentrated
on preserving the virginity of young women. In today's right-
wing America the essence of morality is opposition to abortion,
tax cuts for the very rich, and stopping gay marriage legislation—sounds similar. And seemingly a relationship with Jesus—
whatever that means—is more important than what he actually
preached or what the vast majority thinks he preached. Believe
in the Bible but don't bother to read it or know what it truly says.

Ask a born-again Christian to tell you the Ten Commandments, and only 40 percent can name even four. Some poor
wretches can't name any, but they will tell you with total sincerity
that the moral backbone of America depends on these ten. Since
they don't know them, study them, or understand them, where do
they acquire what morals they have? Like wolves, whales, and
elephants, they get them from their group or social milieu.

I'm happy to say the majority of Americans, and almost all
Canadians and Europeans have a kinder, gentler, and broader
moral code than this. Woman's right to choose, gay marriage,
the abolition of the death penalty, and universal health care—the
golden rule at work—are a few of the signposts you are on a different road in another world.

For both groups, however, there is an inconsistency, more
crucial for the first group than the second. The nearly universal
claim is that God, Allah, or Yahweh gave us our moral code as

delineated in the New Testament, the Qur'an, and the Torah for once, for all, and forever. Yet in the West, at least, we have abandoned many of these commandments—such as stoning rebellious children to death—under personal revulsion and a fear of arrest from authorities. That inexorably implies there must be a moral source other than this triumvirate of desert deities, and this source has made us a kinder and gentler people. We understand that a basic part of our evolutionary heritage is as a group animal. The other part—and I make no claim that this list is exhaustive—is our cultural heritage, but exactly which culture makes all the difference. Is yours Jerusalem or Athens, that is biblical or classical Greek? By taking the better parts of each, some would say it was both. But the best thing about Athens is it isn't Jerusalem, and the best thing about Jerusalem is it isn't Mecca.

In Tennyson's immortal poem *Ulysses* (Latin), a.k.a. *Odysseus* (Greek), expresses the evolution of morality. In the initial lines of the poem, Ulysses complains of his unsuitability for leading his people out of barbarism:

> *It little profits that an idle king,*
> *By this still hearth, among these barren crags,*
> *Matched with an aged wife, I mete and dole*
> *Unequal laws unto a savage race,*
> *That hoard, and sleep, and feed, and know not me.*

Some lines later, he recognizes his son Telemachus as having the right stuff to do what he cannot:

> *This is my son, mine own Telemachus,*
> *To whom I leave the sceptre and the isle—*
> *Well-loved of me, discerning to fulfil*
> *This labour, by slow prudence to make mild*
> *A rugged people, and through soft degrees*
> *Subdue them to the useful and the good.*

As I've shown elsewhere, we in Western civilization are the children of Odysseus, the man who was never at a loss. We are heirs to a cultural past like no other. We have avoided the worst of those dark irrational voices from Zoroastrianism, Pythagoreanism, and Judaism. Yet, just as we are freeing ourselves from a chorus of Christian fanatics, we are being assaulted by similar voices from Islam. Now it's our turn to act as Telemachus to the Muslims and win them over to reason, science, and a shared morality by example and discussion, not guns and destruction. And it could take a hundred years. But judging by our past confrontations, this may be impossible to achieve. We remember the carnage of 9/11; Muslins have longer memories and recall the medieval Crusades. The Internet and the social media, however, are encouraging signs of change. The clash is between knowledge and certainty—science and religion—not Christianity and Islam.

SECOND ROUND: God 0, Humanity 2

VIRTUE ABOVE ALL ELSE

The Abrahamic religions have no tolerance for private vice, none whatsoever! They wish to monitor every bedroom and every thought of every American. This is in accord with the tenth com-

It's kinda chilly. Throw another lawyer on the fire.

mandment* which is a statement of mind control because *covet* is a mental not an observable activity. Christians have a singular and well defined concept of sin as *unbelief* or its twin *disobedience*. This has been quite consistent through the centuries. Thomas Aquinas wrote, "unbelief is the greatest of sins." An identical statement to this could easily come from any monotheistic religion or political dictator. Imagine even questioning the great President for all Eternity, Kim Il-sung—now deceased—of North Korea, or his fat farm failure son, Kim Jong-il—now also deceased, or his son, the clone, Kim Jong-un. You would be imprisoned almost before you had completed your question.

---

* "You shall not covet your neighbor's house. You shall not covet your neighbor's wife, or his male or female servant, his ox or donkey, or anything that belongs to your neighbor." Exodus 20:17 (NIV).

And you would be a foolish person indeed, if you thought born-again Christians wouldn't revert to this missionary position when given political power. Right now from America's wasteland of Ecclesiastistan, you can hear their clamorous calls for control:

> Yes, religion and politics do mix. America is a nation based on biblical principles. Christian values dominate our government. The test of those values is the Bible. Politicians who do not use the Bible to guide their public and private lives do not belong in office. Beverly LaHaye (Concerned Women for America)

> There should be *absolutely* no Separation of Church and State in America. David Barton (WallBuilders)

> Behind this judicial wall of separation there is a tyranny of lies that will fall . . . I say to you, my friends, let it fall!
> A good butt-whipping and then a prayer is a wonderful remedy. Fob James (Governor of Alabama)

> The wall of separation between church and state is a metaphor based on bad history, a metaphor which has proved useless as a guide to judging. It should be frankly and explicitly abandoned. William Rehnquist (Chief Justice of the U.S. Supreme Court)

If—perhaps I should say when—these uni-brain fundamentalists gain political power, the United States of America will become another failed state like Pakistan, Afghanistan, Somalia, and so many others in the Middle East. The First Amendment, "Congress shall make no law respecting an establishment of religion, or prohibiting the free exercise thereof." will be repealed—perhaps the entire Bill of Rights will be thrown out. The schools will indoctrinate creationism, and what little sex education there is will be abolished replaced by the great law of abstinence. Christian prayers will permeate the school day; Bible study will replace Shakespeare, Walt Whitman, and *To Kill a Mockingbird*. Music class and glee clubs will be restricted to the singing of hymns. History will be rewritten and refocused on Jerusalem and the Bible. Illiteracy and innumeracy rates will climb to even higher levels. All the world's great books will be banned and we'll only have Christian fiction and the *Left Behind* series on the rapture. Science and engineering schools will be devoid of students; law schools will mainly study the Ten

Commandments. Every public place will have displays of these laws carved in stone like Roy's Rock[*] in the Alabama State legislature. With no sex education, teenage pregnancy rates will rise, and a woman's right to choose will be annulled—that is *Roe v. Wade*. What little heath care there is for the poor will vanish; social programs will be underfunded, life expectancy will fall, and murder rates will rise even higher. As in the Dark Ages there will be two classes of people: the lavishly rich and the rest of us, the poor riff-raff. Remember, "God helps those who help themselves," and they certainly will. The great American dream founded on the principles of the Enlightenment will be but a flickering candle in a dark and cruel world, and the rest of us will quietly stand and curse the night.

These new Christian sharia-type laws will be vigorously enforced until the prisons burst. As Romans 14:11 (KJV) says and the bumper stickers affirm, "Every knee shall bow to me." Disbelief will be the ultimate crime, and if history is any guide, the greatest virtues will be something to do with the suppression of sex. A few pages back I alluded to the preservation of virginity as the supreme virtue in the disintegrating Roman Empire. St. Jerome, an early church father, wrote many letters to young women and ladies on how they could preserve their virginity— welcome advice I'm sure. In his monumental *History of Western Philosophy* Bertrand Russell comments on this:

> [I]n a letter to a friend who has decided to devote his daughter to perpetual virginity, and most of it is concerned with the rules to be observed in the education of girls so dedicated. It is strange that, with all Jerome's deep feeling about the fall of the ancient world, he thinks the preservation of virginity more important than victory over the Huns and Vandals and Goths. Never once do his thoughts turn to any possible measure of practical statesmanship; never once does he point out the evils of the fiscal system, or of reliance on an army composed of barbarians. The same is true of Ambrose and of

---

[*] Roy Moore, chief justice of Alabama's Supreme Court, had a 5,280-pound granite rock carved with the Commandments and set in the rotunda of the state's judicial building.

Augustine; Ambrose, it is true, was a statesman, but only on behalf of the Church. It is no wonder that the Empire fell into ruin when all the best and most vigorous minds of the age were so completely remote from secular concerns. [2]

Virtue, of course, is a most wonderful thing, but only if it's your virtue—ah there's the rub. We needn't go back to ancient Rome to see examples of this single-mindedness nonsense; it's in the nightly news. Consider the virtues (?) of the Taliban, which are tightly focused on Sharia law. One result is a multifaceted suppression of girls and women. Punishable offenses include such harmless behaviors as wearing socks not sufficiently opaque, showing wrists, hands, or ankles, and not being accompanied outside the house walls by a close male relative. One suspects that any part of an exposed breast could cause the earth to open up and swallow Afghanistan. Girls are not permitted an education even within the home, and NATO built schools are regularly bombed, and some girls have had their faces disfigured with acid as punishment just for attending.

Human behavior is such that we can be impassive to what happens to thousands, but transfixed by the tragedy of one. The story of an Afghan girl Bibi Aisha is such a case and her ultimate triumph of spirit and recovery is inspiring. At 12, Aisha and her younger sister were given to the family of a Taliban fighter to settle a blood feud; at 16 she married this Taliban. She and her sister were treated as slaves and housed with the other livestock. Because of her spirited nature, Aisha escaped, but her husband tracked her down in Kandahar. And with the assistance of his

brother, who pinned her to the ground, he sliced off her ears and then her nose. Bleeding profusely and unconscious from the trauma, she was left for dead. Incredibly, she awoke and crawled to her grandfather's house, and her father took her to an American medical facility. After treatment she was transported to a secret shelter for women in Kabul. Then by pure chance she was

Aisha with Prosthetic
Nose and a Smile

photographed by a *Time* reporter and ended up on the August, 2010, cover issue of that magazine. Never before had *Time* published such a controversial cover of a face—so disfigured, so mutilated that it caused an outrage. Some thought *Time* had gone too far; everyone knew the Taliban had. Although I agree with their decision to use the photograph, I will not reproduce it here. Rather, look above and witness what the kindness and reason of American doctors can accomplish. The prosthetic nose is temporary while the doctors attempt to rebuild a real one. The fate of her younger sister, still with this Taliban family, is unknown.

When the Taliban were in power, they also prohibited kite flying, music, dancing, films, and female voices on the radio and TV. What was allowed? Favorite activities, often staged in soccer stadiums, were beatings, stonings, amputations of hands and feet, and decapitations. When some concept of "virtue" is placed above all else, this is where humans can descend to. Natural feelings of empathy and kindness vanish and a beast emerges to scour the earth be it the Christians in the Inquisition or Muslims during the reign of the Taliban. This is always done in the name of some higher good—political or religious. To paraphrase Mark Twain: when you realize all religions are *mad* and their fervent followers *insane*, then the mysteries disappear and their world stands explained.

THIRD ROUND: God 0, Humanity 3

THE TWO FACES OF JESUS

Forget questioning Kim Jong-un; imagine questioning Jesus on his claim to divinity. This "Savior" must be awarded full credit for starting the Christian cruelty we saw before, during, and after the Inquisition. *See* John 8:24 (NIV):

> *I told you that you would die in your sins; if you do not believe that I am he, you will indeed die in your sins.*

Jesus, however, was often unwilling to wait for the afterlife to punish the disobedient unbelievers. *See* Luke 19:27 (NIV):

> *But those enemies of mine who did not want me to be king over them—bring them here and kill them in front of me.*

Yes, that's actually in the Bible but Saddam Hussein or any other monomaniac could have said it, but instead it was the meek and mild Jesus of Christian mythology. Beyond this wickedness of the "Savior" is something far worse, if possible. Jesus believed in hell, he taught about hell, and he threatened unbelievers and believers alike with hell. But, and you may find this hard to accept, the Old Testament makes *no mention of hell* whatsoever. It is entirely the invention of the Gospel writers reporting (?) Jesus' words. On rare occasions, never in the Torah, the Old Testament uses the word *Gehenna* to refer to a valley outside Jerusalem where apparently in certain sacrifices children were burned alive to appease the gods. Some Bible translators incorrectly substitute *hell* for *Gehenna*. Yet, why do they translate *Jerusalem* for *Jerusalem* and *Nazareth* for *Nazareth*, but they choose *hell* for *Gehenna* and *Hades*? For the same reason these translators chose *servant* over *slave*, theological bias.

Nothing in pagan and Hebrew tradition offers a nightmare equal to the Christian and Islamic hell: the pagans had hades, the Hebrews, Sheol, but these were poorly defined, morally neutral domains.

You should be astounded to learn that the meek and mild Jesus said more about hell than anyone else in the Bible, and continuously warned the hell-bound about their future vacation prospects. Sometimes Jesus liked to cast unbelievers into the fiery furnace himself; other times his angels did it for him. *See* Matthew 13:42 (KJV):

And shall cast them into a furnace of fire:
there shall be wailing and gnashing of teeth.

Like a bad penny, Christ has two faces in the Gospels: the mild and gentle Jesus and the vindictive and daemon Jesus. We have all seen the first face ad nauseam, so let's rent the curtain concealing the second. This face was prevalent during the Inquisition, the burning of heretics, and the endless witch hunts. In the past, this is how they behaved—time, secularism, science, and their loss of political power has given us a kinder, gentler church, at least in Europe and America. All their past incredibly immoral behaviour follows directly from the teaching that unbelief is the greatest of all sins. This behaviour was not a bizarre twisting of the biblical message; it issues directly from the core of the Gospels. Look for yourself. This is how men behave when they believe they have absolute knowledge with no test in reality. When virtue, which is defined as belief in Jesus, becomes the ultimate value, the consequence is the criminalization of sin—in this case disobedience leading to disbelief. Recall John 14:6 (NIV) where Jesus says, "I am the way and the truth and the life. No one comes to the Father except through me."

In *Why I Am Not a Christian* the philosopher Bertrand Russell clearly delineates the moral character of Jesus as revealed in the Gospels:

> There is one very serious defect to my mind in Christ's moral character, and that is that He believed in hell. I do not myself feel that any person who is really profoundly humane can believe in everlasting punishment. Christ certainly as depicted in the Gospels did believe in everlasting punishment, and one does find repeatedly a vindictive fury against those people who would not listen to His preaching—an attitude which is not uncommon with preachers, but which does somewhat detract from superlative excellence. . . .
>
> You will find that in the Gospels Christ said, "Ye serpents, ye generation of vipers, how can ye escape the damnation of Hell." That was said to people who did not like His preaching. It is not really to my mind quite the best tone, and there are a great many of these things about hell. There is, of course, the familiar text about the sin against the Holy Ghost: "Whosoever speaketh against the Holy Ghost it shall not be forgiven him neither in this World nor in the world to come." That text has caused an unspeakable amount of misery in the world, for all sorts of people have imagined that they have committed the sin against the Holy Ghost, and thought that it would not be forgiven them either in this world or in the world to come. I really do not think that a person with a proper degree of kindliness in his nature would have put fears and terrors of that sort into the world.
>
> Then Christ says, "The Son of Man shall send forth His angels, and they shall gather out of His kingdom all things that offend, and them which do iniquity, and shall cast them into a furnace of fire; there shall be wailing and gnashing of teeth"; and He goes on about the wailing and gnashing of

teeth. It comes in one verse after another, and it is quite manifest to the reader that there is a certain pleasure in contemplating wailing and gnashing of teeth, or else it would not occur so often. Then you all, of course, remember about the sheep and the goats; how at the second coming He is going to divide the sheep from the goats, and He is going to say to the goats, "Depart from me, ye cursed, into everlasting fire." He continues, "And these shall go away into everlasting fire." Then He says again, "If thy hand offend thee, cut it off; it is better for thee to enter into life maimed, than having two hands to go into Hell, into the fire that never shall be quenched; where the worm dieth not and the fire is not quenched." He repeats that again and again also. I must say that I think all this doctrine, that hell-fire is a punishment for sin, is a doctrine of cruelty. It is a doctrine that put cruelty into the world and gave the world generations of cruel torture; and the Christ of the Gospels, if you could take Him as His chroniclers represent Him, would certainly have to be considered partly responsible for that.

. . . I cannot myself feel that either in the matter of wisdom or in the matter of virtue Christ stands quite as high as some other people known to history. I think I should put Buddha and Socrates above Him in those respects. [3]

Among the world's many "sacred" texts only the Qur'an dwells more and with more relish on hell than Jesus in the Gospels. All religions are correct and in agreement on one point: each "knows" that all the other religions are *false*. On the subject of hellfire and eternal damnation, however, Jesus and Muhammad are in perfect harmony—so either one is right or both are wrong.

FOURTH ROUND: God 0, Humanity 4

THE SINS OF THE FATHERS

It all begins in an unlikely place for a Darwinian evolutionist: the Garden of Eden that I wrote about at the beginning of this chapter. After a little hanky-panky in the orchard, something bizarrely unexpected happened. God—the creator of the universe, master of a gazillion worlds, a being of infinite existence, an entity living in eternal bliss, happiness, and perfect health—has a monumental hissy fit! He curses Adam to hard labor, Eve to hard childbirth, and both to eventual death, and he sends them east of

Eden out of paradise. Moreover, God laid a multigenerational curse on Adam and Eve's descendants for their parents' sin of disobedience a.k.a. original sin. Two Hail Marys and one Our Father should have been enough.

This was not an isolated incidence of unbridled rage, but a distinct character trait. In Exodus 20:5 (NIV), the second commandment, God brags about his generational punishments:

> *I, the LORD your God, am a jealous God, punishing the children for the sin of the parents to the third and fourth generation of those who hate me.*

I wonder how many of us would be inclined to pay our long-dead grandfather's parking tickets. None I suspect! Therein lies the divide between the *generational guilt* of the Old Testament and modern thought. Why should the son pay for the sins of the father? Clearly the father of Bibi Aisha thought his daughters should for earlier family guilt. Yahweh clearly thinks so too.

There may also be blame over space as well as time. And this results in tribal justice or *group guilt*, another biblical and Qur'anic favorite. Consider the mass extinctions of the men, women, children, and the yet unborn, as in Noah's flood, and you have perfect knowledge of God's "perfect" justice. This is still preached from pulpits and in Sunday schools as a soporific to the already somnolent and a deadening agent to inquiring minds. In his autobiography, Mark Twain commented on this collective guilt concept:

> I was educated, I was trained, I was a Presbyterian and I knew how these things are done. I knew that in Biblical times if a man committed a sin the extermination of the whole surrounding nation—cattle and all—was likely to happen. I knew that Providence was not particular about the rest, so that He got somebody connected with the one He was after.

Tribalism or collective guilt still flourishes in the darker backwaters of the human mind whether you are Jewish, Christian, Muslim, or ideologically indoctrinated. The Holocaust laid collective guilt on all Jews, homosexuals, and gypsies because of an accident of birth. No individuality or nuances here—just kill the bastards! This is the place ignorance and dogma—religious and political—can descend to. The 9/11 terrorists attacks are examples every reader remembers. Reactions in the Muslim world varied from deep and sincere regret to protests that this was not Islam, the religion of peace. Some saw it differently, danced in the streets, and let up the barbaric shout that the dead were all guilty just because they were all Americans.

Well, they weren't all Christian Americans. At least thirty-one were Muslims: one was a seven-month pregnant woman and another was a sixty-five year old janitor. But the apologists would say, "Why worry about that; they're all Americans and therefore guilty." This is the primal mind at work—Qur'anic tribalism. It should terrify the reader to know that someday soon these cretins will have nuclear weapons and no inhibitions on pressing the button and going directly to paradise or elsewhere. After all, we are just infidels. This is the ancient tribal concept of collective guilt, alive in the modern world.

Consider Tariq Ramadan, regarded as Islamic royalty. His maternal father, Hasan al-Banna, founded the influential Muslim Brotherhood. Presently, Ramadan is professor of His Highness Hamad Bin Khalifa Al-Thani Chair in Contemporary Islamic Studies at Oxford University, and he is generally considered the moderate face of Islam to the West. What is his attitude on the 9/11 terrorist attacks? Remarkably, he has denied, along with almost all Islamists, that Bin Laden was responsible for 9/11. Secondly, he publicly calls 9/11 and other such attacks "interventions." Weasel words are an ancient ploy; the Priestess at Delphi used them to have wiggle room to go both ways. Ramadan once called for a "moratorium" on stoning* in Middle Eastern countries—another weasel word to please both sides.

This Islamic scholar's statements, however, were models of thoughtfulness and restraint compared to those of two fundamentalist American toads, Jerry Falwell and Pat Robertson. The following comes from the croaking of the Christian Broadcasting Network's "700 Club," hosted by Robertson. Falwell speaks first:

---

* Rabbinic law based on the authority of the Torah affixes death by stoning to eighteen crimes. The Qur'an never mentions stoning, although the Hadith wallows in such brutality.

"God continues to lift the curtain and allow the enemies of America to give us probably what we deserve."

"Jerry, that's my feeling," Robertson chirped. "I think we've just seen the antechamber to terror. We haven't even begun to see what they can do to the major population."

Falwell, who detests freedom it would seem, said the American Civil Liberties Union has "got to take a lot of blame for this," while Robertson gulped in agreement, "Well, yes."

Then Falwell's throat filled with wind, and he began a rhetorical rant seldom heard but often thought in evangelical wastelands concerning throwing God out of the public square. He began: "The abortionists have got to bear some burden for this because God will not be mocked. And when we destroy 40 million little innocent babies, we make God mad. I really believe that the pagans, and the abortionists, and the feminists, and the gays and the lesbians who are actively trying to make that an alternative life style, the ACLU, People for the American Way—all of them who have tried to secularize America—I point the finger in their face and say, 'You helped this happen.' "

Jerry Falwell

If all the beautiful princesses in Hollywood kissed these two toads until sundown, they would still be toads in the morning.

It seems to me that the Abrahamic religions are impaled on the horns of a dilemma: intellectual falsity and moral turpitude. And it's the latter that concerns us here. Although as Christopher Hitchens has said, "Falsity is part of the wickedness of religion." By accepting generational and collective guilt as somehow justifiable, fundamentalists group themselves by default with Adolf Hitler, Ratko Mladić, Pol Pot, the Rwanda genocides, the Armenian genocide, and all ethnic cleansers. As disturbing as that is, Falwell and Robertson were correct on one point: God agrees with them on every point. The Bible has a tribal perspective thinking in terms of groups not individuals although both Jeremiah 31:30 and Ezekiel 18:20 dissent from this viewpoint, but no one was listening. Falwell and Robertson were more honest and biblically based in their comments as were the Islamic clerics who declared Mohammed Atta and his fellow terrorists to be heroic martyrs punishing the evil Americans, of whom none are innocent.

For all those who aspire to sit in the presence of Almighty God for eternity, ask yourself the following question. Is it possible you may be mistaken? The rest of us are not gods, nor do we aspire to be gods, we are just normal human beings hopefully free of fixed ideologies both political and religious who from the deepest parts of our nature deem generational and collective guilt as overwhelmingly immoral. Ask yourself if you are not merely toadies at the feet of the devil himself. It's not just that religion is false that I contend; it's the other horn—immorality.

FIFTH ROUND: God 0, Humanity 5

JESUS AND JUSTICE

Who says I am not under the special protection of God?

During a debate for the nomination of the Republican candidate for president, George W. Bush was asked to name his favorite political philosopher. This most uncurious of men stumbled around in his vacuous mind to finally blurt out "Jesus." Realizing George had accidentally hit a home run, several other GOP candidates quickly followed suit.

Despite the wisdom of George W. Bush, Jesus was not a philosopher but a Jewish rabbi particular to his time and place. I have clearly shown one of Jesus' moral shortcomings: his implacable fury toward all those who do not accept him as their messiah. Contrast this with the spirit of Socrates in *Plato's dialogues*. The Athenian gadfly serenely accepts those who disagree with him—he even calmly accepted the city's death sentence for corrupting the youth by teaching them to reason and be skeptical. With equanimity, he drank the hemlock and then asked a friend to repay a debt he owed. This is the reason Russell ranked Socrates morally superior to Jesus.

In an earlier chapter, I noted a second moral defect—one common to every Hebrew prophet, including Jesus and Paul of Tarsus. None of them spoke a word condemning the great evil of slavery although the Greek playwright Euripides had done so in the 5th century BCE.

Many of the wonderful maxims of the Gospels can be found in earlier Jewish writing—much of it from Rabbi Hillel. The Golden Rule is in every culture (*see* pages 96-97 of Chapter 4), and its first appearance in the Bible is in Leviticus 19:18. What is original with Jesus? Let's examine God's "perfect" justice, a foundational element in every animal group, especially primates.

In the previous section, "The Sins of the Fathers," I dissected generational and tribal guilt. Nevertheless, today's Christians will quickly dismiss this with a supercilious wave of their hand. While doing this they pronounce that Jesus came to replace the rigidity of the Old Testament with its "eye for an eye" with the New Testament's "love your neighbor as yourself." Let's examine this claim in light of what Jesus actually said—I would think that should matter.

The scribes, also called the teachers of the law, and others frequently questioned Jesus on his position regarding the prophets of the Torah. He pronounced on this immediately after delivering the Beatitudes in Matthew 5:17-18 (NIV):

> *"Do not think that I have come to abolish the Law* or the Prophets; I have not come to abolish them but to fulfill them. For truly I tell you, until heaven and earth disappear, not the smallest letter, not the least stroke of a pen, will by any means disappear from the Law until everything is accomplished.*

The above is a sweeping general statement of *total* agreement with the Torah. But just so the reader may know in what harmonic resonance Jesus was with the details of these "laws" consider the following from Mark: 7:9-10 (NIV):

> *And he [Jesus] continued, "You have a fine way of setting aside the commands of God in order to observe your own traditions! For Moses said, 'Honor your father and mother,' and, 'Anyone who curses their father or mother is to be put to death.'*

---

* Christians refer to the Torah as the Pentateuch, meaning five books, or as the Law, or Law of Moses while Muslims call the Torah "Tawrat."

You may wish to reread this. Yes, Jesus is criticising the Jews *for not killing* their disobedient children according to Old Testament law; he repeated this demand to murder in Matthew 15:3-4. Of all the horrific decrees from the Old Testament to be in perfect harmony with, the "gentle" Jesus chose the worst. If anyone said that today, the state wouldn't be able to afford him the years of necessary psychotherapy. Clearly, Jesus was just a Jewish rabbi—albeit a troubled one—particular to his time and his place. The fault lies not so much with him but with those who still follow these Bronze Age ravings just because they're from an ancient book. But, of course, *civilized* people don't follow them; they have moved on to higher moral ground.

Stone throwers have a well-developed technique to prolong the pain of their wretched victims. Start with your smallest stones, gradually working your way up to the rocks. That way the target will remain conscious for as long as possible.

Some years past, I was with a group of Christian and freethinker friends. The topic of stoning was raised by a nonbeliever who proceeded to read Leviticus 20:9 on killing disobedient children. Naturally he asked the Christians if they could endorse this, but they pointed out this was from the Old Testament that Jesus had come to replace. The sceptic then read Matthew 5 from the previous page pointing out that Jesus was speaking. The true believers again emphasised that Jesus would not condone the stoning to death of children. The sceptic's paradox trap was now set, and so he read Mark 7 where Jesus reveals himself as a lifetime member, in good standing, of the stonethrowers.

Two Christians, realizing what had happened, quickly left, but the remainder stayed and offered various explanations or ways to extricate the "gentle' Jesus from the stoning Jesus. The first was to be expected: you are reading this out of context—to which someone replied what possible context could justify this. And then like the oysters in *The Walrus and the Carpenter* the excuses trotted forth, "And thick and fast they came at last, and more, and more, and more." *Occasionally* we get these weird statements in the Bible—maybe this person hasn't read the whole book. If such an order were enforced today, we wouldn't need our prisons or legal system—much like North Korea with its political labor camps. He deserved to be killed because he was over fourteen and drunk—new criteria for the death penalty. The people had to kill him, or God would punished the entire country—collective guilt. And so it goes to its dreary close.

A paradox is a powerful tool; it can force you to choose between two incompatible viewpoints. There are, however, alternatives. You may leave the room, or you may be so indoctrinated politically or religiously that you cannot make a logical deduction. Yet truth is a potent element in our lives and most of us want our beliefs to be proven true by reason and logic. So is he the gentle Jesus we have all been led to believe or the stonethrowing killer of children? If we accept that Matthew 5 and Mark 7 are the very words of Jesus, then it's the stonethrower. The scribes, whom the "Savior" was haranguing, had progressed morally beyond the Torah while Jesus had not.

The proposition that men and women are rational animals is false; rather they can be in normal circumstances with a little training. Reichsmarschall Hermann Göring said of Hitler, with some exaggeration, "If the Führer wants it, two and two makes five!" At the beginning of this section on JESUS AND JUSTICE was the following unidentified quote, "Who says I am not under the special protection of God?" Perhaps you thought Jesus said it or some saint or other. But no, it was Adolf Hitler. Delusions are everywhere. George Orwell in *Nineteen Eight-Four* wrote:

> In the end the Party would announce that two and two made five, and you would have to believe it. It was inevitable that they should make that claim sooner or later: the logic of their position demanded it. Not merely the validity of experience, but the very existence of external reality, was tacitly denied by their philosophy. The heresy of heresies was common sense.

How far can propaganda take you? Much further than we might have feared in our saner moments in the morning. Recall the Milgram experiment and its terrifying results—truly we are more sheep than goat. With sectarian schools, Madrassas, seminaries, political boot camps, youth rallies, and endless religious TV programming, we can be led to almost any belief: the wine and the wafer are the blood and the body of Christ; condoms cause AIDS; Jesus rose from the dead; if I send sounds into the air the creator of the universe hears them; Muhammad flew on a winged horse from Mecca to Jerusalem and back, and he regularly spoke to the angel Gabriel; God gave Moses two tablets and said call me in the morning. How far can propaganda take you? Far enough to see black is white or white is black or 2+2=5 if you start young and keep at it. Far enough to believe God's justice is perfect rather than perverted!

SIXTH ROUND: God 0, Humanity 6

THE SCAPEGOAT

Crucifixion was a common Roman method of prolonged execution. As noted in Chapter 4, the remnants of Spartacus' army, some 6,000 captives, were crucified along the Appian Way from Rome to Capua in a single day. According to Will Durant in his *Caesar and Christ*, their rotting bodies hung there for months as a warning to all slaves and a comfort to all masters. Legend says they were killed because none would identify Spartacus. And so, in a demonstration of collective punishment, the Roman general Crassus commanded his legions to crucify all of them. From the perspective of the slaves, they were willing scapegoats in order to protect the identity of their leader. As unlikely as this story is it has a higher probability of being true than the passion and crucifixion of Christ. We at least know there was a Spartacus and that 6,000 of his followers were crucified. In the case of Christ we are certain neither of his existence nor his crucifixion. For the sake of the discussion at hand, however, let's *assume* both are historical events.

The centerpiece of Christianity was never the fish but always the cross of crucifixion. Jesus was the sacrificial lamb whose blood would wash away the sins of all the ages. This most terrifying symbol of human sacrifice deserves close inspection. For those who haven't read all 39 books of the Protestant Old Testament—and who could blame them—they might be startled to learn how common human sacrifice was. Abraham was certain he was to sacrifice and burn his son's body; he even brought along the necessary wood for the fire—recall Yahweh loves the smell of burning flesh*. In a veritable *deus ex machina* an angel appears in the final seconds of this atrocity and stops Abraham from killing Isaac. Yet some scholars maintain this is a redacted tale and in the original, the "good" patriarch did cut his son's throat. Let's grant Christians the survival of the now traumatized Isaac and the suggestion that God was just testing Abraham's depth of faith. Now ask yourself what kind of a God or devil could demand—to prove your love for Him—that you sacrifice and burn your son? Even Freud didn't delve into such depths of depravity.

An American soldier returning to his hometown in the Midwest considers himself fortunate to be alive after having killed so many Taliban warriors. When he arrives home in his small town, his daughter—his only child—is overjoyed to see her father and runs to greet him with hugs and kisses. Nonetheless he cuts her throat and burns her lifeless body in a bonfire.

At trial, his "defense" is he gave a solemn vow to almighty God that if he were allowed to slaughter as many Taliban as possible and return home alive, he would sacrifice whoever came out the door of his home to greet him *first*.

This appalling tale is a modern retelling of the story of Jephthah from Judges 11:29-40. Read it for yourself; weep and be astonished! The obvious question for believers is why didn't God intervene and save her as he had Isaac. Do girls not have as much value as boys in the Bible? Like many others of her gender in the Old Testament, she was nameless. How stupid was Jephthah? Of course someone he loved would come out the door of his home to greet him, and become a scapegoat for his ignorant vow. And by the way, the New Testament thought this monster to be one of the great heroes of faith—see Hebrews 11:32.

Had I the powers of Shakespeare, I could not describe the depth of my disgust—not just for Jephthah—but all those present-day Christians who attempt to justify this ghastly act. Jephthah was a Bronze Age brute, but what excuse can today's believers possibly have? And this is where we are to get our morality?

---

* The aroma of burning flesh is a "sweet savor unto the lord"—so sweet, that this phrase occurs in the Old Testament twenty-three times. The slaughter demanded by Yahweh was truly monumental.

These wars between the Israelites and the neighboring peoples were all about land. As Sam Harris says, the Israelites thought they had hired an omniscient real estate broker in Yahweh, and this gave them the right—as long as they were totally obedient to his laws—to massacre with a clear conscience all those living on these lands. Jephthah said as much to the Amorite kings before he slaughtered them. This is the identical problem in the Arab-Israeli conflict today: Orthodox Jews believe God gave the land to them. This real estate broker from Jephthah's day is the same one in tonight's newspaper—Religion Ltd.

It's too dreary, too sickening to list any more of these atrocities from the Torah. They are easy to find if you look, but impossible to see if you don't wish to. As the famous Greek philosopher Anonymous said, the mind of the fundamentalist is like the pupil of the eye: the more light you pour in the more it will contract. These blind beings are like the priests who wouldn't look through Galileo's telescope less they see something to upset their minor cosmologies—such as the moons of Jupiter. Remember everything was to rotate around Earth, the center of all God's creation, and not another planet.

Jesus is alleged to be the second person in the Trinity: God incarnate during his time on earth. John 1, 14 (NIV) proclaims:

In the beginning was the Word, and the Word was with God, and the Word was God. . . . The Word became flesh and made his dwelling among us.

In John 10:30 (NIV) Jesus says, "I and My Father are one."

Jesus the avatar has two major problems: the first is intellectual limitations; the second, moral imperfections. Let's consider his limitations. He was convinced the Jews of his day were living in the End Times. This belief* and no other would seem to account for his declaration in Matthew 16:28 (KJV):

Verily I say unto you, There be some standing here, which shall not taste of death, till they see the Son of man coming in his kingdom.

---

* This conviction gave rise to the curious legend of the Wandering Jew.

Jesus was running all over Palestine telling the people not to worry about the material world or their relationships saying things such as consider the lilies of the field, they neither spin nor weave. Leave your father and your mother and follow me! Take no thought of the morrow! These are morally irresponsible statements unless . . . unless you firmly believe you are living in the End Times. The Jews did believe the apocalypse was at their door, and clearly Jesus did as well, and in this he was mistaken and therefore intellectually flawed.

There is no cogent reason to believe Jesus' statements listed above are not similar to those of Harold Camping who entertained us in the previous chapter. Also, there is no reason to believe Jesus was lying. Like Camping, he was simply deluded as were vast numbers of the Jewish population in those days. I can't seem to discover how many followers Camping had—post apocalypse few are willing to admit accepting his nonsense—but surely tens of thousands, maybe a million. Fundamentalists will tell you, however, that was Camping not Jesus. Without apprehending the incongruity of their words, Christians will say what does it matter if Jesus was wrong on the time of the Apocalypse/the Second Coming/the rapture, after all, he is God.

We have previously shown Jesus' many moral limitations: he said nothing against slavery, yet he preached vigorously on the horrors of hell. You could say the gentle Jesus invented hell. Here we'll consider another moral deficiency.

Consider the crucifixion, the *sine qua non* of Christian iconography—the impetus behind a million road signs declaring, "He died for your sins," the lamb as the scapegoat. Give up your personal responsibility, sin as you please, but in the end just cast all your iniquities on Christ and you will be forgiven by God's grace. As Jesus said to the penitent thief, "Today you will be with me in paradise."

This concept of saved by grace or baptism or whatever can have unexpected consequences. Consider how St. Constantine used this notion to his service—recall that Constantine was the first *Christian* Roman Emperor. The circumstances of his conversion are most curious and illustrate the unusual fallout of being "saved by baptism." It was a favorite practice of Constantine to kill or have killed whoever annoyed him. At times that included his wife, his son, various relatives, and most of his in-laws. Somehow it dawned on his serpentine mind that he had been a naughty, naughty boy, so he went to the Mithraic Holy Father to ask forgiveness. Unfortunately for Western civilization, this religious leader bluntly told him his crimes were unpardonable. Ever the opportunist the emperor turned to Christians who informed him all his sins could be washed away by baptism. And since Jesus differed from Mithras in name only, Constantine promptly converted.

Since baptism with its sin-removal quality can be performed only once, the cunning emperor delayed the event. For the remainder of his life he kept a priest at his side with instructions to immerse him the moment his death appeared imminent. In years thereafter he could sin with great abandonment with his free ticket to heaven close by. And as far as anyone knows, it worked. After his blessed departure—according to a particularly perceptive Church Father named Lactantius—Constantine was deemed "a model of Christian virtue and holiness." So the church had to make him a saint even without the obligatory two miracles. The concept of *saved by grace* abrogates personal accountability and so does an end-run around individual responsibility.

Innumerable ancient societies practiced human sacrifice through various means on an irregular or seasonal basis. Believers know there are gods or godlets and we should have dealings with them. All such deities are modelled in the minds of the faithful on earthly dictators and potentates. And how do you propitiate these ever-angry beings? Apparently by the most brutal act conceivable—human sacrifice. The ancient Jews and Romans did not rise above this barbarism because their crucifixion of Jesus stands astride this tradition as its apotheosis.

The crucifixion of Jesus was an immoral act done for immoral reasons. With the wink of his eye or a wave of his hand, God the Father could have said all the sins of all the ages are forgiven and that would have been that. He chose, however, to have his son crucified for his own sadistic reasons. He chose this outcome rather than wave his hand or wink his eye. He chose to do this passion. He chose to have Judas betray Jesus. He then chose to punish Judas in hell for all eternity because he correctly followed the script. In the Garden of Eden, he chose to be offended. Free men and free women everywhere should choose not to accept such foolishness!

As for Jesus, the scapegoat, his immorality comes from accepting the ridiculous concept of generational guilt for original sin—*disobedience*, the one thing all dictators, bullies, and gods cannot tolerate. Jesus took it for granted that every man, woman, and child of every age was guilty because of a minor act of freedom by Adam and Eve. And then Jesus allowed himself to be crucified for reasons, as part of the Trinity, he made to happen. This is not a father-son relationship; it is sadomasochistic bondage.

SEVENTH ROUND: God 0, Humanity 7

SUMMARY DECISION OF THE JUDGES

In light of the deity's loss of all seven rounds in this morality boxing match the pseudo-Dostoyevsky question, "If God does not exist everything is permitted" must be reworded. The question should be "Where do Muslims, Christians, and Jews get their morality?" Surely it can't be from Allah, Jesus, or Yahweh who clearly have little or none. The answer is as apparent as the eyeglasses you are searching for that are resting on your forehead. Abraham's followers and freethinkers alike get their morals from their animal and cultural heritage of living in groups. As Aristotle said man is a social animal.

Walk into any nomadic encampment in central Asia, and you will be welcomed with tea and a meal. Meet some Inuit on the frozen tundra of northern Canada, and you will be fed and clothed. Stumble into any impoverished village in southern India, and you will be treated as a long-lost son. People everywhere are overwhelmingly kind and generous. A universal compassion exists among all peoples[*] who recognize the adversity of the human condition. The concept of original sin is diabolical nonsense and it has inflicted immense pain for millennia.

---

[*] This does not exclude the fact that most of these societies had their own dark cults, practices, and beliefs.

This common humanity existed before these people learned about the "joys" of Abrahamic submission. Religion divides, humanity unites.

What follows are the judges' summaries and further comments.

ROUND 1: God versus Humanity

Where does God get his morals? He's not a social being; he has no group. Either morals exist independently of him, or he makes them up. If they stand outside him, then we can have a morality without God, so let's consider the second alternative. If God gives us our morality, would you commit murder if he made it the eleventh commandment? This is usually referred to as the "Euthyphro dilemma" after Plato's dialogue of the same name. The philosopher phrased it as "Is the good loved by the gods because it is good? Or is it good because it is loved by the gods?" Since the Abrahamic god(s) love so many actions that are clearly evil, the first alternative is the only possible conclusion. Amazing isn't it that all the Hebrew prophets never thought of anything as simple as the Euthyphro dilemma. It took Socrates, a henpecked Athenian philosopher, who *never said* believe in me or you will go to hell. He just presented the logic to carry his argument, and for this, the state put him to death.

ROUND 2: Morals and the Old Testament

Now kill all the boys. And kill every woman who has slept with a man, but save for yourselves every girl who has never slept with a man.
Moses speaking in Numbers 31:17-18 (NIV)

ROUND 3: Virtue above All Else

Any society that places freedom above other values will always have individuals who abuse that freedom. Take a deep breath and look the other way at all such abuses so long as they harm no one. Religions must stay out of the bedrooms of humanity. All enlightened people have acknowledged this, but none so quickly as the ancient Greeks. Alfred North Whitehead once said that the Funeral Oration of Pericles should have been the final book of the Bible rather than the Book of Revelation. The following three sentences from that famous speech—delivered in 431 BCE—are taken from Thucydides' *Peloponnesian War*:

> And, just as our political life is free and open, so is our day-to-day life in our relations with each other. We do not get into a state with our next-door neighbor if he enjoys himself in his own way, nor do we give him the kind of black looks which, though they do no real harm, still do hurt people's feelings. We are free and tolerant in our private lives; but in public affairs we keep to the law. [4]

Fundamentalist Christians, all Muslims, and some Jews still wish to know what goes on in your bedroom and to control any sexual activity as much as possible. Incredibly, they think the creator of the universe is equally interested—but surely it can't be that interesting.

ROUND 4: The Two Faces of Jesus

In his youth, Charles Darwin studied to be a country parson; in later years, he was a world-class freethinker. His rejection of Christianity—indeed of all religions—was as much moral outrage against its dogmas as intellectual acumen about its doctrines. The following passage from page 87 of his autobiography makes this clear:

> Thus disbelief crept over me at a very slow rate, but was at last complete. The rate was so slow that I felt no distress, and have never since doubted even for a single second that my conclusion was correct. I can indeed hardly see how anyone ought to wish Christianity to be true; for if so the plain language of the text seems to show that the men who do not believe, and this would include my Father, Brother and almost all my best friends, will be everlastingly punished.

Then there are those wretches who claim they would enjoy watching the damned writhe in hell. Aquinas was one such sadist. He wrote, "The blessed will rejoice over the pains of the impious." This is an inhumane, sickening thought of a profoundly disturbed person who nonetheless is honored as the greatest

Catholic philosopher. And remember, Jesus invented hell to make converts and keep them. And it did, and it does.

The concept of hell has inflicted immense agony on millions for centuries—especially children. Mark Twain wryly remarked how pitiful were the poor Hawaiians who had gone to their graves for centuries before the missionaries arrived without knowing the least thing about hell. Christianity claims it will save us from hell, the very hell it invented in the first place. At least in Nazi death camps you could die only once.

ROUND 5: The Sins of the Fathers

When Adam and Eve practiced free will, God called it sin and like a small child having a temper tantrum he was angry for all the ages. Authoritarian structures whether religious, political, or military distrust freedom and believe it ultimately leads to decadence and disorder. The church thinks we are far too wicked to be free—the sheep need a shepherd and the shepherd needs dogs. Robert Browning caught the essence of this in four lines from his poem "The Italian in England":

> *"Freedom grows license," some suspect*
> *"Haste breeds delay," and recollect*
> *They always said, such premature*
> *Beginnings never could endure!*

Freedom has no greater enemy than religion, and when merged with politics, its power is inexorable. Consider collective guilt in the context of a theocracy. If the entire group will be punished for the sins of the few, then the group has a vested interest in the misdeeds of everyone. And inevitably that diminishes freedom by introducing morality police and peepholes in the bedrooms. Collective guilt is anathema to freedom.

ROUND 6: Jesus and Justice

None! The punishments of hell are too terrible to be just. And the eternal boredom of heaven is no better. Life becomes meaningless with infinite time just as diamonds would be valueless if they were as common as coal.

ROUND 7: The Scapegoat

Many have exploited the potential for profit by pandering to sado-masochism, but none so well as Hollywood actor and producer Mel Gibson in *The Passion of the Christ*. As an extreme right-wing Catholic, Gibson realized that with this subject he truly had found El Dorado. Perhaps Mel missed the verses where Jesus angrily drove the merchandisers out of the temple. The film is universally recognized by critics as anti-Semitic. Yet Pope Benedict XVI diplomatically side-stepped that issue by saying "it is as it happened." Gibson comes by his anti-Semitism through his father Hutter Gibson who said publicly that the Holocaust didn't happen. The apple didn't fall too far from the tree; in fact, it landed on its roots. The film also ranks as one of the violent and gory ever made. Except for the first 20, the remaining 106 minutes are just brutal, bloody, and bestial. Movie critic Roger Ebert said it was the most violent film he had ever seen. When the huge spikes were driven into Jesus' palms, an off-camera turkey baster spurts blood. The film is shot, not for any scintilla of truth, but to match the iconography of the Catholic Church. For example, the scene of Mary at the cross conforms to the overall layout of Michelangelo's *La Pietà*. Also Mary came to Jesus and kissed his foot, then blood poured into her mouth and dripped from her lips, and she appeared rather satisfied. A scripture flashed on the screen, it was about Jesus being the "water of life." This is, of course, the Catholic mass but it's also vampirism. Mel made millions, but millions of viewers of all ages were traumatized, and this is still happening in church basements and auditoriums all across America. Even more despicable is the abuse of this trauma to proselytize. Tim LaHaye said, "No film in my lifetime has the potential of impacting more people with the world's greatest story than *The Passion*. It could be Hollywood's finest achievement to date."

EPILOGUE

Mark Twain enjoyed pointing out that he was born with Halley's Comet in 1835, and he hoped to go out with it in 1910—and he did. Emperors and gods couldn't ask for a more illustrious entrance and exit. In 2010, Volume I of his *complete* autobiography was finally published. These are dictated ramblings, whims, non-sequiturs—a stream-of-consciousness technique long before its time. Most of this writing was left to his only surviving daughter Clara Clemens with directions not to publish it for a century. He thought the material was far too controversial for its time, but he need not have worried. During his lifetime, he had written such things and promoted such ideas before. With his complete mastery of language, dialogue, and humor, his packaging was so brilliant that America would take almost any medicine he prescribed. This closing quotation below sums up much of this chapter with such power and elegance, that I couldn't make a shadow on it. It's taken from chapter 11 of *The Mysterious Stranger*:

> A God . . . who mouths justice, and invented hell—mouths mercy, and invented hell—mouths Golden Rules and foregiveness multiplied by seventy times seven, and invented hell; who mouths morals to other people, and has none himself; who frowns upon crimes, yet commits them all; who created man without invitation, then tries to shuffle the responsibility for man's acts upon man, instead of honorably placing it where it belongs, upon himself; and finally, with altogether divine obtuseness, invites his poor abused slave to worship him!

CHAPTER—8

CULTURES IN COLLISION

Reason should be destroyed in all Christians.
Martin Luther

*If you give up on reason, you might as well
been born a plant.* Anonymous

When the earth was young and the summers green and carefree, my cousin and I would roam the fields in search of whatever we might find. We had no pre-scribed duties, except perhaps bringing the cows to the barn at dusk; we were rather the keepers of berry patches and bluebird nests. Since we weren't in search of rare animals like moose, wolves, or bears, we were never disappointed. Hollow fence posts had to be inspected for birds' nests, ponds for tadpoles, swamps for turtles, pools for gilled salamanders, and special hidden places we alone knew for snakes and the occasional blue skink.

We were unfettered in our natural interests. As far as we knew, the adults in our lives had little interest or knowledge of the world outside. Rarely did they speak about it—never a bird's name or a flower's location. Infrequently an aunt would express some fear or other, especially about poisonous snakes (we never found one), or skinks that might run up inside your pant leg to do great damage, or the ever-vicious wolves. On one occasion, a not too likeable aunt with an ugly goiter asked my cousin and me to capture a snake large enough to wrap around her neck twice, and then to release it before sundown. Local "wisdom" affirmed this would cause the goiter to shrivel up and disappear. Since she feared snakes, and we didn't particularly like her, we quickly granted her wish. Trusting adult wisdom, we fully expected the wretched disfigurement to vanish, but that never happened. So I learned grown-ups were not always wise.

In the two years following the snake debacle, my aunt tried various faith healers and herbalists, but by the time she sought proper medical treatment the growth had turned cancerous and spread. She died at forty-seven. Unfortunately, my cousin was ensnared by a belief in hucksterism and herbalism as well. As we grew up our roads diverged, his to the occult, mine to the more scientific, although we were and always will be friends. It's these two divergent paths—ways of thinking about the world—that I will concentrate on in this final chapter. The road of my aunt and cousin is more traveled and generally called idealism; mine is a newer and less worn trail usually termed realism. I would ask the reader to reflect on which household he or she was raised in: occult or rational. You may be unable to answer this question immediately. The differences are usually subtle and not often verbalized, and no one is entirely one or the other.

These words *idealism* and *realism* come in several nuances expressed by the antonyms in the chart below. Each describes a general thread but with different emphasis. The table could easily be expanded to *particular* antonyms such as creationism versus evolution, but more on that shortly.

TABLE OF ANTONYMS	
Idealism	Realism
Religion	Science
Non-rational	Rational
Occult	Science
Supernatural	Natural
Paranormal	Science

Everyone has a worldview even if they have never consciously thought about it. These will be a set of ideas, thoughts, and opinions you learned almost insentiently—they were in your mother's breast milk. Plato called this the unexamined life. Inevitably your worldview is the result of the culture you were raised in. Idealists believe ideas—even bad ones—are more important than the facts; these bad ideas could be bizarre folk wisdom or the thoughts of Hitler or Marx. Don't bother me with evidence, they would say, my mind is made up. So, if your parents were Christians almost certainly you will be too, a fortiori for Muslims and Jews. As the Jesuit motto says, "Give me a child until he is seven and I will give you the man." Or consider the words of another pope, the Soviet Communist Party Chairman, Vladimir Lenin, "Give me a child until he is five years old and I will own him for life."

Recall the Milgram experiment. Even with only a *single* authority figure 66 percent of the test subjects complied with outrageous instructions. And if they witnessed the previous subject conform, then the compliance rate rose to an astonishing 95 percent. Now consider the coercive power of an entire culture with thousands of authority figures and millions of conformists. It's a wonder anyone can revolt, but they always do. There is a little Prometheus in each of us.

The other road, the one less traveled, usually has to be pointed out by a mentor or teacher or you might never know it existed. It's a consciously *chosen* path that leads, I think, to a healthier, happier, and more fascinating world.

The idealism you defend comes from your particular culture, and since there are hundreds of cultures, so correspondingly there are hundreds of diverse idealisms. This explains the plethora of religions. Realism, on the other hand, in the guise of science, comes in a single form because it's based on a single observable reality at the macro level.

Idealists may reach for the stars, but realists know how to get there.

DEBATING A CREATIONIST

Some years ago, I unwisely debated a Young Earth Creationist for the entertainment of an educated audience. This person had written several books attempting to destroy Darwinian evolution. Rather than provide proof for their position—it's difficult to know what that would be—creationists try to demolish the opposition's assuming theirs is the only default position remaining. Putting that false assumption to one side, we each spoke for thirty minutes followed by a heated exchange. In any debate I have two general rules: make positive points and rarely ask questions. Peppering your opponent with questions only gives him the microphone while you're left standing there like a schoolboy waiting to be chastised.

The centerpiece of my talk was the speed of light—Einstein's foundational constant. The Danish astronomer Roemer made the first determination of light's velocity in the 1670s. Since then many scientists have measured this speed, and within the limits of the method used, they all got the same result to increasing decimals of accuracy. In Chapter 3, I showed how scientists used this constant speed to help determine the age of the universe at 13.7 billion years. To my debating opponent I simply noted that the light from the great Andromeda galaxy took 2.5 million light-years to reach Earth, and so the creation could not have happened 10,000 years ago.

His response was as unexpected as it was unanswerable. For him, God had caused the light *to go faster* in the past to allow creationist "theories" to come out correct. This makes "creationism" an unfalsifiable notion and therefore it doesn't qualify as a scientific theory. For an explanation to be scientific there must be the possibility, however remote, of proving it false. My opponent, by introducing God to solve his factual contradiction, had exited this possibility. Almost all idealistic theories are unfalsifiable while all the realistic ones are. This is a most human and honest position to adopt. Incidentally, Creationism is presently baptized "intelligent design," but formerly it was called "scientific creationism"—a perfect oxymoron.

AN ALLEGORY ON SCIENCE

". . . this place is sacred—thick-set with laurel, olive, vine;
and in its heart a feathered choir of nightingales makes music.
So sit thee here on this unhewn stone . . ."
Sophocles, Oedipus at Colonus

It's dark. Although the first gray mists of morning fill the east, sunrise seems a long way off as you huddle in the cold rocks with two fellow hunter-gatherers. From the plain below, the dark roars of the predators and the cries of their prey fill your mind with terror. This is the second night on the same hillock. The previous morning a pride of lions had killed a wildebeest near the base of the rocks; they had feasted on it all morning. After that, the jackals and vultures took what was left as the lions rested under a nearby acacia tree. The quickly rising sun was about to break over the eastern ridge while the roar of lions could still be heard in the distance. One old male returned to the bare bones of the beast in the hope of finding a forgotten fragment. Finally the moment has come, and with the sun shining full on your face, you and your friends break like a whirlwind from the rocks in an all-out running assault on the male lion. Your numbers, and the stones and sticks you carry, chase him from the standing rib cage. You don't slacken your pace until you reach the worthless prize. Even though you have driven the lion away, it seems you're a day late. But the older man takes a large wildebeest femur, places it on a flat rock, and smashes it with another rock. It splits revealing the rich marrow within—the prize you have been waiting for. Only wolverines, hyenas, and some wolves can crush bones with their jaws and reach this precious food source. Man does it with his brain. Welcome to the world of ideas.

Science probably began on the African plains through the developing ideas, tools, and animal tracking skills for survival, but the origins of the scientific method (SM) are a different matter. By the SM, I mean testing statements, beliefs, and ideas against the real world and having the willingness to change your mind depending on the results of these tests. The SM rests on honesty and truth; any scientist who breaks this moral code is drummed out. The SM is not some dry, stuffy idea mouthed by wimpy teachers terrified to offend anyone. It's the most powerful idea humankind has ever discovered—the sacred omega point of our brain development over millions of years. It can build skyscrapers, incredible aircraft, or rockets to the moon. It saves millions with antibiotics and vaccinations. It feeds the poor and comforts the afflicted. It entertains the planet with incredible electronic devices. It can bring down empires and send the religious scampering to their catacombs. When it questioned the divinity of kings, the rotation of the sun, and the origins of man, all hell broke loose. By using simple genetic markers, the SM has proven humans left Africa only 75,000 years ago—not long enough for any significant genetic diversity. And this makes racists into fools. The history of science should be taught in all the world's schools, and replace the sorry spectacle of kings, wars, dates, and the dreadful indoctrination of religious texts. Teach students the SM and to doubt and autocrats will tremble. Science offers freedom.

Enter two elderly Greeks, Epios and Phemios.

"Epios, have you ever wondered why we've lived so long?"

"Yes. Often! We have much in common, you and I, artist and scientist. Odysseus blessed you for keeping the suitors entertained and so distracting them from his wife, Penelope. As I recall, you sang so often of the Achaean heroes that Penelope herself asked you to sing a different song. And on that terrible, triumphant day after the returning hero had slaughtered everyone in the great hall except you and the priest, what did you do? You placed your lyre carefully on a table. If you were to be slain, you didn't want this instrument damaged. That's a lesson only a poet would teach. What did Odysseus do? He slew the priest and spared you saying he could not kill a man of God."

"Nothing in all these years," said Phemios "has dimmed your passion. You speak and think as clearly as when you designed and built the great wooden horse. Its construction ended the war, and Odysseus blessed you for your skill. I suppose in a way we're both the blessed sons of the wandering hero. Is that what you meant when you said we have much in common?"

"That's part of it. But it's impossible to recollect everything for a full comparison. Even though I've lived three millennia, there are vast periods—occasionally whole centuries—I don't recall. How can you think about what you can't remember?"

"I know what you mean," said the poet. "I wonder if the periods we recall and the ones we don't are the same."

They each got a mug of coffee from the kitchen and went to the solarium of their seniors' residence. In the morning sunlight, with coffee and oranges, they recalled their lives at leisure. The best remembered, sometimes the only remembered times, were ancient Greece to late Alexandria, the Renaissance, Modern Europe, and America. Their lives outside these periods were blurred, and the Dark Ages were indeed dark. Early Greece and the Renaissance, the two greatest periods of art, literature, and sculpture were also the times in which science was born, the times when the two men felt most alive.

"The biggest discovery of science is science itself," said Epios. "I mean humanity has for centuries—millennia even—looked for ways to influence nature to increase the food supply and cure disease. Before science we vainly prayed, performed sacrifices, and used other forms of magic, some still do. After all, the only purpose in praying to the gods is to have influence over them."

"But why wasn't the structure of science born all at once, full-grown and in complete armor, like Athena from the head of Zeus or art in the caves of Lascaux and Chauvet?" asked the poet.

"The deductive side of science—the part we call mathematics—was born with Pythagoras and Thales, nourished on the Greek islands, reached maturity on the mainland, and found its apotheosis in Alexandria with Euclid's *Elements*. Everything in the *Elements* was meant to be a deduction from ten axioms. This was the Greek way and their gift to science. The second part— the induction—was born during the Renaissance with the Scientific Revolution."

Phemios asked his friend if he would explain the difference between these two faces of science. Which is more powerful, which more certain?

"How long, my friend, have we lived in North America?"

"At least a century," replied the poet.

"And during all that time we've walked and hiked over most of this continent. Even here at this seniors' residence, we stroll the grounds and the nearby roads. Throughout these decades, we must have seen thousands of red squirrels."

"Epios, what's your point? I asked you to explain deduction and induction, and you're telling me about squirrels. Where has your legendary directness gone?"

"I'm getting to a definition of induction. Be patient, we have the time. . . . After collecting some information from our random walks on these noisy mammals, I now propose a 'theory' about them: all these squirrels are colored red. I propose this statement because I've noticed these squirrels to always be the same rufous color. That's induction: you reason from the particular to the general. Since I haven't seen every such squirrel, the theory goes far beyond the facts of my observations, yet it seems reasonable wouldn't you say?"

"It's more than reasonable; it's true, but trivial. I need another coffee to stay awake."

"You're being impatient again; maybe you've had too much coffee. What would you say if I now told you that my theory—based on induction—is false, plainly false? I can prove it. Here's

a photograph of a 'white' red squirrel, and by its eye, it isn't an albino either nor has this picture been altered in any way by an editing program. So, all red squirrels are not red. One counterexample kills any theory based on induction," concluded the scientist.

"Now you're confusing me. First, you set up this induction process and then you shoot it down. Why are you attacking your passion, or bliss as I call it?"

"White" red squirrel

"I'm attempting to be honest, a virtue as important to science as it is to your art, but not to religion. As I said, we have much in common, you and I."

"Let me see if I understand this," reflected Phemios. "You're saying that all the theories in science—regardless of the number of confirming instances—are never, and never can be, 100 percent confirmed. And that extends even to, say, universal gravitation, so things might *fall up*."

"The short answer is yes, but that incredibly remote possibility doesn't merit consideration. All the same, the fact that the sun has always risen doesn't mean it will always rise.

"People commonly view scientists, myself included, as a little arrogant, know-it-alls as they say. Paradoxically, any sense of superiority we may have rests on induction, which, as the philosopher David Hume said, is logically indefensible. But it reflects the way the world is. Induction gives us the power to predict the future and therefore control small parts of it."

The poet reminded the scientist that he had asked two questions concerning deduction and induction: which is more powerful, which more certain?

"Deduction isn't about this world," Epios continued, "it's about internal consistency. If a triangle is right-angled, then the sum of the squares on the two shorter sides equals the square on the longest side. Pythagoras proved this once and forever." Epios recalled how the sage had shown him the proof when they were together on the Island of Samos. "Within the rules of mathematics, his proof is 100 percent certain. Deduction speaks of an ideal world and most mathematicians tend to be idealistic; induction talks about the real world. The first is certain, the second is not; in some sense, the first is powerless; the second is not. The Greeks discovered the former; the Renaissance created the latter."

"Good," said Phemios, "I understand this now. Let's get out of here and go for a walk. We need to keep fit or the staff will transfer us to the nursing-home section of this place. They already think we're senile."

The Greek aristocracy, the only ones with enough leisure to speculate about anything other than the source of their next meal, preferred the abstract worlds of geometry, lyric poetry, and heroic sculpture. Not for them the things of this world—raw reality. Plato's Dialogues speak about the abstract concepts of truth, justice, the good life, and the ideal state ruled by philosopher kings. Euclid's edict to use only straight edge and compass was partly an injunction against the measuring instruments of artisans and slaves. Ancient Greece was barren ground for any theory requiring detailed observation and measurement of the natural world.

Enter Leonardo da Vinci! Born an illegitimate child in the tough and tumble of the Renaissance he was the right person, at the right time. He wasn't educated in the curriculum of the upper classes of Italian society. Largely self-taught, he learned Latin only in middle age but never Greek.

"Epios, do you remember the time we both worked for Leonardo? We built those striking wooden models of the five regular solids that the master painted for Pacioli's *De Divina Proportione.*"

"Those were the great days, the best in a thousand years. I recall Pacioli afterward hired you to do the dropped-letter calligraphy for his book. And Jacopo de Barbari even included you as Pacioli's student in his famous portrait of the friar. Some student! But with your good looks, you seemed a mere boy. So there you are, immortalized, forever staring directly into the viewer's eyes[*]."

---

[*] *Google* "Barbari Pacioli painting" to see this famous picture.

"What I remember about Leonardo was his unrivaled attention to detail—for him nothing seemed too great an effort. Even

as Andrea del Verrocchio's apprentice, assisting on the *Baptism of Christ*, Leonardo displayed that trait. Do you recall the story about the two angels in this painting [shown to the left]?"

"No, I don't—now it's your turn to teach me."

"Well, Epios, the apprentice painted one of these two angels. Can you point out which one? . . . Look carefully. Yes, yes, that's right; your artistic sense seems as well developed as your scientific. It's the one on the left. Leonardo's angel is more finely drawn."

Detail from the
Baptism of Christ by
Andrea del Verrocchio

"The other angel," the scientist noted, "appears to need the immediate attention of a skilled oculist—I hope this judgment isn't too harsh."

Exeunt Epios and Phemios.

Jacob Bronowski commented on this painting:

It is usual to say that Leonardo's angel is more human and more tender; and this is true, but it misses the point. Leonardo's pictures of children and of women are human and tender; yet the evidence is powerful that Leonardo liked neither children nor women. Why then did he paint them as if he were entering their lives? Not because he saw them as people, but because he saw them as expressive parts of nature. We do not understand the luminous and transparent affection with which Leonardo lingers on a head or a hand until we look at the equal affection with which he paints the grass and flowers in the same picture. [1]

Giorgio Vasari, Leonardo's biographer, says Verrocchio never touched colors again, being most indignant that a boy should know more of art than he did.

Phemios pointed out that if induction needed the particulars of nature for its birth, then Leonardo was its godfather. The master distrusted all large theories; he saw that nature displays herself in detail—the small features he put into the rocks and grasses that the angels are kneeling on. Other Renaissance artists had this view, unlike the artists of the Dark Ages. But Leonardo went further. He understood that science as well as art has its expression in particulars. It's not just the devil that's buried in the details; it's the origins of induction. More than a century passed after Leonardo before Francis Bacon laid out the intellectual basis for induction. As previously mentioned, *the greatest discovery of science is science itself.*

Medieval "scientists" didn't examine nature for answers; instead they looked to Aristotle. And so, they continued to repeat his every error. One often-quoted example of this was that women have fewer teeth than men. A cursory examination by Aristotle of Mrs. Aristotle's mouth would have easily dispatched this blunder, but he never bothered, and neither did anyone in the Dark Ages. Fortunately, Leonardo couldn't read Greek.

SCIENCE AND SOCIAL CONSCIOUSNESS

The role of science in society has changed over time. For Galileo and Newton it was solely a method for unlocking the secrets of nature, in their cases the movement of the heavenly bodies. By the time of the Industrial Revolution, it was an organ for social change and the betterment of humankind as well as a seeker of truth. The men behind these massive transformations were not university-educated, some could barely read. Nonetheless, they were skilled at harnessing water and steam power. So they built better mills to grind grain and sharpen flints, better canals to transport goods, and ultimately steam-powered machines to change the world. This was more technology than science, but its practical inventions were ingenious and eased the pain of workers while increasing the abundance of goods available for their homes and tables.

312 / Allah, Jesus, and Yahweh

Consider, for example, Josiah Wedgwood, famed potter to the poor, the rich, and the famous who lived during the heart of the Industrial Revolution. He had orders for his china wares from Queen Charlotte and Empress Catherine the Great of Russia. But the vast majority of his plates, pots, pitchers, and bowls were sold to lowly workers' homes, the identical ones that queen and empress purchased. The difference was the "nobility" paid handsomely for these wares to be elaborately decorated while the workers' were plain, functional, but beautiful nonetheless.

The Wedgwoods and the Darwins were friends. Josiah was the grandfather of Emma who married Charles. The abundance of every conceivable thing during the Industrial Revolution made both sides of their family rich, which gave Charles Darwin the leisure to develop the best idea anyone had ever had.

Josiah Wedgwood and others like him set in motion a revolution that quickly swept Europe and America and since then has engulfed the rest of the world. These ingenious, vigorous men had no awareness of how powerful their inventions would be. They created a large leisure class—other than the mostly effete nobility—that resulted in a blooming of genius never witnessed before.

Regrettably, when Josiah was a boy he contracted smallpox, which at that time was killing approximately 400,000 people a year in Europe. He survived, but the disease left him with a weakened right knee; in later life that leg had to be amputated. He died in 1795, the year before another of the Industrial Revolution's bright men Edward Jenner demonstrated the effectiveness of cowpox in protecting humans from smallpox.

In one of the greatest triumphs of modern science, smallpox has been eradicated from the face of the Earth. This was done by men and women everywhere working in concert for the greater good. It was not done by gods, saints, faith healers, or other frauds. After all, if God created the universe, he is responsible for this most hideous virus that has killed and mutilated millions—mostly children. What evil God has done good people everywhere can undo.

The world-wide eradication of smallpox was certified by a committee of distinguished scientists on 9 December 1979 and afterward endorsed by the World Health Assembly on 8 May 1980. The first two sentences of resolution read:

Having considered the development and results of the global program on smallpox eradication initiated by WHO [World Health Organization] in 1958 and intensified since 1967 . . . Declares solemnly that the world and its peoples have won freedom from smallpox, which was a most devastating disease sweeping in epidemic form through many countries since earliest time, leaving death, blindness and disfigurement in its wake and which only a decade ago was rampant in Africa, Asia and South America.

Three-year-old Bangladeshi girl, Rahima

The last naturally occurring case of the most deadly form of the smallpox virus was in a three-year-old child in one of the poorest countries on earth, Bangladesh. Incredibly, she lived through this horror—such is the human spirit—but unfortunately we have lost track of her. *See* her picture to the left. We can only hope that her later life was better than its beginning.

The total eradication of this plague is a tribute to modern science and human cooperation even between enemies. The major opponents during the Cold War, the Soviet Union and the United States, were the early major manufacturers of the smallpox vaccine. As a matter of record, the Deputy Minister of Health for the USSR first called on WHO to undertake a global eradication of this scourge. What God wouldn't do man did!

When I use the word *miracle*, I mean it in a figurative sense. As Albert Einstein said "The miracle is there are no miracles." Place all the trivial miracles reported by the faithful in a pile: tears flowing from statues, blood dripping from paintings, images of Jesus in pancakes, and what do you have? Nothing, absolutely nothing! Pile on all the paltry miracles of the saints, and what do you have? Still nothing. And now finish your anthill with the miracles from the Bible and the Qur'an, and what do you have? Still nothing, not even a man "behind the curtain"—nothing but delusion, fraud, and the groveling minds of the faithful sheep.

Consider a second "miracle." On the morning of September 28, 1928, in the laboratory of Scottish biologist Alexander Fleming, he noticed a phenomenon in a culture of lethal staphylococci bacteria; many were dead from an accidental fungus infection. From this simple observation came the discovery of penicillin and our world changed forever. Many of my readers, including myself, are alive today only because of this miracle of science.

To recognize the 100 Most Important People of the 20th Century, *Time* magazine, in 1999, named Fleming for his discovery of penicillin. The citation read:

> It was a discovery that would change the course of history. The active ingredient in that mold, which Fleming named penicillin, turned out to be an infection-fighting agent of enormous potency. When it was finally recognized for what it was, the most efficacious life-saving drug in the world, penicillin would alter forever the treatment of bacterial infections. By the middle of the century, Fleming's discovery had spawned a huge pharmaceutical industry, churning out synthetic penicillins that would conquer some of mankind's most ancient scourges, including syphilis, gangrene and tuberculosis.

Newton told us that in the physical world for every action there is an equal and opposite reaction. This is often, and unexpectedly, true in human culture as well. Almost immediately after Jenner's brilliant successes with his cowpox vaccine an anti-vaccination movement arose. Among the ignorant and the fundamentalists—but I repeat myself—people feared they would be transformed into cows.

The reaction of the religious communities, however, has been varied. Many have helped with mass vaccinations. In Iceland, almost since Jenner's time, the clergy have been responsible for smallpox vaccinations and record keeping. Some of the darker elements of the churches, mosques, and synagogues thought vaccination was against God's plan; they were probably correct. The Jehovah's Witnesses thought it was a crime against humanity, not God. Even among Protestant sects the Jehovah's Witnesses stand out as extra weird: they are forbidden to buy Girl Guide cookies, celebrate their own birthday, and they must not own wind-chimes—we all know how dangerous they are. And, as we shall see, the anti-vaccination movement flourishes among the Taliban and right-wing politicians.

Thomas Jefferson took a keen interest in smallpox inoculation, especially ways to protect the vaccine from heat damage while being transported to the South. With present-day Republicans their position is unclear—some think this party has adopted an anti-science attitude. Many are creationists, some dismiss the evidence for global warming, and a few even have the need for vaccinations—specifically the human papilloma virus (HPV). This vaccine is given to young girls to prevent sexually transmitted cervical cancer, a devastating disease killing 4,000 Americans per year and a quarter million worldwide, and crippling many more. By fifty, at least 80 percent of American women will have contracted at least one strain of genital HPV.

Michelle Bachmann, who ran in the 2012 Republican presidential primaries, has grave doubts about the HPV vaccine. In an interview[*] she preached:

This new STD vaccine shouldn't hurt a bit.

"The problem is, again, a little girl doesn't get a do-over: once they have that vaccination in their body, once it causes its damage, that little girl doesn't have a chance to go back." Later, Bachmann *clarified* her remarks on the *Today* show, saying that the HPV vaccine "can have very dangerous side effects," including perhaps mental retardation, and that the vaccine "could potentially be a very dangerous drug." (*See* the above cartoon by Ben Lansing.)

Well there clearly is a problem here! What drives this deadly nonsense are three words, *sexually* and *young girls*. Fundamentalists such as Bachmann believe this vaccine like sex education will cause uninhabited promiscuity among the young. And if they do have sex, they should suffer the full consequences—it's God's will. This reminds me of the latter days of the Roman Empire, when instead of solving massive

[*] *Google* "Bachmann on anti-vaccination".

governmental problems officials concentrated on the preservation of virginity. (*See* pages 273, 277)

Some Islamic countries have vigorously combatted the polio immunization programs believing it was a plot to sterilize them. The Taliban issued fatwas opposing vaccination as being against Allah's will; they are probably correct. And to prove their perfect logic, they assassinated the head of Pakistan's vaccination program. The situation in Nigeria is worse; they seem wary of vaccinations. In 2006 this country accounted for 50 percent of all new polio cases, and it's Africa's most populous. In 2007, two hundred of their children died of measles in just one province. Like fundamentalist Christian and Muslim groups, the above have a motivation based on religion and anti-science.

Some gentle folk dream of a "golden age" before the Industrial Revolution. Teachers taught us about our economic slavery during this period to the infernal machines in the dark, dreary factories. Yes, the factories were appalling places in which to work yet relative to what the people had been doing, this was a step forward. The rose-colored glasses version of the past is a myth, a false, pernicious myth. The Industrial Revolution, however, did not come to all countries as early as it did in England—some places are still mostly pre-industrial. And because of this, we can have firsthand experience of this life.

My mother and father grew up in the backwoods of Ontario, and I can tell you this life is only for the strong and the tenacious. Our home had no electricity, no running water, no indoor plumbing, and no central heating—just a box stove and stove pipes weaving through the rooms. In winter, the blankets weighed so heavily on me as a boy that I had to be extracted from the bed like a sardine from a can. And try going to an outhouse a hundred yards from the house at -30° F with an Eaton's or Sear's catalogue for toilet paper.

The average farmer was consuming 7,000 to 9,000 calories a day just to be able to do the necessary work to survive. These "farms" on the Canadian Shield yielded two crops, spring rocks and summer mosquitoes and blackflies. The rocks seemed to jump out of the ground pushed upward by the frost, and the bug crop was terrible day and night because the windows had no screens. Every spring my grandfather picked these stones and arranged them in intimidatingly lengthy rock fences.

A short section of my grandfather's rock fences

No one in a fully industrialized society can comprehend the sheer physical labor and daily drudgery of these pioneers. No one! It's notable that in photographs from this period, no one *ever* smiled. Nonetheless, they were the most kind and caring people imaginable. With no social net for support, everyone depended on his or her neighbors. During the deadly Spanish flu outbreak after WWI, my grandfather—who seemed to have a natural immunity—did the chores on five nearby farms. As children, my cousin and I had many idyllic summers roaming the fields completely shielded from this grim reality. Not only did the adults endure, but they did so with quiet dignity.

Jacob Bronowski in his timeless *The Ascent of Man* describes this pre-industrial golden age myth in a more poetic way:

We dream that the country was idyllic in the eighteenth century, a lost paradise like The Deserted Village that Oliver Goldsmith described in 1770.

Sweet Auburn, loveliest village of the plain,
Where health and plenty cheared the laboring swain.

How blessed is he who crowns in shades like these,
A youth of labour with an age of ease.

This was a fable, and George Crabbe, who was a country parson and knew the villager's life first hand, was so enraged by it that he wrote an acid, realistic poem in reply.

Yes, thus the Muses sing of happy Swains,
Because Muses never knew their pains.

O'ercome by labour and bow'd down by time,
Feel you the barren flattery of a rhyme?

The country was a place where men worked from dawn to dark, and the labourer lived not in the sun, but in poverty and darkness. [2]

Since the Industrial Revolution, there have been many others. The vast vaccination programs were a medical revolution that saved more lives and prevented more human misery than all the prayers ever mumbled. Perhaps the greatest revolution—one so profound its full consequences will never be known—is the electronic one, and its spearhead the Internet. Access to it opens the door to the entire world's knowledge and *accurate* knowledge is freedom and power. We have come a great distance since we first fashioned a femur into a tool or weapon on the African savannah a million years ago.

The Industrial Revolution laid the groundwork for all these later revolutions. And it in turn was based on three principles:

- Fate or the stars do not rule us. Shakespeare said it best in his play *Julius Caesar*, "The fault, dear Brutus, is not in our stars, but in ourselves, that we are underlings."
- Unlike the French and the Swiss, who constructed elaborate automated toys for the entertainment of the idle rich, the vigorous men of the Industrial Revolution believed inventions should be useful for the farmers and workers.
- Lastly, science is not just about truths of the natural world as it was for Galileo and Newton, but about improving society.

These principles are a tripod or a three-legged barn stool. No matter how uneven the terrain, they are always a firm basis to advance society materially and socially. The heroes of the Industrial Revolution, Watt, Wedgwood, Jenner, and others, looked to the future, not to the past. As we shall see in the next section, this was not always so.

SCIENCE AND ISLAM

In short, all sciences are included in the works and attributes of Allah, and the Qur'an is the explanation of His essence, attributes, and works. There is no limit to these sciences, and in the Qur'an there is an indication of their confluence. Dr. Abu Hamid al-Ghazali, Islamic scholar

The sacred truth of science is that there are no sacred truths. Carl Sagan, *The Demon-Haunted World*

A legend persists that during Europe's Dark Ages the Roman Catholic Church was so backward it had to send envoys to the Islamic world to find the date of Easter. Many people in the West are surprised that Islam had a Golden Age in mathematics, science, art, medicine, and architecture from approximately 750 to 1250 CE. At its height this Islamic Empire stretched from southern Spain to east of Iran. And all their major cities had hospitals and universities. In particular, the city of Baghdad was then a famous center for learning and the translation of books.

Like the ships of ancient Greece scouring the Mediterranean and Black Seas, the great caravans of Islam fanned out over Asia to trade and gather knowledge from every corner of that continent. Islam during its Golden Age had two great accomplishments. First, it conserved and translated the wisdom and knowledge of India and Classical Greece. The Muslim preservation of many Greek classics by translating these works into Arabic saved them from extinction. In Moorish Spain—where Christian met Muslim—many of these texts were translated into Latin and helped kick-start the Renaissance. Their second major achievement was original contributions to the sciences—we will concentrate on mathematics here. Note that the words *algebra*, *cipher*, *zero*, and *algorithm* are all of Arabic origin.

The mathematical contribution we all know: our society, business, and computer worlds are built on it. It's the Hindu-Arabic numeration system with a zero and place-holder structure; before this we used Roman numerals. To realize the power of this transformative world event *try* multiplying XXVI by CLXXXI. Take your time, maybe a week[*]. The answer is MMMMDCCVI.

---

[*] In the Hindu-Arabic system, this means 26 times 181 or 4,706.

Arabic mathematics contains several examples of deep originality—the second point. Consider the still famous polymath Omar Khayyám (d. 1123). Bertrand Russell in his *History of Western Philosophy* writes, "Omar Khayyám, the only man known to me who was both a poet and a mathematician, reformed the calendar in 1079." In quatrain 57 of the Fitzgerald translation of his poem the *Rubáiyát*, Khayyám refers to his mathematics and astronomy in the following self-deprecating manner:

> *Ah, but my Computations, People say,*
> *Reduced the Year to better reckoning? — Nay,*
> *'Twas only striking from the Calendar*
> *Unborn Tomorrow, and dead Yesterday.*

In truth, he had calculated the length of the year to an impressive four decimals.

0	1	0							
0	1	1	0						
0	1	2	1	0					
0	1	3	3	1	0				
0	1	4	6	4	1	0			
0	1	5	10	10	5	1	0		
0	1	**6**	**15**	20	15	6	1	0	
0	1	7	**21**	35	35	21	7	1	0

Khayyam's Triangle

To solve certain problems, the renowned Omar used the above array of numbers, so to this day in modern Persia (Iran), it's still referred to as Khayyam's triangle while in Europe we know it as Pascal's. Neither man discovered it, but both found new and intriguing properties in it. Among other things, Khayyám used it to find what we would call today Newton's binomial coefficients. Consider the third column from the left (disregard the ghost zeroes). The reader will recognize these as the number of relationships among wolves relative to pack size that we saw in Chapter 7, page 258.

You can easily find every entry in this table by adding the number directly above and the one to its left. So the first 21 in the bottom row is the sum of the 15 directly above and the 6 to its left (I've highlighted these numbers in the array). The interested reader may wish to find the next row; the answer is in the Chapter Notes. The ghost zeros on two sides of the triangle demonstrate how we arrive at the *bordering* ones, but are usually omitted.

We in the West know him through his remarkable poem the *Rubáiyát*. It's a series of 99 quatrains written in later life praising wine, women, and song:

> *Here with a Loaf of Bread beneath the Bough,*
> *A Flask of Wine, a Book of Verse—and Thou*
> *Beside me singing in the Wilderness—*
> *And Wilderness is Paradise enow.*
> Quatrain 11

> *And much as Wine has play'd the Infidel*
> *And rob'd me of my Robe of Honour—well,*
> *I often wonder what the Vintners buy*
> *One half so precious as the Goods they sell.*
> Quatrain 71

The poet could almost have said, "I spent my money on wine, women, and song, and the rest I wasted."

The *Rubáiyát* has another more profound theme—much denied by the faithful—on the foolishness of theology and those who prattle on about God and the hereafter. Consider the following two quatrains and judge for yourself:

> *Why, all the Saints and Sages who discuss'd*
> *Of the Two Worlds so learnedly, are thrust*
> *Like foolish Prophets forth; their Words to Scorn*
> *Are scatter'd, and their Mouths are stopt with Dust.*
> Quatrain 25

> *And that inverted Bowl we call The Sky,*
> *Whereunder crawling coop't we live and die,*
> *Lift not thy hands to *It* for help—for It*
> *Rolls impotently on as Thou or I.*
> Quatrain 52

Howard Eves in his entertaining book *Great Moments in Mathematics before 1650* tells a strange and intriguing story about Khayyam's youth:

> In the second half of the eleventh century, three Persian youths, each a capable scholar, studied together as pupils of one of the greatest wise men of Khorasan, the Imam Mowaffak of Naishapur. The three youths—Nizam ul Mulk, Hasan Ben Sabbah, and Omar Khayyám—became close friends. Since it was the belief that a pupil of the Imam stood a good chance of attaining fortune, Hasan one day proposed to his friends that the three of them take a vow to the effect that, to whomever of them fortune should fall, he would share it equally with the others and reserve no preeminence for himself. As the years went by, Nizam proved to be the fortunate one, for he became Vizier to the sultan Alp Arslan. In time his school friends sought him out and claimed a share of his good fortune according to the school-day vow. [3]

Hasan claimed a high governmental post, and the Sultan at the Vizier's request granted this. Omar asked for nothing so grand, but the Vizier approved him a yearly pension to pursue his mathematics and astronomy. Within a short time, Hasan attempted to replace his old school mate as the Vizier. The Vizier and Sultan saw through his schemes and plots and banished him in disgrace.

Now Hasan joined a band of religious fanatics and soon became its leader. They successfully proselytized a previously large unconverted region south of the Caspian Sea, and with this as their home base, they conducted raids upon passing caravans. His growing gang of terrorists initiated dread in the Islamic world and Hasan became known as "the old man of the mountain." Much of this terror arose from their tactic of assassination by a dagger to the throat. One of the first to be killed in this fashion was the Vizier Nizam, his boyhood friend. Hasan's dedicated followers called themselves the Assassins, the name deriving from either *Hasan* or the *hashish* they smoked to arouse their frenzy before battle. These terrorists are the model for all later suicide bombers, the ones in the nightly newspapers.

Two more disparate lives than Hasan's and Omar's are difficult to imagine, Hasan the crazed religious fanatic ready to kill
and sacrifice at the identical moment and Khayyám the studious
intellectual and infidel. In Islam—as in all societies—there have
always been two paths through life exemplified by the extremes
of these boyhood friends. During the magnificent Golden Age,
Khayyám's vision was in the ascendancy for 500 years, and their
civilization blossomed.

The situation was the reverse of what it is today where the Islamic countries are tragically backward. *What happened to cause
this titanic shift?*

THE DESCENT

Civilizations are pendulums swinging inexorably between extremes. We must remember that Galileo, although persecuted by
the Roman church, was a devout Catholic. He said, "The Bible
teaches us how to go to heaven, not how the heavens go." John
Paul II[*] repeated those words when he exonerated Galileo in
1979. In those days, the pendulum swung between wildly devout
and just religious. American society swings between the enlightened principles of the founding fathers with their deism to the
fundamentalism of a thousand crazed televangelists. The latter is
increasing today. Muslim civilization fluctuates between fanaticism and devoutness. During Islam's Golden Age the so called
more rational Mutazilites dominated politics; they interpret parts
of the Qur'an metaphorically rather than literally as do the dogmatic Asharites who mostly rule today.

ISLAM AND SCIENCE		
Pre-scientific	Golden Age	Anti-scientific
610-750 CE	750-1250 CE	1250 to Present

If you wish to destroy your mind with meaningless trivialities, *Google* "Mutazilites versus Asharites," and see what their
quarrels were about. It's as if two sides of a debate decided to
murder each other because one knew Allah's Creation took six
days and the other was certain it took seven. I feel someone

---

[*] The pope forgave Galileo for being right, but who forgives the pope?

would have to pay me a large amount of money to read this paralyzingly dull material a second time.

When religion takes a country over completely you get failed states like present-day Pakistan, Somalia, and Afghanistan—other theocracies in this region are on a life support system of crude oil. By a failed state, I mean ones with female mutilation and subjugation, lack of proper medical care, few doctors and fewer hospitals, short life expectancy, low educational standards, high illiteracy and innumeracy, inadequate nutrition, and a general absence of freedom. And you could add lack of proper sanitation—it was the historian Will Durant, I believe, who noted that ages of faith were also ages of filth*. All these items and more speak clearly of an anti-science attitude and every failed state has little or no science, but some technology. This is where the nonsense of creationism flourishes or "intelligent design" as its proponents call it today, but it's just Qur'anic or biblical literalism.

In the table above, I called the period from 610 to 750 pre-scientific because Muslims believe the archangel Gabriel dictated the first verses to Muhammad in 610. And the Qur'an knows nothing, absolutely nothing, about science beyond what any camel trader of that time knew. But what an opportunity this was for Allah to convert the whole earth if only he could think of something, anything, original to say. Not a single scientific fact is revealed. All the Qur'anic statements I have read, purportedly of a scientific nature are either false or trivial like those of Genesis. It wasn't until Islam met Greek culture that this changed.

Consider a Qur'anic example of this falsity from Surah 25:53 of the Pickthall translation:

> *And He it is Who hath given independence to the two seas (though they meet); one palatable, sweet, and the other saltish, bitter; and hath set a bar and a forbidding ban between them.*

That's right, fresh water and salt water will not mix. If you imagine for even an instant that any Muslim today would

---

* Saint Anthony the Great never bathed, and despite his bodily stench attracted many followers to his austere life—he was easy to find.

contradict this "sacred truth," you are profoundly mistaken. For a shrill and fast-paced defense of this position—to the point of hilarity—watch the YouTube videos* in the footnote. More importantly do what any scientist would—test it yourself. Take a glass of fresh and a glass of salt water; pour together in a single container. Now remember, it's shaken, not stirred. Voilà, brine!

Consider a second Qur'anic example of this falsity from Surah 21:33 of the Pickthall translation (PT):

> *And He it is Who created the night and the day, and the sun and the moon. They float, each in an orbit.*

Yes, the Qur'an, just like the Bible, does say the sun goes around the Earth. This pre-Copernican viewpoint was fine for Muhammad's time 1400 years ago, but it's difficult to know what Gabriel's and hence Allah's problems were. And furthermore, the sun went down every evening into a muddy pond, presumably to extinguish the fire. Surely, you say, no present-day Muslim would interpret this passage literally, but you would be wrong. Sheikh ibn Baaz, the supreme religious authority of Saudi Arabia, also preached that the sun rotates around the Earth. He revealed his geocentrism as vice-president of the Islamic University of Medina in 1966. I quote:

> The Holy Qur'an, the Prophet's teaching and the majority of Islamic scientists, and the actual facts all prove that the sun is running in its orbit . . . and that the earth is fixed and stable.

These ultra-conservative views were not enough for Osama bin Laden who criticized ibn Baaz for being too liberal.

After this foray into astronomy, ibn Baaz—cited just above for his deep insights on the sun's rotation around the Earth—decided again in 1993 to correct errant scientists:

> Ibn Baaz issued a fatwa that the world is flat. He ruled anyone of the round [spherical] persuasion does not believe in God and declared them infidels.

---

* *Google* "Qur'an fresh and salt water don't mix".

The Sheikh's astronomical degree derives from reading and rereading the Qur'an, which he eventually memorized. Consider these passages supporting his flat Earth claims:

And the earth have We spread out [like a carpet], and placed therein firm hills, and caused each seemly thing to grow therein. Surah 15:19 (PT)

Have We not made the earth an expanse, And the high hills bulwarks [anchors]? Surah 78:6-7 (PT)

Allah knew that earth was flat like a carpet and mountains are there to anchor the earth so that earth does not shake with us. Allah is a most merciful scientist and most wise.

We cannot rightly censure Muhammad for any of these scientific bloopers. He was of his time and culture, not of eternity and the universe. We can censure those who *still* teach such foolishness in the name of Islam. You will not be surprised that such is taught everywhere in the Muslim world. You may be surprised that Muslim schools in Europe teach this today. If you demonstrate anything to be true and contradictory to the Qur'an, you are promptly informed you haven't interpreted the Qur'an correctly, or your evidence is mistaken. Yet, if all the phenomenal advantages of modern science have to conform to the Surahs of the Qur'an, then you will be mired in the sands of 7th century Arabia, and the European Dark Ages will seem like the Age of Enlightenment. Recall the opening quote to this section by Carl Sagan: "The sacred truth of science is that there are no sacred truths."

Without the benefit of Allah's or Sheikh ibn Baaz's wisdom, the "ignorant" Greeks knew the Earth was a sphere[*] more than two millennia ago. The evidence—now there's an idea—comes from the real world, not sacred texts. Aristotle (384–322 BCE) proposed a spherical earth on the basis that the shadow of the earth on the moon during a lunar eclipse is round, since only a sphere *always* casts such an outline. Furthermore, the Greeks being sailors knew that the last part of a ship to disappear over the horizon is the top of its mast, and this can only happen if the Earth is curved.

---

[*] The Farnese Atlas is a 2nd-century Roman copy of a Greek statue of Atlas holding a *globe* on his shoulders. Evidence exists that the original dates from circa 150 BCE.

These two pieces of evidence convinced educated Greeks of the Earth's spherical form. A few years after Aristotle, a Greek named Eratosthenes did an ingenious experiment to calculate the Earth's circumference. His estimate varied only a few percent from the modern value of 24,902 miles at the equator. Remember, Columbus had convinced himself that Asia was only 2500 miles west of the Canary Islands rather than 12,500 miles—an error of 80 percent. The explorer thought he was in India proper when he was in the West Indies. Nonetheless, he had no doubt, as did all educated Europeans that the Earth was a sphere.

More than three centuries after Eratosthenes, Matthew, the author of the gospel bearing that name, was still ignorant of the Earth's form. This was doubly strange because Matthew wrote in Greek—koine Greek—yet knew nothing of their scientific advances. Recall chapter 4, verse 8 (KJV) of the first Gospel:

Again, the devil taketh him up into an exceeding high mountain, and sheweth him all the kingdoms of the world, and the glory of them;

However, you cannot *see all of a sphere* from anywhere in the universe, least all from on Earth. The author of Matthew assumed the Earth was flat, and his writing reflects that as did all the authors of the Bible and the Qur'an.

There is a timeless intractable ignorance about religion, a certain determination to shut out the world of knowledge and learning. If the churches, mosques, and synagogues had the power, they would deny our crowning glory as humans, our ability to reason and correction. In more than 700 years, since the end of the Islamic Golden Age, Muslims haven't discovered a single important scientific invention or idea. [4]

Consider the curious case of Abdus Salam who has won virtually every scientific award of note including the Nobel Prize in physics with Steven Weinberg and Sheldon Glashow. And by the way, did I mention he was Muslim? This seems to contradict what I just wrote in the paragraph above—so let's look closer. Although Salam received a M.A. in mathematics in Lahore, Pakistan, he did his advanced education in Cambridge, England. Here he redid a B.A. in both mathematics and physics receiving

double first-class honors. Ultimately, he earned a Ph.D. in theoretical physics from the famous Cavendish Laboratory at Cambridge, and the rest is history as they say. Salam is the first Paki-
Pakistani and the first Muslim Nobel Laureate in the sciences.
It's striking to note that none of the Muslims who have won the
Nobel Prize lived under the numbing yoke of Islam, except for
the dead "terrorist" Yasser Arafat.

What is so curious about the case of Abdus Salam? Quite
simply he was honored everywhere in the world except in his native Pakistan and the Muslim states. Even though he had won a
Nobel Prize in 1979, Salam was not allowed to set foot in any of
Pakistan's universities. The Ahmadi religious sect, to which Salam
belonged, had earlier been declared non-Muslim by the government, and therefore its members were heretics. During this period,
intolerance and conservative elements were sweeping through the
Islamic world. Their universities are sub-standard, their curriculum confused, and little research is accomplished. Most of their
"universities" have many mosques but no bookstores.

In the heart of Pakistan's capital, Islamabad, the head cleric
of the government-funded mosque-cum-seminary proclaimed the
following frightening warning to Quaid-i-Azam university's
female students and professors on April 12, 2007:

> The government should abolish co-education. Quaid-i-Azam
> University [Pakistan's "best"] has become a brothel. Its female
> professors and students roam in objectionable dresses. . . .
> Sportswomen are spreading nudity. I warn the sportswomen of
> Islamabad to stop participating in sports. . . . Our female stu-
> dents have not issued the threat of throwing acid on the uncov-
> ered faces of women. However, such a threat could be used for
> creating the fear of Islam among sinful women. There is no
> harm in it. There are far more horrible punishments in the here-
> after for such women.

The suppression inflicted by the full veil does make a difference. Perhaps this is why France has banned it. Teachers have
noticed that over time most veiled female students lapse into silent note-taking, become increasingly timid, don't ask questions,
or take part in discussions. The majority of all Muslim university

students refer to themselves as girls and boys rather than women and men. Suppression now, suppression later!

Some Westerners may object to this characterization of Islamic universities. They protest that they know people who have gone to Saudi Arabia and the Gulf States to teach science. And these protesters would be correct, yet that's not the full story. These countries and their clergy welcome technology of all descriptions: clothes washers, refrigerators, cell phones, and airplanes and so on. But what they do not want are the *methods of science* necessary for advanced research, that openness to question everything and to base answers on real world evidence not "sacred" texts.

Steven Weinberg clearly expressed all this in an interview[*] he gave to TV personality Jonathan Miller. The host asks him why he addresses himself to the topic of religion more than his colleagues. Weinberg responds:

> I have a friend—or had a friend, now dead—Abdus Salam, a very devout Muslim, who was trying to bring science into the universities in the Gulf States, and he told me that he had a terrible time because although they were very receptive to technology, they felt that science would be corrosive to religious belief, and they were worried about it.
>
> Damn it, I think they were right. It is corrosive of religious belief, and it's a good thing too.
>
> Miller: That's terrific!

After Salam died in 1996, his body was finally brought home to his Ahmedi community in Pakistan to be buried beside his parents; approximately 30,000 people attended the funeral. His tombstone (in part) read "The First Muslim Nobel Laureate." In an act of small mindedness, only fanatics are capable of, the police arrived with a magistrate to grind off the word *Muslim*. Now the tombstone inscription nonsensically reads "The First ###### Nobel Laureate."

Perhaps Steven Weinberg was thinking about his old friend Abdus Salam when he told the following to *The New York Times,* on April 20, 1999:

---

[*] To see the entire interview *Google* "Weinberg religion YouTube".

> With or without religion, you would have good people doing
> good things and evil people doing evil things. But for good
> people to do evil things, that takes religion.

The arrested scientific development of the Middle East lays fertile ground for the sidelining of Islam outside the modern world.
In this soil grows a well-founded sense of injustice and victim-
hood. In failed states like Pakistan, they interpret this as Allah's
anger for straying from a strictly religious course. Accordingly,
as with all Muslim idealists, they further tighten Sharia Law, and
turn inward to the Qur'an for answers, which only worsens their
problems—like the preservation of virginity did for the late Roman Empire. Somalia is the endpoint for such folly.

I wish to thank Pervez Hoodbhoy for much of the information
above on Abdus Salam and Pakistani universities. I've taken it
from his article "Science and the Islamic World" found in *Free
Inquiry* magazine for February/March 2008. Hoodbhoy is chair
and professor in the department of physics at Quaid-I-Azam
University, where he has taught for more than thirty years.

POSTSCRIPT: Abdus Salam was fond of quoting a few sayings
of Muhammad from a weak Hadith. In particular, "Seek
knowledge even as far as China." For Salam this seemed a justification of science from Islam. And I suppose the passage could
be interpreted in that manner in the present time, but that's not
what the Prophet meant when he wrote it. A Saudi, who goes
under the pseudonym Ibn al-Rawandi, is an Islamic scholar and
critic who put this word *knowledge* in its proper context:

> Islam never really encouraged science, if by science we mean
> "disinterested inquiry." What Islam always meant by
> "knowledge" was religious knowledge, anything else was
> deemed dangerous to the faith. All the real science that occurred
> under Islam occurred despite the religion not because of it. [5]

This Islamic apostate is now living under the above pseudonym in some Western country to protect himself from assassination. To my knowledge, he is the only outspoken Saudi atheist.

SAVONAROLA

*It would be good for religion if many books
that seem useful were destroyed.*
Savonarola (1452-98 CE)

When secularism retreats, religion and superstition fill the void. The Middle East is less secular today than it was a few decades ago even with the Arab Spring. As I write, Libya has just won its freedom from the lunatic Gadhafi, and the very first act of the provisional government is to reimpose Sharia law. And Sharia is required in the constitution of neighboring Egypt as the main source of legislation. We in the West could hope that their interpretation of Sharia is milder than that of the Saudis or the Taliban. The first new law proposed, however, is to allow the men to have four wives because the Qur'an permits it in Surah 4:3—not a very auspicious beginning. What are all the young women who endangered their lives in the revolution to do? They fought for freedom but gained a new servitude. Will they share this joy with friends on Facebook? I think not. The revolutions in Libya and the rest of the Middle East aren't over yet. That celestial thug Allah and his henchman Muhammad must be intellectually overthrown.

When religion and superstition retreat, secularism fills the void. Western Europe and Canada are much less religious today than they were a few decades ago. The USA is a special case; it always has been and much of this difference has been marvelous. But large parts of the new America are radical, irrational, and anti-scientific—much like parts of the Middle East.

No member of the British House of Commons ever mentions God in a speech, and it's a rare event to hear the name of the deity in the Canadian Houses of Parliament unless as an expletive. An American politician, on the other hand, would feel naked unless wrapped in the fabric of religion. Americans speak of their faith as if it were a merit badge rather than an admission that they will believe anything regardless of the evidence. It's difficult to get consistent statistics but somewhere between 18 and 33 percent of all Americans believe the sun goes around the earth—that's their faith. Perhaps the flat-earth society will return as well. After all, the Bible and the Qur'an support both of these positions.

Christians and Muslims whine and complain all over the world that they are under attack. After centuries of murdering and discriminating against freethinkers, Christians brim over with contempt toward Dawkins, Hitchens, Harris, and Dennett and their books. Muslims are consistent; they just keep on with the killing whenever possible. Christians call these books shrill, repetitive, and any other pejorative within mental grasp, but seldom tackle the arguments they present. According to the Pew Research Center 16.1 percent of Americans say they are unaffiliated with any faith today; that's double the number of just a decade or so ago. The younger their age the greater the chance they are unaffiliated. Why don't we hear from them more often? Because it's not politically or economically wise to speak out and just say, "I'm a nonbeliever through and through." Ronald Reagan Jr., the former president's son, said, "I would be unelectable. I'm an atheist. As we all know that is something people won't accept." I encourage all freethinkers to come out of the closet, and stand proud and free. You are in a magnificent tradition. In this clash of cultures, those freethinkers who have outed themselves need more colleagues.

Something similar to the fall of the Islamic Golden Age during the 11th and 12th centuries could happen here. It's happened before. Germany was a great, creative culture before Hitler. I have emphasized before that Nazism was the state religion in all aspects of its behavior where der Führer was God and top officials were his henchmen. I must repeat that he caused the deaths of millions and left us with the horror of the Holocaust as an everlasting memory. The vast majority of Germans were just normal people, but as Steven Weinberg said, "for good people to do evil things, that takes religion."

All the foremost scientists and artists, except Werner Heisenberg, left Germany when they saw what was happening. Oh, the Nazis had excellent technologists during the war but no original researchers. That great master of the English language—a Polish Jew—Jacob Bronowski expressed this brilliantly:

If you want to know what happens to science when it allows itself to be dominated by authority, political or scientific [or religious], let me take you to a field of which I have some special knowledge: German research during the war. We went into the war very much afraid of German science: it had once had a great reputation. Yet the Germans all through the war never took a fundamental step, whether in U-boat research, in radar bombing, or in nuclear physics. Why were they, the professional war-makers, outclassed by us? One example will tell you. About the time that we had our first atomic pile working, Himmler's director of war research was sending an investigator to Denmark to discover believe it or not how the Vikings knitted. By one of those exquisite strokes of irony, which dogged the Nazis, the name of this investigator believe it or not was Miss Pifil [sounds like piffle]. [6]

Despite the initial fears of the Allies, Nazi Germany never got close to making a nuclear weapon. And the rocket scientist and creationist Wernher von Braun was applying known technologies using slave labor.

The 1490s are justly both famous and infamous because of two men: Christopher Columbus and Girolamo Savonarola. One led us to a new, beautiful world and the other tried to take us to its

Savonarola

antipodes. One will always be remembered while the other is nearly forgotten except for one significant event. Savonarola was a fanatical Italian Dominican friar and a powerful contributor to the politics of Florence until his execution in 1498. He behaved like an Old Testament prophet full of condemnation and the fires of hell. In Florence—the center of the Italian Renaissance—he convinced many of the eternal pain to come if they didn't reform their ways.

In supreme arrogance that he was doing God's holy bidding, Savonarola sent his followers door to door collecting items *he associated with* moral laxity. These included classical Greek books, mirrors, cosmetics, lewd pictures, sculptures, chess pieces, lutes, and other musical instruments, fine dresses, women's hats, and the works of "immoral" and ancient poets, and he burnt them all in a huge pile in Florence's Piazza della Signoria. Numerous beautiful Florentine Renaissance artworks were lost in these notorious Bonfires of the Vanities—including some paintings by Sandro Botticelli, which he threw into the fires himself. *Sic transit gloria mundi, sed omnia fecimus!*

Savonarola had a large following, but he made the fatal mistake of condemning priests, cardinals, and even the pope for corruption and debauchery—all of which were undoubtedly true. Had this fanatical friar prevailed, Europe would have plunged back a millennium into a deep new Dark Age. And Western civilization would have sunk into the useless, meaningless servitude that happened to Islam after its Golden Age.

However, the pope's soldiers captured Savonarola and tortured him and his two closest associates on the rack—a favorite church activity—because at that time they could get away with such cruelty. After confessing to heresy, the friar and his friends were hung in chains from a single cross surrounded by an enormous pile of wood. Since the church believed in an eye for an eye, they gave him his own bonfire of the vanities in the Piazza della Signoria—the fire burned for hours.

There have been and will be more fanatics like Savonarola who challenge Western civilization's intellectual and rational traditions. Religions start as cults, and sometimes grow large enough to be considered religions; eventually die and become myths. Some are just frauds created to make money for the *founder and his supporters*. Mormonism is an example of this. Some, however, are just frauds created to make money for the *founder*. Scientology, formerly known as Dianetics, is example of this.

L. Ron Hubbard (the *L* stands for *Lafayette* or "liar" if you like) told Isaac Asimov that he was going to found a religion based on his science fiction writings. And damn it, he did! He didn't hide his intentions; once in a speech he said, "Writing for a penny a word is ridiculous. If a man really wanted to make a million dollars, the best way would be to start his own religion." Hubbard wrote for *Astounding Science Fiction* under the direction of its editor John W. Campbell during the 30s, 40s, and 50s who appropriately introduced the dianetic theories of Hubbard in *Astounding's* May 1950 issue. Much to the dismay of Asimov,

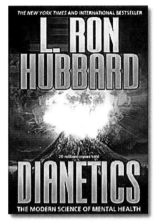

Campbell was one of the first converts. Dianetics is a psychological theory that later evolved into a full-blown religion, Scientology. Both titles along with a piece of expensive gadgetry he sold called the electropsychometer are words invented by Hubbard—a true sign of quackery. Scientology is so bizarre, so totally ridiculous. *Google* this word, but be aware that many of the links are covers for recruiting sites.

I'll give an outline of its basic dogma. Scientology centers around Xenu, a galactic ruler, who 75 million years ago brought billions of people to Earth, stacked them around volcanoes and blew them up with hydrogen bombs—hence the cover of *Dianetics* shown above. The by now well traumatized spirits of these dead—Hubbard called them "thetans," another of his neologisms—were stuck together at special "implant stations" and forced to watch a 36-hour-long movie which implanted in them destructive thoughts and feelings about God, the universe, and everything. And these became plastered onto human bodies, yours and mine. Enter $cientology, which for large sums of money and L. Ron's "auditing system," will allow you to shed these pesky thetans or in their terminology become "clear" of them. I assure the reader I didn't invent this space opera, Hubbard did. PS, I left out the parts about the *clams*.

This cult, as well as being hilarious, is cruel to its converts and rapacious of their money—at his death, Hubbard's personal net worth was in access of $600 million US. Seemingly, like lemmings, his followers give up any rationalism they may have had and smilingly rush headlong toward brain annihilation. As proof of this, read L. Ron's death announcement by Scientology leaders. They proclaimed his form had become an impairment to his work so he had decided to "drop his body" to continue his research on another planet, having "learned how to do without a body." In the jargon of their cult, this world is now "clear" of him. According to his former friends and at least one of his three wives, Hubbard had severe psychological problems.

Religion appears to have always been with us. Yet, there is no glory in geographical distribution or longevity. Scientists have found dinosaur fossils everywhere, even in Antarctica, and by studying these fossils can tell they had arthritis. I know of no group of people without some aspects of religion. Historians of the world's religions tell us that competing belief systems have only two dogmas in common: higher being(s) exist and we should have dealings with them. Neanderthals buried their dead painted in red ocher to imitate life and surrounded by items the deceased would need in the next world. Various hypotheses have been advanced to show some utility for religion, reasons for its continued existence such as an evolutionary advantage for the true believer. Richard Dawkins and Daniel Dennett plus others have put forward a few cogent ideas. But whatever these reasons may be, I side with Bertrand Russell who couldn't see how anything ultimately good or worthwhile could come from a false doctrine.

If you wish to find the origins of religion, then you must look hundreds of thousands or even a few million years deep into prehistory. By virtue of a common ancestor four to six million years ago, humans, chimpanzees, and bonobos share 98.5 percent of their DNA. From this, it's reasonable to expect that we also share much similar behavior. Chimps mourn their dead, notice things that have only esthetic value such as sunsets, have a sense of self and are not deceived by their reflection in a mirror. They will even use mirrors as an aid in personal grooming. Amazingly, they help strangers without obvious expectation of personal gain—a behavior thought unique to humans and a level of conduct *above* the golden rule. We have perhaps a genetic and behavioral debt to our near animal ancestors.

With all the above behavior in common with *Homo sapiens*, it should come as no surprise that chimps have a "primitive" form of religion. Readers can see this for themselves by watching the YouTube video[*] in the footnote—this film is almost better with the sound off. Theirs is strictly a hierarchical society maintained by the alpha male. To show their obedience to his

---

[*] *Google* "chimpanzee religion".

authority his subjects kiss his hand in a manner reminiscent of Catholics doing the same to the Pope's or Cardinal's ring. The alpha male must in turn protect his subjects from all dangers. His is a dangerous position! Periodically, younger, virile males challenge his dominance as they try to access his harem. Near the end of the video, an unexpected danger arises and the hero swaggers out to encounter this thunder and lightning threat as best he can. While his subjects cower in fear, like your dog under the bed, he contests with this sky challenger. He beats his chest and runs about at great speed shaking smaller trees and waving large sticks to the sky. What are we to make of this strange behavior?

Alpha chimp looks up to challenge a sky god

The alpha male "knows" there is someone in the sky growling thunderously and throwing lightning bolts. Moreover, by going forth like all classic heroes the chimp is attempting to confront this sky deity and drive him away. This video clearly shows that chimpanzees believe in a sky god, and are interacting with him; therefore, their behavior qualifies as religious.

The chimp's reaction to these meteorological events is eerily reminiscent of two religions now called myths where the gods threw lightning bolts followed by thunder: Thor of Norse paganism and Zeus of Greek mythology. Much later, some wag noticed that the deity who tossed these bolts had a peculiar distaste for tall trees and taller church steeples. Incredibly, this belief in a deity casting lightning bolts continued into the first years of the 19th century. These sky events were considered tokens of God's displeasure. It was thought impious to prevent their doing damage; this despite the fact that in a period of three decades, almost 400 German towers were smashed killing 120 bell ringers. Ultimately, everyone accepted Ben Franklin's unholy lightning rod thereby preserving thousands of buildings and saving hundreds of lives. Because science has explained them, no one today regards these meteorological activities as anything other than natural phenomena.

Religion was born of terror when our fellow primates fought with sky gods, and will maintain itself on a diet of ignorance and fear until science drives the demons out. Lucretius wrote, "Fear was the first thing on earth to make gods." And this basic truth is as valid today as when this Roman poet wrote it two millennia ago. Truths are like that, not limited by space and time.

A LIGHT IN THE LABYRINTH

We are on the African savannah; it's 100,000 BCE. Game is extremely scarce during the dry season, and two men who haven't eaten in several days are examining the spoor of an animal in the dusty soil. By its tracks and the terrain they decide it's a kudu. Furthermore, the depth of its split hoof prints, plus the stride and straddle indicate it's a large kudu. The mid-morning sun has already dried the prints of the overnight ground mist, yet they contain no dust or sand signifying aging. The men conclude the tracks are fresh, and this antelope passed through here at about sunrise, so they commit themselves to the chase. This was a wise decision. But, first, they must find the animal.

Their only visible weapons are one spear, one bow, and some arrows; furthermore, their method of hunting seems unbelievable if not impossible. Once they have sighted the kudu, they pursue it to exhaustion—either its or theirs! Runners call this "racing the antelope"; we call it persistence hunting. On the African savannah this is the preferred—really the only method of killing a large, swift kudu. And unless they find a carcass to scavenger, this will be their final hunt.

Why is a large, swift antelope* a good choice to race to exhaustion; it seems counterintuitive. But the larger the animal the longer it retains heat, and this is what will surely bring it to its knees. Just as a large cup of coffee cools slower than a small cup or the reason we cut hot potatoes into pieces—size does matter. Fortunately, humans have sweat glands over their entire body while kudus lose heat mostly from their mouths by panting, and it's impossible to pant while running. Moreover, the kudu is covered in heat retaining hair, plus the full length of its back is

---

* Kudus can weight 600 lbs. or more, the hunters, at most, 150 lbs.

Art of the San People, Kalahari Desert: undated

exposed to the intense savannah sun. Contrast this with the hunters. They are almost hairless, and what hair they do have on their
heads is short, sparse, and well-spaced. Also, they run upright,
exposing little of their small bodies to the sun. Only the younger
man will begin the chase while the other follows at a half trot. If
the first man collapses before the kudu does, the second man will
take the spear and continue the chase at a full run. Both men are
very lean and fit with thin lithe frames, long fingers and toes to
allow body heat to dissipate quickly. And the San hunter has at
least three times the body surface per unit mass as the kudu. As I
said, this was a wise choice. To see a modern example of this
hunting, *Google* website in the footnote[*].

After they killed the kudu, they ate its liver. Then one man
quickly skinned the animal with some crude stone tools while the
other constructed a fire to smoke the meat and fend off predators
seeking a free meal; already a few vultures were circling overhead. Having done this, the less exhausted man raced back to the
group's encampment to enlist anyone able to return to the kill
site and help carry the meat home for everyone.

The African night is large and full of wonders. The mighty
roar of lions and the unnerving "laughter" of hyenas can fill a
heart with terror. The remaining man stoked his fire high to protect himself and his prize. After two nights alone on the savannah guarding his group's survival, he saw a few women and two
older men coming toward him. His companion was leading the

---

[*] *Google* "persistence hunting".

way. That evening under the intense starlight of a moonless night, they all feasted—everyone laughed at fear and hardship; life was good. Yet in two weeks, the hunters would have to go out and kill another kudu!

These Savannah hunters were unconsciously using the correspondence theory of truth (*see* page 165). There was extreme natural selection pressure against false conclusions—the hunters starved to death. Evidently, the better you were at tracking, the more you and your hunter-gather encampment ate, flourished, and multiplied. This was a major impetus shaping us to be capable of rational thought and science—our light in the labyrinth.

Who were these San people? They were our ancestors; we are their descendants. In 100,000 BCE and millennia afterward, Africa was mostly desert and scrubby savannah with little water and less game. This was the time of last ice age and much of the world's water was locked up in glaciers and snow. Seeking new grazing, Africa's large game crossed the wide land bridge into Asia and never returned. At that time, the San people numbered only a few thousand, so the human race teetered on the brink of extinction. Something drastic had to be done so the San trackers followed the game out of Africa. We are all Africans, and the world's peoples form one gigantic extended family. The San didn't leave Africa empty-handed; they took bows, arrows, and their rock painting skills. But they also brought something vastly more important, something intangible: the ability to reason and arrive at true conclusions. And although we have no direct evidence, they almost certainly were burdened with some forms of superstition and religion, as were our primate cousins.

There are those, and they are many, who would say religion is valuable even though it is false. To them I would say look at history, look at social justice, look at morality, and you will find little or none of these in churches, mosques, synagogues, or any rigid ideology. Systems of thought that have no touchstone in reality lead to the darkest places in the human heart. As Jacob Bronowski said, "Science is a tribute to what we can know even though we are fallible." The values of science are human values: truth, tolerance, independence, common sense, and a willingness to change your mind on the presentation of new evidence.

Whether your belief system is robustly ideological—Nazism, Communism, Fascism—or passionately theological—Judaism, Christianity, Islam—the results are the same. Look for yourself! The evidence lies all around us in lost lives, ruined civilizations, vanished opportunities, sexual repression and aberrations, genocides, and meaningless decades of prayer mumbling. In the *pantheon of a single god*, his messengers all bring the same commandment, "Fall on your knees."

Enter another pantheon, one without gods: no prayers, no lost years, no submission, no sacred texts, no fawning adulation, no kissing of rings, no infallibility. Enjoy the unfettered freedom of an untethered mind. Explore without fear! Question without reprisal! Live without guilt! And love unconditionally! This is the true home of the brave and the land of the free. This is the rational landscape of science, reason, Western culture, and the Enlightenment. This is a free man's or woman's worship. Come, stand with us in the light and enter a new paradise.

Science is proof without certainty.
Religion is certainty without proof.

CHAPTER NOTES

The following entries are referenced in the main text by the words *see Chapter Notes* or by a numerical superscript [#].

CHAPTER—1

1 Herodotus: *The History of Herodotus*, Volume 2, translated by G. C. Macaulay (EBook #2456: The Gutenberg Project, 2001), Book VII, p. 38.

2 Ibid., Book VII, p. 109.

3 *Google* "Shelley on the literature and the arts".

4 Lucien Price, *Dialogues of Alfred North Whitehead* (New York: The New American Library, 1954), p. 143.

5 Bertrand Russell, *History of Western Philosophy* (London: George Allen and Unwin Ltd., 1946), pp. 49-50.

6 Ibid., p. 55.

CHAPTER—2

1 Stanley Milgram, "The Perils of Obedience" from *Harper's Magazine*, (1974), abridged and adapted from *Obedience to Authority*.

2 Stephen Jay Gould, *Wonderful Life: The Burgess Shale and the Nature of History* (New York: W. W. Norton & Company, 1989), p. 320.

3 Salman Rushdie, *the Portable Atheist: Essential Readings for the Nonbeliever selected* by Christopher Hitchens (Philadelphia: Da Capo Press, 2007), p. 383.

CHAPTER—3

1 Stephen Jay Gould, "Fall of the House of Ussher" in *Eight Little Piggies* (New York: W.W. Horton & Company, 1993), pp. 181-93.

2 Bertrand Russell, "On the Value of Scepticism" in *Sceptical Essays* (London: Allen & Unwin, 1928), Introduction.

3   Paul Feyerabend (1924-94) studied science at the University of Vienna, but moved into postmodernist philosophy where he was a critic of Karl Popper's "critical rationalism." He became a detractor of science, particularly of "rationalist" attempts to lay down or discover rules of the Scientific Method.

4   Richard Dawkins, *The God Delusion* (New York: First Mariner Books, 2006), pp. 320-21.

5   David Hume, *An Enquiry Concerning Human Understanding* (EBook #9662: The Gutenberg Project, 2006), Section X, "Of Miracles," Part II, 101.

6   Ibid., Section X, "Of Miracles," Part I, 91.

7   Lucian (2nd Century CE), *Alexander the False Prophet*, translated by A.M. Harmon, *Lucian*, Volume IV (Cambridge, Mass: The Loeb Classical Library is published and distributed by Harvard University Press #162), p. 207.

8   Carl Sagan, *Cosmos* based on Sagan's 13-part television series (New York: Random House, 1980), pp. 335-36.

CHAPTER—4

P. 120 *Google* "Model Circumcision Informed Consent Form" for a list of possible surgical complications.

P. 121 *Google* "Neonatal Circumcision Complications".

P. 127 To hear a 100-year-old recording of the Bach/Gounod *Ave Maria*: *Google* "Moreschi Castrato Ave Maria".

1   Thomas Paine, *Age of Reason*, Part II, Section 5 (New York: Dover Publications, 2004), p. 102.

2   Plutarch, *The Lives of the Noble Grecians and Romans*, translated by John Dryden and revised by Arthur Hugh Clough (United States: The Modern Library, Random House, Inc. undated), p. 655.

3   Ibid., p. 658.

4   From the John Jay Report, a 2004 account by the John Jay College of Criminal Justice, commissioned by the U.S. Conference of Catholic Bishops.

CHAPTER—5

P. 138 Timothy Freke and Peter Gandy, *The Jesus Mysteries: Was the "Original Jesus" a Pagan God?* (New York: Three Rivers Press, 1999).

P. 141 To read David Ulansey's complete *Scientific American* article: *Google* "The Mithraic Mysteries in Scientific American".

P. 162 Martin Gardner, *Did Adam and Eve Have Navels? Debunking Pseudoscience* (New York, W.W. Norton & Company, Inc., 2001), pp. 274-87.

P. 174 This entire document is on the Vatican website. *Google* "Vatican on Limbo".

P. 183 This website is a repository of biblical dilemmas and a fatal indictment for any book aspiring to be revealed truth: *Google* "Fatal Bible Flaws by Morgan".

P. 190 Get the *Loose Canon, a Holy Book of the Church of the FSM* by *Googling* "the FSM consortium PDF".

1 Elaine Pagels, *The Gnostic Gospels* (New York: Vintage Books, 1981), p. 57.

2 Martin Gardner, *Order and Surprise* (Buffalo, New York: Prometheus Books, 1983), p. 355.

3 Martin Gardner, *Did Adam and Eve Have Navels? Debunking Pseudoscience* (New York, W.W. Norton & Company, Inc., 2001), p. 249.

4 Ibid., p. 276.

5 Sam Harris, *The End of Faith: Religion, Terror, and the Future of Reason* (New York: W. W. Norton & Company, 2004), p. 38.

6 Jacob Bronowski, *The Ascent of Man* (United States: Little, Brown and Company, 1973), pp. 367 & 374.

7 Sam Harris, *Letter to a Christian Nation* (New York: Vintage, 2008), p. 66.

8 Jack Huberman, *The Quotable Atheist* (New York: Nation Books, 2007), p. 25.

9 Mark Twain, *Mark Twain Speaking* edited by Paul Fatout (United States: University of Iowa Press, Iowa city 1976), p. 290.

CHAPTER—6

1 Carl Sagan, "Science's Vast Cosmic Perspective Eludes Religion" in Volume 31.2, March/April 2007 of the *Skeptical Inquirer* magazine.

2 Richard Dawkins, *Unweaving the Rainbow* (Boston, New York: Houghton Mifflin Company, 1998), p. 1.

3 David Samuel Margoliouth, *Encyclopedia of Religion and Ethics, Volume 8* (published by T&T Clark in Edinburgh, and Charles Scribner's Sons in the United States), p. 878.

4 For the interview with Michael Persinger: *Google* "Persinger telepathy Skeptico".

CHAPTER—7

P. 264 Pericles intervened to save the philosopher Anaxagoras from death for saying the gods are myths we created in our own image. Compare Pericles actions to those of George Bush senior, and try not to weep.

1 Bertrand Russell, *Why I Am Not a Christian* (London: George Allen & Unwin Ltd., 1958), pp. 14-15.

2 Bertrand Russell, *History of Western Philosophy* (London: George Allen and Unwin Ltd., 1946), p. 363.

3 Bertrand Russell, *Why I Am Not a Christian* (London: George Allen & Unwin Ltd., 1958), pp. 12-14.

4 Thucydides, *History of the Peloponnesian War*, translated by Rex Warner (London: Published by the Penguin Group, 1972) Book 2, p. 145.

CHAPTER—8

P. 321 The next row of Khayyam's Triangle is
1 8 28 56 70 56 28 8 1.

1 Jacob Bronowski, "The Creative Process," *Scientific American*, September 1958, p. 62.

2 Jacob Bronowski, *The Ascent of Man* (United States: Little, Brown and Company, 1973), p. 160.

3 Howard Eves, *Great Moments in Mathematics before 1650* (United States: The Dolciani Mathematical Expositions, 1980), p. 148.

4 Pervez Hoodbhoy, "Science and the Islamic World" from *Free Inquiry*, February/March 2008, Vol. 28 No. 2.

5 Jack Huberman, *The Quotable Atheist* (New York: Nation Books, 2007), p. 249.

6 Jacob Bronowski, *A Sense of the Future* (United States: The Massachusetts Institute of Technology, 1977), p. 4.

INDEX

Page numbers in *italics* refer to photographs.

J

Jefferson, Thomas, 56, 315
Jeffs, Warren, 94-95, 215, 217
Jehovah Witnesses, 162, 170, 227, 242
   anti-vaccination and, 314
Jenner, Edward, 312, 314, 318
Jephthah, 291-92
Jerome, St., 277
Jesuit motto, 302
Jesus, 58, 71, 78, 80, 93, 98, 110, 122
   castration, 116
   character defects of, 281-82
   circumcision of, 119
   crucifixion of, 140, 179, 290, 293,
     294, 295
   earthly father of, 76
   End Times and, 295-96
   environment and, 263-64
   fury of, 281, 286
   Gadarene swine and, 219
   hell and, 280-82, 293, 294, 301
   moral character of, 281-82, 286,
     287-88
   Muhammad and, 78-79, 93, 282
   Ossuary of James and, 75-76
   sign of fish, 153
   slavery and, 105, 289, 296
   Socrates and, 282, 286
   Torah and, 289
   two faces of, 279-82, 289
Jews, 42
   Adolf Eichmann and, 37-38
   Danes and the, 45
Jim (a runaway slave), 131-34
Johnson, Lyndon, 11
Johnson, Dr. Samuel, 81
Jonah, 197, 204
Jones, Jim, 95
Joshua, 182-183
Judaism, 138-39, 144, 180, 275
Judas, 265, 294
Judgment, Day of, 268
Jung, Carl Gustav, 190

K

Kaaba, 30, 248
Karpinski, Janis, 52

Kepler, Johannes, 59, 73
Khalifa, Rashad, 206-07
Khayyám, Omar, 34, 77, 196
   Howard Eves on, 322-23
   theology of, 321
   triangle of, 320-21
Khomeini, Ayatollah
   Salman Rushdie and, 245-46
Kimball, Spencer W., 217
King James Version (Bible), 158, 164
Klement, Ricardo, 36-38
   see also Adolf Eichmann
Kolob 214, 248
   Battlestar Galactica (TV series)
     and, 214
   Kobol (anagram), 214
Koresh, David, 95
Krishna, 137, 179
Kubrick, Stanley, 101, 102, 103

L

LaHaye, Tim, 163, 164, 262, 299
Lamanites, 212, 213, 216
Larson, Glen A., 214
laws, religious dietary, 28
Leavitt, Henrietta Swan, 65-66, 69
Lee, Robert E., 129
legal codes, ancient, 90, 95
Lenin, Vladimir, 303
Lennon, John, 54
   "Imagine" (song), 54-55
Leno, Jay, 270
Leonardo da Vinci, 309-11
   detail from the *Baptism of Christ*,
     310
Leonidas at Thermopylae, 22
Leviticus
   sexual laws in, 236-37
Lewis, C. S., 137
Lightfoot, John, 57-59
light-year (definition of), 64
   Cepheid variables and, 65, 67
Limbo, 173-74
Lincoln, Abraham, 53, 217
   Gettysburg Address, 156-57
   slavery and, 250
Lindsey, Hal, 163-64

White, Ellen Gould
   144,000 and, 227
   TLE and, 227, 228, 229, 239
Whitehead, Alfred North,
   Christian theology, 24
   Funeral Oration of Pericles, 296-299
   humor in the Bible, 155
WHO, 313
witches, 91, 267, 280
women and the church, 116-18, 126,
   127, 135, 138, 144, 145
Women's Bible, 118
wolves, 262, 273, 301, 305, 320
   Algonquin, *258*-59
   deer and, 263
   morality of, 259
   pack size of, 258
Wollstonecraft, Mary, 118

X

Xerxes, 12-13, 22, 24

Y

Yahweh
   bizarre commandments of, 239
   burning flesh and, 243, 290-91
   fury and rage of, 42-43, 250, 282-83
   morality and, 250, 273, 295
   real estate broker, 292
   recognizes other gods, 243-44
Young, Brigham, *215*, 216

Z

Zeus, 25, 67, 107, 233, 247, 307, 337
   Prometheus and, 86
Zimbardo, Philip, 41-45, 46, 50
   banality of heroism and, 45
   Stanley Milgram and, 51
Zodiac, 141, 143
Zoroastrianism, 23, 31, 138, 274
   symbols of, 22